Karen Brown's
Mexico

Charming Inns & Itineraries

D1716744

Written by

Clare Stevenson Brown and Jane Stevenson Day, Ph.D.

Illustrations by Barbara Tapp
Cover Painting by Jann Pollard

Karen Brown's Guides, San Mateo, California

Karen Brown Titles

Austria: Charming Inns & Itineraries

California: Charming Inns & Itineraries

England: Charming Bed & Breakfasts

England, Wales & Scotland: Charming Hotels & Itineraries

France: Charming Bed & Breakfasts

France: Charming Inns & Itineraries

Germany: Charming Inns & Itineraries

Ireland: Charming Inns & Itineraries

Italy: Charming Bed & Breakfasts

Italy: Charming Inns & Itineraries

Mexico: Charming Inns & Itineraries

Mid-Atlantic: Charming Inns & Itineraries

New England: Charming Inns & Itineraries

Pacific Northwest: Charming Inns & Itineraries

Portugal: Charming Inns & Itineraries

Spain: Charming Inns & Itineraries

Switzerland: Charming Inns & Itineraries

Dedicated to the memory of
Steve
Whose love of Mexico and joy of travel
Have been passed down through the generations,
and to
Bill
Your book on Mexico—Finally

Cover painting: Antigua Villa Santa Monica, San Miguel de Allende

Editors: Karen Brown, June Eveleigh Brown, Clare Brown, Jane Stevenson Day, Kim Brown Holmsen, Iris Sandilands,   Tony Brown, Lorena Aburto Ramirez, Suzanne Young, Rosalina Hernandez.

Illustrations: Barbara Tapp.

Cover painting: Jann Pollard.

Webmistress: Lynn Upthagrove.

Technical support and graphics: Michael Fiegel.

Maps: Michael Fiegel.

Distributed by Fodor's Travel Publications, Inc., 280 Park Avenue, New York, NY 10017, USA.

Distributed in Canada by Random House Canada, 2775 Matheson Boulevard. East, Mississanga, Ontario, Canada L4W 4P7, phone: (905) 624 0672, fax: (905) 624 6217.

Distributed in the United Kingdom by Random House UK, 20 Vauxhall Bridge Road, London, SW1V 2SA, England, phone: 44 20 7840 4000, fax: 44 20 7840 8406.

Distributed in Australia by Random House Australia, 20 Alfred Street, Milsons Point, Sydney NSW 2061, Australia, phone: 61 2 9954 9966, fax: 61 2 9954 4562.

Distributed in New Zealand by Random House New Zealand, 18 Poland Road, Glenfield, Auckland, New Zealand, phone: 64 9 444 7197, fax: 64 9 444 7524.

Distributed in South Africa by Random House South Africa, Endulani, East Wing, 5A Jubilee Road, Parktown 2193, South Africa, phone: 27 11 484 3538, fax: 27 11 484 6180.

A catalog record for this book is available from the British Library.

ISSN 1540-2983

Contents

Foreword

This book is a sentimental journey. My grandfather, Louis Carr Stevenson (Steve), lived part of each year in Mexico, which he called his "second home." Steve had a deep appreciation for the beauty and culture of the country and a genuine love and admiration for its people. By hosting family celebrations there, he instilled in his children and grandchildren his enthusiasm and love for Mexico and we have thought for many years of writing about it, but were concerned that there weren't sufficient hotels of charm and quality to make such a book feasible. How wrong we were! In the past few years, superb inns and hotels have been popping up all over the country—properties that rival in romantic ambiance and service the finest hotels in the world. The idea of a book became too good to resist when my aunt, Dr. Jane Stevenson Day, an archaeologist and renowned authority on pre-Columbian civilizations, retired as chief curator of the Denver Museum of Nature and Science and generously offered to contribute her profound knowledge to our project. This book reflects the efforts of two sisters, Steve's daughters: my Aunt Jane and my mother, Clare, my partner and my best friend. Together, through their writing of *Mexico: Charming Inns & Itineraries*, they continue Steve's legacy in sharing his love for Mexico with an even greater audience, the readers of our guides. This is truly an exceptional book because of Clare and Jane's extensive research and blended talents: Jane's archaeological expertise and Clare's ability to find the most wonderful places to stay. Consequently, this guide to Mexico is unique in that it has a strong focus on archaeology while recommending a wide variety of exceptional lodgings, from sumptuous 16th-century haciendas on vast estates to alluring thatched huts on secluded beaches. Easy-to-follow itineraries encompass a wealth of fascinating attractions—from whale watching in Baja to exploring the country's Colonial heart. Naturally, we include descriptions of Mexico's famous beaches, but our real target is the traveler who wants to have an in-depth experience of this incredible country just "south of the border."

We welcome you to Mexico.

Karen

Introduction

Mexico City, Cathedral

Mexico is an incomparable destination, a stunning country that includes such a wealth of wonders that whatever your interests, you are bound to have your dreams fulfilled. There are marvelous hotels, archaeological treasures beyond belief, breathtaking beaches, soaring mountains, deep canyons, fascinating 16th-century Colonial towns, cosmopolitan cities, quaint Indian villages, colorful markets, fine golf courses, divine snorkeling, whale excursions, outstanding bird watching, butterfly reserves, tropical forests, dense jungles, superb deep-sea fishing, chic boutiques, cute shops featuring native handicrafts, and, for all of us who love to eat, culinary delights. To add the final touch of perfection, the weather in Mexico is excellent. However, Mexico is not for everyone. If it bothers you when service isn't instant, if you are upset when everything isn't totally tidy, if you are disappointed if your hotel doesn't have Internet access, then perhaps you should stay closer to home. But the things that may seem like faults to some are in our estimation exactly what make Mexico so special. Here you step back into another time where people are not rushed, where friendliness prevails, where cultural differences enrich your travels. We have always loved Mexico. Now, after spending an extended period of time there, we are more captivated than ever by its charms. We know that our readers who are young in heart will share our enthusiasm for this fabulous country with its extraordinarily warm people and amazing culture.

The purpose of this guide is to help you plan your trip. Mexico is an incredibly diverse country with a bewildering selection of sightseeing and hotel accommodations. Our goal is to help you sort out all the options so that you can discover the ideal destination to fulfill your dreams and to choose just the right accommodations so that your holiday will be memorable. There are four sections in the book. This first section, *Introduction,* begins with a bit of history, delving into Mexico's legacy of the past and laying a foundation for what you will be seeing, then follows with practical information that should be useful in your travels. The itinerary section lays out routings that cover the highlights of Mexico; the third section provides descriptions and pertinent details of recommended hotels; the fourth section contains maps that pinpoint each hotel's location and outlines the routes of each featured itinerary.

Archaeology & the Legacy of the Past

Chichén Itzá, Temple of the Warriors

To visit Mexico without including at least one of its archaeological wonders would be a pity since its history cannot be understood or appreciated without a journey into the past. Mexican archaeology has revealed one of the most fascinating and splendid chapters in all of world prehistory. Mexico has been inhabited for thousands of years, during which time a stunningly sophisticated culture emerged. During the peak of this civilization, awesome cities were constructed, a superb network of roads was built, and massive pyramids emerged in honor of the gods. Today throughout Mexico there are archaeological sites that attest to the profound grandeur of this era. These sites are dotted throughout every part of Mexico and are described in depth in our itineraries. The archaeological and Colonial sites, and various museums recommended here are not in any way a complete inventory. Instead, they are places we consider very special that conveniently blend into our itineraries and are close to excellent accommodations.

The archaeological record in Mexico begins thousands of years ago at the end of the last ice age (c.10,000 B.C.) when Paleo-Indian bands hunted now-extinct animals such as bison and mammoth. However, the great civilizations of pre-Hispanic Mexico have their beginnings about 2500 B.C. with the development of a rich agricultural tradition based on a triad of crops: corn, beans, and squash. Interestingly, this change from hunting to village-based agriculture occurred not only in Mexico, but also all over the world. The establishment of a stable food supply allowed for an increase in population, growth of settled communities, and eventually the development of cities and sophisticated cultures.

The first great civilization of Mexico developed on the hot Gulf Coast at around 1500 B.C. among a group of people known as the Olmecs. The majority of traditions and traits that characterize the many succeeding Mesoamerican cultures have their origin with these very early people. In fact, one of the most amazing aspects of pre-Hispanic Mexico is the continuity of these cultural traits across time and space. Most of the hallmarks of pre-Columbian Mesoamerica had their beginnings in the Olmec period, but were still present 3,000 years later among the Aztecs, a civilization well documented for us by the Spanish conquistadors. Some of these clearly recognizable characteristics are: a dependence on the basic crops of corn, beans, and squash; a preference for green jade over all other materials for royal or ceremonial objects; the making of fine ceramics; the creation of specialized architecture such as stone pyramids, palaces, temples, and ball courts; the carving of massive stone sculptures depicting gods and rulers; the use of solid rubber balls for playing a ritual team sport; a large pantheon of gods whose names, but not necessarily their characteristics, changed over time; and the use of human sacrifice to placate these gods. Perhaps the greatest achievement, however, was the construction of great urban centers containing plazas, pyramids, ball courts, roadways, monuments, and massive stone architecture, all carefully finished with cut stone and white plaster. These amazing ancient cities still survive throughout Mexico and today offer visitors a glimpse of the extraordinary world of pre-Columbian Mesoamerica.

This continued survival of ancient traditions from past into present is one of the most intriguing aspects of a visit to modern Mexico. Travelers to Mexico today become quickly, if unconsciously, aware of this through the food—the basic foods are the same as they were 3,500 years ago. Corn, beans, and squash still form the basic triad of a rural diet and even in sophisticated Mexico City tortillas are preferred to bread. In addition, tomatoes, avocados, chocolate, potatoes, chilies, popcorn, papaya, yams, peanuts, turkeys, and much more are all popular survivors of the pre-Hispanic world. Associated with this are centuries-old agricultural techniques that are still used in rural Mexico. Large-scale agriculture is now more common, but in many small farming communities, fields are still ritually marked out just as they were long ago and a *coa*, or digging stick, is used to plant the corn kernels—three in each hole: one for the gods, one for the birds and one for human needs.

Another modern continuance from the past can be traced to a ritual pre-Columbian game played with a solid rubber ball by two opposing teams. In fact, the actual concept of playing to win as a team, rather than as an individual, and the use of rubber to form a bouncing ball were unknown in the Old World until the Spanish reached Mexico in 1519. On his first return journey to Spain, Cortés took players and rubber balls to play at the royal court of Charles V. The skillful players and the rubber balls amazed the European spectators. Today ball games played around the world clearly have their origin in this 3,500-year-old team sport with its colorful rituals, stone courts, specialized equipment, and bouncing rubber balls. Happily, no longer is the losing captain sacrificed to the gods!

Also reflecting their pre-Columbian origin are the colorful local markets you find in Mexico today. Everything imaginable is laid out in its own section of the vibrant, noisy marketplace and an incredible variety of merchandise can be purchased. Shoppers can wander from vendor to vendor to select the freshest produce, strongest baskets, fine jewelry, and even medicinal herbs and the services of the local healer. Today, as in the past, markets are the heart and pulse of daily life. When Cortés arrived in Mexico, he found that markets flourished throughout the country. Riches such as feathers, gold, and jade from far-flung frontiers of the empire were available for purchase as well as locally produced agricultural crops and goods such as baskets, pots, clothing, and services of all types. Shoppers strolled through colorful rows of fruits, flowers, and vegetables, listened to merchants hawking their wares, and enjoyed a snack amid the noise, odors, and confusion—a scene still typical of Mexican markets today.

Current religious beliefs and activities also hark back to the past, blending ancient pre-Columbian gods with 16th-century Spanish Catholicism. Indeed, the Spanish Colonial churches and cathedrals were often built on the same sacred spot as the original ancient temples and pyramids that preceded them. Pilgrimages are still made to these hallowed places, and the timeless odor of copal incense rises from the altars as the feasts and rituals of past and present blend in the current church calendar.

ARRIVAL OF THE CONQUISTADORS

To understand Mexico today, it helps to be familiar with one of the most dramatic events in all history: the meeting of the Old and New Worlds in the Americas during the early 16th century. Of these many events, the encounter between the Spaniards under Cortés and the Aztecs under Montezuma is probably the most astounding, a tale culminating when Cortés's forces finally took over the Aztec capital, Tenochtitlán (now called Mexico City).

The story began on February 18th, 1519, when Hernán Cortés set sail from Cuba to search for gold and glory. He was accompanied by 500 soldiers, 50 sailors, 200 islanders from Cuba, several black servants, and a few Indian women. Also on board his 11 ships were 16 horses, 14 pieces of artillery, supplies of food, and trinkets and clothing for trading. Cortés's ships sailed along the Gulf coast of Mexico. At stops along the way he heard of the power of the Aztecs and of an empire rich in gold ruled by the feared emperor Montezuma. On Good Friday, April 18, 1519, he and his men landed near the site of the modern city of Veracruz.

Cortés's arrival in Mexico on the Aztec calendar date *ce acatl* (one reed) prompted Montezuma to consider that Cortés might actually be the god *Quetzalcoatl,* returning as promised in legend, to reclaim his kingdom in the year one reed. This coincidence of the date of Cortés's arrival, coupled with uncertainty produced by the evil omens, left Montezuma perplexed as to Cortés's identity and purpose. Although originally Montezuma thought Cortés might be a god, it would have been impossible for a few scraggly Spanish soldiers to have ever been able to defeat the powerful, mighty army of Montezuma without help. Luckily, Cortés had one great windfall—after a successful battle against a Mayan village, the chief presented him with 20 Indian maidens. One of these, La Malinche, was an exceptionally bright young woman who not only became his mistress, but who also was able to act as translator and advisor. With her aid, Cortés enlisted the assistance of thousands of Tlaxcalan warriors, who were passionate enemies of the Aztecs and joined forces with him.

Maya Nobles

By the time Cortés crossed the snows of the last great mountain barrier and descended into the rich valley below, his entourage consisted of several thousand well-equipped Tlaxcalan warriors along with his own still surviving 350 Spanish soldiers. His troops entered Tenochtitlán where the final battle was fought in the great marketplace of Tlatelolco. There the Aztec nobles and warriors, assisted even by the women, according to legend, made a valiant last stand for the city, but the forces of the Spanish and their thousands of Indian allies were too powerful. The end came on August 13th, 1521. Of the 300,000 warriors who had defended the city only 60,000 were left. Mexico had fallen; the glorious city of Tenochtitlán was destroyed and neither the New World nor the Old would ever be the same again.

Once the Aztecs surrendered, the quest for gold was on. The Aztecs and their contemporaries were amazed at the Spaniards' unquenchable thirst for gold. To them objects of rich green jade, with their connotation of rain, water, and fertility, were far more beautiful and valuable than the shiny metal. But the Spanish hungered for the treasure, plundered it, fought over it, and after the fall of Tenochtitlán tortured their captives for information of its whereabouts.

The aesthetic beauty of the gold ornaments created by Aztec artists held little interest for Cortés and his soldiers. Only a handful of the splendid objects described by the chronicles remains today. Most of the magnificent pieces were immediately thrown into the melting pots. Once it was cast into ingots, standardized weights were made to establish the king's fifth, that rich share of New-World wealth that was conscientiously set aside for the Spanish throne. These bars of gold, along with carefully selected examples of the finest jewelry, were sent by ship to Spain where they were displayed with great pomp at the courts of Charles V. In Seville, Valladolid, Brussels, and Barcelona the undreamed-of splendor of Montezuma's gifts to Cortés and the plundered golden treasure of the Aztecs dazzled the world of Renaissance Europe.

The search for treasure exploded. Soon adventurers, priests, bureaucrats, and soldiers flocked to New Spain (Mexico) to look for fame, fortune, and the conversion of souls. A few came to make Mexico their home; some to convert the Indians to Christianity; but most simply to pillage the wealth of the new land. The population was decimated by disease and bondage. For almost 300 years the Aztecs and other indigenous peoples lay under the colonial yoke of Spain. Finally revolutions broke the bonds that tied New Spain to Europe and Mexico rose as a new country, a nation that blended the genes and customs of the Old and New Worlds in a new tradition unique to the Americas.

About Hotels

BASIS FOR SELECTION

This guide does not try to appeal to everyone—it is definitely prejudiced: we visit hundreds of hotels and select only those few we think are special. The place that captivates us might be a 17th-century hacienda surrounded by vast acreage, a simple thatched hut nestled under palm trees, or an appealing beachfront hideaway accessible only by boat, but there is a common denominator—they all have charm. So if you prefer to travel spending your nights in romantic accommodations, this book is for you. For some of you, cost will not be a factor if the hotel is outstanding; for others, a budget guides your choice. What we have tried to do is to indicate what each hotel has to offer and describe the setting, so that you can make the choice to suit your own preferences and budget. We feel that if you know what to expect, you won't be disappointed, so we have tried to be candid and honest in all our appraisals.

BED & BREAKFASTS

Those of you who like the intimate bed-and-breakfast style of travel will be happy to know that this type of accommodation is an increasingly popular concept in Mexico. Some of the ones we feature in this guide are extremely elegant—rivaling the amenities in the finest hotels. Others are more simple, sweet, and appealing. But they all have the common denominator of great warmth of welcome and delightful personal attention.

CHILDREN

Most places in Mexico accept children with open arms. However, in some hotels, especially those that cater to adults who want a romantic get-away, children are not appropriate. Even for the hotels that do welcome children, their policies and stipulations may vary widely: some will accept only infants, some will accept children over 12, some accept children over 16, etc. Therefore, if you will be traveling with your family, be sure to ask the hotel what their policy is concerning children when making reservations.

FINDING YOUR HOTEL

Many hotels in Mexico are difficult to find. In towns, street names frequently change from block to block or the signs continue to use an outdated name that no longer exists— many times you cannot find a street sign at all! If there is no street number, the address reads s/n (which translates "without number"). The situation doesn't improve much in the countryside. Some of the hotels (especially the haciendas on the Yucatán Peninsula and the beach hideaways along the Costa Alegre) are not in any town at all and their addresses only hint at a nearby location. However, some things make finding your hotel easier. In cities, most hotels are marked by signs pointing you in the right direction. In the countryside, your life is made easier if you watch the signs that mark the kilometers along the roads (these are much like the old "milestones" in England). Some hotels use these signs in their addresses, such as "located at Km 12," which makes finding the hotel very simple. When making reservations, ask for the closest kilometer sign to the hotel. In all cases, buy a detailed map in advance of your arrival and mark your hotel. To supplement your map, ask the hotel to send exact driving directions and, if possible, a local map.

ICONS

Supplementing each hotel's description is a series of icons that provide additional information about each property. When using our website to supplement the guides, positioning the cursor over an icon will in many cases give you further details. For easy reference an icon key can be found on the last page of the book.

We have introduced these icons in the guidebooks and there are more on our website, *www.karenbrown.com.* ❄ Air conditioning in rooms, ☎ Archaeological site nearby, ▣ Breakfast included in room rate, ✅ Children welcome, ♨ Cooking classes offered, ▦ Credit cards accepted, ☎ Direct-dial telephone in room, ⌂ Dogs by special request, ⛲ Elevator, ⚒ Exercise room, Υ Mini-refrigerator in room, ⊘ Non-smoking rooms, P Parking available, ⑆ Restaurant, ≈ Swimming pool, ⚡ Tennis, ▣ Television, ⚘ Wedding facilities, ♿ Wheelchair friendly, ⊥ Beach nearby, ⚐ Golf course nearby, ⚐⚐ Hiking trails nearby, ⛷ Horseback riding nearby, ⚡ Skiing nearby, ⚓ Water sports nearby, ⚑ Wineries nearby.

PLUNGE POOL

You will notice in the hotel description section that we mention some hotels have "plunge" pools. Several people unfamiliar with the term have asked what this means. This is a term frequently used in Mexico and designates a small pool that was never intended for swimming, but is used for relaxing and dips to cool off while sunbathing. Most of these romantic plunge pools are in deluxe hotels and are private to the room.

RATES

In our other guides we quote room rates in the currency of the country but we have made an exception in the case of Mexico since almost all hotels quote rates in U.S. dollars instead of pesos (though the final bill is calculated in pesos). The rates shown are approximate, based on a double room for two persons in the high season. There might be special surcharges added during Christmas, Easter, or festival times, while sometimes rates are substantially lower during the off season. The rates cover the range of room prices from standard to deluxe but there might be a few special rooms such as a presidential suite offered at substantially higher prices than those shown. Some of the hotels include breakfast in their quoted room rate; some include breakfast and dinner; some include all meals. This is noted in the details for each hotel. When some or all meals are included, you are generally receiving very good value. Some hotels charge extra for parking. We indicate if the hotel has parking available but you will need to ask when you make your reservation if there is a charge.

Be aware that hotel taxes are high in Mexico, varying between 12% and 17%. Some hotels include this tax in their quoted tariff. If not, we indicate that tax is added and the percentage since this is very important when comparing values. Also, be aware that some hotels add an extra service charge to their rates. We find this trend growing, especially in deluxe hotels in popular resort areas. We have noted when hotels add a service charge and the percentage so that you won't be surprised at your final bill.

It is very important to remember the rates shown for each hotel are approximate. Be sure to ask exactly the rate for the period when you are traveling and what the rate includes (such as meals) and what extras are added (such as tax and service charge).

RESERVATIONS

We recommend advance hotel reservations. If you are traveling off-season, you can probably do fine by calling ahead the day you want a room, but don't expect to just stop en route: there are very few choices of places to stay except in major cities or resort areas. There are almost no motels, and hotels off the beaten path are rare and usually offer very basic accommodations. If you are traveling during peak travel periods (Easter, Christmas, and mid-July through mid-August), you will find hotel space very scarce. When you make advance reservations, most hotels will want a deposit and if you cancel, you might not be able to get your money back, so, when making a reservation, ask what the penalty is. To protect yourself in case you have to cancel due to illness, we recommend cancellation insurance. A link on our website (*www.karenbrown.com*) will connect you to a variety of insurance policies that can be purchased online.

HOW TO MAKE RESERVATIONS

E-MAIL: This is our preferred way of making a reservation. Many hotels have an e-mail address, which can be found by going to the hotel's page on our website, *www.karenbrown.com*. You can link directly to a property from its page on our website using its e-mail hyperlink. (Note: Not all hotels choose to be included in our website.)

FAX: If faxing, be aware that even if the hotel has a fax number, the fax machine is sometimes turned off (especially at night) and fax lines are sometimes shared with phone lines, making connections difficult. If faxing from the United States, dial 011 (the international code), then 52 (Mexico code), then the city code and local number.

LETTER: Mail service is slow; letters sometimes take up to one month to be delivered.

PHONE: If dialing from the United States, dial 011 (the international code), then 52 (Mexico code), then the city code and local number.

TRAVEL AGENT: A travel agent can be of great assistance, particularly if your own time is limited. The majority of travel agencies charge for their services.

UNITED STATES REPRESENTATIVES: In the back of the book there is a page giving information on KB Travel Service, a company that specializes in hotels recommended by Karen Brown.

WHEELCHAIR ACCESSIBILITY

If an inn has *at least* one guestroom that is accessible by wheelchair, it is noted with the symbol ♿. This is not the same as saying it meets full disability standards. In reality, it can be anything from a basic ground-floor room to a fully equipped facility. Please discuss your requirements when you call your chosen place to stay to determine if they have accommodation that suits your needs and preference.

About Itineraries

Mitla, Vendors in Front of the Church

We have put together itineraries covering Mexico's many fascinating towns, rich archaeological sites, remarkable natural wonders, and delightful beach resorts. These itineraries tie in with suggestions for romantic places to stay. If possible, try to combine one or more itineraries. As an example, top off a week climbing pyramids in the Yucatán Peninsula with several days stretched out on a hammock on one of the unsurpassed beaches of the Riviera Maya. For those who are apprehensive about driving, we begin our selection of itineraries with *Colonial Gems: Charming Towns by Car or Bus,* designed for those who want to get off the beaten path but prefer not to drive. This itinerary gives two ways to get to each destination: one by car and one by bus. Contrary to the situation in Europe, deluxe or first-class bus transportation is the preferred means of public transportation between towns within Mexico.

In addition to Colonial gems, our itineraries cover Mexico City and the surrounding valley, Oaxaca and its nearby archaeological sites, the Yucatán Peninsula with its Mayan ruins, and the natural wonders of whale watching, the Monarch butterfly, and the Copper Canyon. For those whose idea of a holiday is to head for the beach, we also offer itineraries that feature places to play in the sun, including beach resorts on both coasts of Mexico and on the Baja Peninsula.

In the back of the book in the map section the itineraries are marked in different colors on the same maps where hotel locations are shown. The first map gives an overview of all the itineraries.

COMMERCIAL MAPS

If you are driving, you will need to buy detailed maps. The most comprehensive maps for Mexico are called *Guia Roji* or Red Guides, though we have found that even the very latest of these maps do not always show the most recently opened roads (especially on the Yucatán Peninsula). In addition to a map of the country and individual state maps, the *Guia Roji* has an excellent atlas that includes almost all of the towns mentioned in this book. For where to buy *Guia Roji* maps, look on our website, *www.karenbrown.com*.

General Information

CAR RENTAL

Many major U.S. car rental companies operate in Mexico. It is best to stick to well-known companies, as many of the lesser-known franchises are not properly supervised. Rental fees are in general higher than in the United States, Canada, and Europe. A compact car will cost about $85 per day and the car will probably not be delivered to you with a full tank of gas. You must return the car only to the office where you rented it or an additional fee will be added. Often during high season there are not enough cars to meet demand so it is best to make reservations in advance.

CREDIT CARDS

HOTELS: Most major hotels accept credit cards but many of the smaller ones will accept payment only in cash. Whether or not a property accepts credit cards is indicated in the list of icons at the bottom of each hotel description by the symbol ▭. We have also indicated the specific cards accepted by using the following codes: AX–American

Express, MC–MasterCard, VS–Visa, or simply, all major. Note: Even if an inn does not accept credit card payment, it will sometimes request your account number as a guarantee of arrival.

RESTAURANTS: In large cities that cater to the tourist trade credit cards are generally accepted; however, once off the beaten path, be prepared to pay in cash.

SHOPPING: Large stores usually accept credit cards, but small boutiques and street vendors with whom you negotiate a price usually accept cash only.

SERVICE STATIONS: *Very* few service stations accept credit cards as payment for gas. Since fuel is a major expense while on the road, be sure you have sufficient cash.

DRIVING

BORDER CROSSING: Allow at least an hour to cross the border. Since September 11, the time can be much greater. Expect delays, especially during peak hours of the day or holidays when traffic is more intense. If you are driving across the border, be aware that there are several requirements. These are listed below:

1) Proof of Ownership: A visitor bringing a car into Mexico must have proof of ownership (title or registration). If your car is financed, you must have a notarized letter from your financing institution on the company's letterhead giving you permission to drive into Mexico. You may not take someone else's car into Mexico.

2) Forms: You need to fill out two forms: a *Temporary Vehicle Importation* permit, and a *Promise to Return Vehicle* form. These forms are available at the border or at AAA club offices in Arizona, California, or Texas.

3) Administration Fee: At point of entry, an administration fee of $21 plus tax must be paid with a credit card. The credit card must be in the registered owner's name and issued by a U.S. or Canadian bank or lending institution. *Cash or checks are not accepted.* A sticker is applied to your windshield after you pay the administration fee. If you do *not* have a credit card, you must purchase a bond valid for 6 months (based on the value of your car) from a bonding company at the border.

4) Mexican Insurance: You must have Mexican car insurance. You can buy insurance at the border or in advance from AAA clubs in Arizona, California, or Texas.

5) Additional documents that must be presented at the border:

Proof of citizenship
Valid driver's license
A tourist permit
Current vehicle license/registration receipt

6) Children under 18 years of age, if traveling with only one parent, must have a notarized letter from the other parent allowing them to travel. If traveling without either parent, children need a notarized letter from both parents allowing them to travel (see Entry Requirements below).

After crossing into Mexico, there are two stops where inspectors will check to be sure you have the proper permits and the stickers.

Note that there are certain "free zones" that do not require all the permits listed above. These are generally border towns (within 25 kilometers of the border), the Baja Peninsula, and the state of Sonora. You will encounter checkpoints south of these free zones so do not try to cross without the proper paperwork if you plan to travel farther south.

CUOTA: (TOLL HIGHWAY) Mexico has developed an extensive system of new toll highways, designated by the letter "D" following the route number. Although tolls can be expensive (Mexico City to Acapulco is approximately $125 one way), we recommend taking these toll roads whenever possible. They are very fast and efficient with very little traffic (trucks usually take the free roads). Non-toll roads are usually slow two-lane roads, which might not be in good condition. Toll roads also have the added bonus of solar-powered emergency telephones every 2 kilometers. Most are four-lane roads greatly resembling U.S. interstate highways, though sometimes they have only two lanes. (The roads are privately financed and therefore can vary from region to region.) Tolls are calculated by distance and number of axles on the vehicle and only cash (pesos and sometimes U.S. dollars) is accepted. You enter through a control gate and are given a ticket then at various points along the highway you come to toll stations where money is collected.

DRIVER'S LICENSE: You need a valid driver's license issued by your home country to drive in Mexico. A Mexican driver's license is not required.

DRIVING AND ALCOHOL: Driving under the influence of alcohol is illegal in Mexico. You can be arrested and taken to jail for drunk driving. If you are involved in an accident and found to be under the influence of alcohol, your insurance will become invalid and you will go to jail.

EMERGENCIES: If you have an emergency while driving, the equivalent of "911" in Mexico is "060." You can also call the Green Angels (see below) for help: (01) 55-250-8221, ext. 130. Toll roads have solar-powered emergency phones for your convenience.

GASOLINE: Gasoline in Mexico is expensive. There are gas stations along all the highways, but be aware that they rarely accept payment by credit card. Also, many gas stations are closed at certain times of the day or on holidays, so be sure you always have plenty of gas in the tank. Gasoline is sold by the liter. Remember to have the attendant "zero" out the pump (meaning starting from zero) to be sure you are not overcharged. It is customary to give the attendant one or two pesos as tip. You should always tip the attendant who washes your window about two pesos.

GREEN ANGELS (*Angeles Verdes*): These are trained bilingual mechanics traveling the nation's highways from 8 am to 8 pm in 275 green trucks to provide emergency service and first aid. They carry car parts and gasoline and charge only for the parts; their service is free, thanks to Mexico's Tourism Secretariat. Just open your hood all the way and hope one drives by or call their toll-free number (in Mexico only) (01) 800-903-9200 or (01) 55-250-8221, ext. 130. Tips are greatly appreciated.

INSURANCE: U.S. insurance is *not* valid in Mexico—you must obtain insurance from a Mexican insurance company, either on the Internet or at the border. Mexican liability insurance is not required by law but highly recommended. Insurance companies are a wealth of information and can help you with all the paperwork required for crossing the border. Be sure your insurance includes claims adjusters who will come to the scene of the accident and an attorney. Mexican insurance is not valid if you are found to be under the influence of drugs or alcohol. Mexican law follows the Napoleonic Code, which means you are guilty until proven innocent. Also note that theft and vandalism are usually not covered by insurance.

NIGHT DRIVING: We recommend that you avoid driving after sunset whenever possible, unless on a toll road. The danger of driving greatly increases at night due to poor street lighting combined with donkeys, dogs, children, potholes, and unknown objects that are commonly in the road. Also, be aware that it is not unusual for cars to have broken taillights, etc.

PARKING: When in cities, it is always safest to leave your car in a parking lot with an attendant or in a parking garage. The cost is reasonable and worth the extra expense for peace of mind. If you are driving, when you make your hotel reservation, ask them if they have parking available and the cost. Many hotels have their own parking lot or, if not, they usually have an arrangement with a nearby garage.

RESTRICTED DRIVING DAYS IN MEXICO CITY: In an effort to reduce pollution, vehicular traffic is restricted in Mexico City on certain days of the week. The restriction is based on the last digit of the vehicle license plate (see following page). Since Saturday and Sunday are the only "free" days for access into the city, if you are driving, plan to arrive on a weekend. Note: Our suggestion is *not* to drive into Mexico City at all—wait until the day you leave before picking up a rental car. You will find a car a nuisance while in the city. The best way to get around is to walk or take a private taxi that is recommended by your hotel.

Prohibited Days & Corresponding License Plate Numbers

Monday: no driving if license plate ends with 5 or 6
Tuesday: no driving if license plate ends with 7 or 8
Wednesday: no driving if license plate ends with 3 or 4
Thursday: no driving if license plate ends with 1 or 2
Friday: no driving if license plate ends with 9 or 0
Saturday and Sunday: all vehicles may be driven.

ROAD SIGNS: Road signs are a mix of international picture symbols and signs in Spanish. Signs on smaller roads are often poorly maintained or absent so it is easy to get lost. Make sure you have a good map. The major roads and toll highways will have good signage displaying the highway number, kilometer marker, and mileage for upcoming cities.

SEATBELTS: By law everyone in the car must wear seatbelts.

ELECTRICITY

The standard voltage in Mexico is 110. For those traveling from the United States, no converters or adaptor plugs are needed.

ENTRY REQUIREMENTS

Unless you are traveling to one of the free zones within 25 kilometers of the border, everyone (including children) entering Mexico must have valid proof of citizenship (passport or birth certificate), a picture ID (if age 18 or older, driver's license or passport), and a tourist card. A tourist card is required upon entering and leaving Mexico for those visiting for up to 180 days. Tourist cards are free and can be obtained at border crossings, Mexican consulates, and tourist offices, and through most airlines serving Mexico. Be sure to keep your tourist card in a safe place. You may want to write down the number and keep it separate in case you lose it. If you wish to stay longer than 180 days, contact the Mexican embassy or consulate to obtain a visa.

Children under 18 traveling without their parents *must* have a *notarized* authorization letter from both parents giving the adult permission to take their child to Mexico. A child traveling with just one parent needs a notarized letter from the absent parent. You will be turned away at the airport or at the border if you do not have the proper paperwork.

Make sure you can return to the United States with the proof of citizenship you take with you. Although some countries require only a birth certificate to enter, United States law now requires that you document both your U.S. citizenship (for example, passport or birth certificate) and identity (valid driver's license or government picture ID) when you re-enter the United States.

ETIQUETTE

Mexicans are gracious, friendly, welcoming hosts. Business is done leisurely and greetings drawn out, so for those used to rushing through the day, things seem to move at a snail's pace. Probably the reverse seems true to Mexicans: they must wonder why their foreign guests dash about without incorporating the charm of genuine courtesy into their human interplay. So, why not slow down a bit? Savor meeting people. If doing business, don't launch into practical matters immediately—instead, do as Mexicans do: shake hands, look at each person, and speak individually to each, asking questions about their family and health. Do the same with informal meetings. Don't rush. Display the same courtesy the Mexicans show to visitors and friends: it can't be faulted.

FACTS

BANK HOURS: Most banks are open Monday through Friday from 9 am to 1:30 pm. In larger cities the banks may reopen from 4 pm to 6 pm and open Saturday from 10 am to 1:30 pm. For currency exchange you usually get a better rate at a *casa de cambio* (money exchange) than you do at a bank, and the transaction is faster.

BUSINESS HOURS: Shops are generally open Monday through Saturday from 10 am to 7 pm. Some smaller stores may close for a few hours' siesta in the afternoon.

CAPITAL: Mexico City, D.F.

CURRENCY: The monetary unit is the peso. The exchange rate as this book went to press was about 9.7 pesos = 1 U.S. dollar. Please note the rate is subject to daily fluctuations.

GOVERNMENT: Federal Republic.

LANGUAGE: Spanish, with some 50 Indian languages and dialects being spoken outside major cities and towns. English is also widely spoken.

POPULATION: 101,879,000 (July 2001 estimate). Mexico City and the surrounding metropolitan area are home to nearly 40% of the nation's population.

FESTIVALS & HOLIDAYS

Festivals and holidays are a time for celebration in Mexico and frequently music, colorful costumes, dancing and parades can be enjoyed, especially in smaller villages. On the majority of the holidays, banks and commercial offices are closed.

Año Nuevo (January 1): New Year's Day.

Día de los Santos Reyes (Day of the Kings, January 6): This day ends the Christmas festivities. Gifts are exchanged, symbolizing the gifts brought to Jesus by the three wise men. There is usually a party with food, drink and candy-filled piñatas for the children.

Día de la Constitución (February 5): The commemoration of Mexico's Constitution.

Carnival (February/March): The days preceding the rigors of Lent are celebrated nationally with extravagant parades, floats, confetti, dancing, and the burning of effigies.

Natalicio de Benito Juárez (Birthday of Benito Juárez, March 21): This commemorates the birthday of Benito Juárez, one of Mexico's national heroes.

Semana Santa (Holy Week, March/April, Good Friday through Easter): A very important time that is celebrated all over Mexico. Many parades and passion plays are performed, especially in the southern states and in the Colonial towns.

Cinco de Mayo (May 5): The commemoration of the Battle of Puebla, a Mexican victory over the invading French army in 1862.

Día de la Independencia (Independence Day, September 16): Father Miguel Hidalgo's cry to arms to free Mexico of Spanish rule in 1810 is commemorated all over Mexico. Fiestas take place in every town square on the evening of the 15th, including fireworks, music, and the throwing of eggshells filled with confetti. Children wear national costumes or dress as Independence heroes and many parades take place.

Descubrimento de América (Discovery of America by Columbus, October 12): Commemorates Columbus's arrival in the Americas.

Día de los Muertos (Day of the Dead, November 1 to 2): Mexico's most colorful fiesta, celebrating the belief that once a year the dead have permission to return to earth and visit friends and relatives. During the Day of the Dead the living welcome the souls of the departed with special foods, flowers, candles, and incense. This is an occasion for gaiety and parties. To celebrate the day, artists often portray death with humor, making rather gruesome yet whimsical skull and skeleton artifacts.

Día de la Revolución (Day of the Revolution, November 20): This day celebrates the Mexican Revolution of 1910.

Fiesta de Nuestra Señora de Guadalupe (December 12): The appearance of Mexico's patron saint in 1531 on the Cerro del Tepeyac hill is remembered in every town and village. Thousands of pilgrims flock to her shrine in Mexico City. In the rest of the country Las Mañanitas, an early-morning birthday song, is sung at dawn and special church services are attended.

Las Posadas (Christmas Season): This begins December 16 with the reenactment of Mary and Joseph searching for a place to spend the night while Mary delivers her baby. For nine nights people carry lighted candles and figures of Mary and Joseph as they travel between homes begging for a place to lay their heads. They are greeted at each house with gifts of food.

Navidad (Christmas Day, December 25).

GUIDES (LOCAL)

A local guide is of great value. To select a knowledgeable, reputable guide, we recommend asking at your hotel for recommendations and rates. We particularly recommend that you hire a car with an English-speaking driver/guide when you are in Mexico City because there is a higher incidence of crime there, some involving cabs. But safety isn't the only reason: a guide can greatly enhance your sightseeing experience. If you have several people in your group, then a car and driver is frequently less costly than a package bus tour, and much more personal.

HEALTH

WATER: Because some people get sick when drinking any water that is different from what they are used to at home, we suggest you use bottled water. Many of the deluxe hotels purify their water and if so, it is safe to drink. If your accommodations have a kitchenette, you can always boil water before using it. Almost all hotels serve their drinks with ice made from purified water. If in doubt, ask. When driving, it is a good idea to buy some bottled water to drink along the way. When visiting arcaheological sites, be *sure* to carry a few bottles of water with you. It is not always available to buy and you will need a refreshing drink while exploring the ruins and climbing pyramids!

FOOD: Don't buy food at roadside stands. Although you might be tempted because the aroma is usually bewitching, just remember there is little sanitation available at these stands so it difficult to wash hands or utensils to meet high standards of sanitation. Avoid seafood, fruits, and vegetables that you have not peeled yourself or that cannot be cooked. Also avoid unpasteurized dairy products.

INFORMATION SOURCES

If you have questions not answered in this guide or need special guidance for a particular destination, the Mexican National Tourist Offices can assist you. If you have access to the Internet you may want to visit their websites, *www.visitmexico.com* or *www.mexico-travel.com*. The Mexican Tourist Office's general information line, toll-free from the United States and Canada, is (800) 446-3942. For electronic (print-ready) information, send an e-mail to contact@visitmexico.com.

In an emergency, contact the Mexican Ministry of Tourism's 24-hour hotline: within Mexico, toll-free (91) 800.90.392; from the United States, (800) 482-9832.

MEXICAN TOURIST OFFICES

Los Angeles: Mexico Government Tourist Office, 2401, West 6th Street, 5th Floor, Los Angeles, CA 90057, USA, Tel: (213) 351-2075, Fax: (213) 351-2074, E-mail: losangeles@visitmexico.com

New York: Mexican Tourist Office, 21 East 63rd Street, New York, NY 10021, USA, Tel: (212) 821-0314, Fax: (212) 821-0367, E-mail: info@mexicantourismboard-ny.org

Montreal: Mexican Tourist Office, Place Ville Marie, Suite 1931, Montreal, Quebec H3B 2C3, Canada, Tel: (514) 871-1052, Fax: (514) 871-3825, E-mail: turimex@cam.org

London: Mexico Government Tourist Office, 41 Trinity Square, Wakefield House, London EC3N 4DJ, Tel: (207) 488 93 92 or (207) 265 07 05, Fax: (207) 265 07 04, E-mail: uk@visitmexico.com

TOURIST OFFICES IN MEXICO: Almost all towns throughout Mexico have a local tourist office. We strongly recommend that, during your travels, you make a beeline for the closest office for current information on local events. The tourist offices, which are generally located on, or near, the central plaza, usually have maps and information on what to see in the town and the surrounding area.

LANGUAGE

Spanish is the official language in Mexico. In cities or popular resort areas, almost all of the hotels have English-speaking staff available to help you. In some of the more remote areas, you might encounter situations where English is not spoken. Under Vocabulary we have given a few common words to help you get along. However, the best bet is to carry a small pocket-sized dictionary and point to some of the words if you need assistance. There should never be a problem checking into your hotel because the receptionist will have your name if you have a reservation. Carry your confirmation with you to make check-in easier.

MAPS

There is a map section in the back of the guide with the following maps:

OVERVIEW MAP: The first page of the map section shows an overview map with the route of each itinerary indicated in a different color.

MAP OF STATES: This map shows the states of Mexico.

New York: Mexican Tourist Office, 21 East 63rd Street, New York, NY 10021, USA, Tel: (212) 821-0314, Fax: (212) 821-0367, E-mail: info@mexicantourismboard-ny.org

HOTEL LOCATION MAPS: On the top line of each hotel's description there is a map number which corresponds to one of the four numbered maps in the back of the book where the towns with recommended hotels are marked in red.

ITINERARY MAPS: Itinerary routings are superimposed on the same maps that show hotel locations at the back of the book. Each itinerary is highlighted in a different color.

MONEY MATTERS

The peso is the unit of currency in Mexico. The *nuevo peso* (new peso) was introduced in 1993 and comes in 10-, 20-, 50-, 100-, 500-, and 1,000-peso notes. The symbol for the peso is the same as the dollar sign used in the USA, which can be a little confusing. In the information given for each hotel, the dollar sign represents U.S. dollars. In our other guides we show the hotel rate in the currency of the country but Mexican hotels are so geared to the American tourist that their rates are always quoted in dollars.

ATM MACHINES: It is very quick and easy to get money through one of the ATM machines that are found throughout Mexico, often even in small towns. They are usually located at a bank or on one of the main shopping streets. Try to use ATM machines inside banks and avoid using them at night. Note that some U.S. banks are now charging an exchange fee for obtaining money abroad (you might want to check with your bank before you go).

MONEY EXCHANGE: Contrary to the situation in many countries, in Mexico you can usually get a better rate of exchange at a *casa de cambio* (money-exchange booth) than at a bank. Also, banks are usually crowded and frequently closed, making the money exchange even more user-friendly. Most hotels will also usually exchange your money, but the rate is generally a bit higher.

PHOTOGRAPHY

In any country one should show common courtesy when photographing people. Blatantly photographing people can be intrusive and should never be done without asking.

However, in some of the remote villages in the state of Chiapas taking photos is more than just impolite: it is actually against the law.

SAFETY

Some people are concerned about safety when visiting Mexico, but we have traveled there several times a year for many years and have had less of a problem with crime than we have had in other countries. Basically, it is a very safe place to visit. However, the same logical safety precautions should be taken as when traveling anywhere. Don't tout your wealth by wearing expensive jewelry. Don't leave valuables within sight in your car. Lock your car and park it in an attended parking lot or parking garage. If traveling by bus, take a first-class (*primera*) or deluxe (*lujo*) bus. When cashing money in a bank or at an exchange or ATM, be discreet and don't flaunt your pesos. When in Mexico City, ask the concierge at your hotel to call you a taxi—don't pick one up on the street. When arriving at airports, never just pick up a random cab, but take one of the taxis or vans that are authorized by the airport and for which you can buy a prepaid ticket at the airport transportation counter. Always use a government-approved guide when sightseeing. Keep your valuables locked in the hotel safe or in the safe in your room. Don't keep your wallet in your back pocket. When in crowded tourist areas, always be watchful of your purse and preferably use a purse with a strap over your shoulder or else a pouch around your waist.

Unfortunately, Mexico City has received adverse publicity about safety problems— undoubtedly some of it justified. However, the government is working diligently to make the tourist feel more secure. Everywhere you go there are many policemen about, which makes one feel especially safe. One of the most recent innovations is the use of policemen who double as tourist "helpers" and not only graciously give advice, but also are at hand in case of an emergency. The one area that we consider a bit "iffy" is the state of Chiapas where political discontent and poverty have resulted in more crime than in other parts of the country. If traveling in Chiapas, be cautious about using public transportation and if you are driving, stay on the major roads and drive only in daylight hours.

SHOPPING

ITEMS TO BUY: Mexican handicrafts are very popular and various regions or towns excel in one or more crafts. These items have often been made for generations are great gifts to bring home.

Woven goods such as *ponchos* (woolen blankets worn by men), *serapes* (woolen shawls worn by women), rugs, colorful tapestries, and blankets are easy to find in assorted styles, qualities, and prices.

Silver jewelry is sold almost everywhere in Mexico, but Taxco is the most famous town for beautiful designs by skilled craftsmen.

Hand-blown glass is made in Guadalajara, Monterrey, and Mexico City. *Wooden furniture, guitars*, and beautiful *copper items* are commonly found in the Colonial areas. Oaxaca and the Copper Canyon are noted for their *woven baskets* and *leather goods*.

Pottery is one of Mexico's biggest craft industries. The most famous is gorgeous Talavera pottery, which principally comes from two places, Puebla near Mexico City and Dolores Hidalgo near San Miguel de Allende.

Archaeological artifacts: At some archaeological sites you may find people selling objects they have supposedly found. Refuse these offers. Mexican law states that it is illegal to export antiques or items that can be described as national treasures.

TAXES

Mexico levies a 15% value added tax (IVA) on all goods and services (10% in some areas such as Baja and Cancún). The tax is supposed to be included in the posted price.

TELEPHONES

OVERSEAS CALLS: Making calls from Mexico is not the hassle it once was, but there are a few things to keep in mind. Most hotels have a phone system but we advise *not* charging calls to your room as charges can quickly soar to over $100. This is not because the hotel is trying to take advantage of you, but because long-distance calls are extraordinarily expensive in Mexico. It is more economical to charge your calls to your AT&T, MCI, or SPRINT calling card (you can request one from your telephone company before leaving home). Each of these companies has a local number in Mexico that will connect you to the USA. AT&T: (001) 880-462-4240; MCI: (001) 880-674-7000; SPRINT: (001) 880-877-8000.

Another option is to buy a Ladatel card. Most public phones are labeled Telemex (the national telephone company) and are part of the Ladatel (long-distance) phone system. You can purchase these cards in different peso denominations at most pharmacies and gas stations or vending machines at airports and bus stations. You swipe the card, enter the access number on the card, and place your call. It is very easy and efficient.

CALLING WITHIN MEXICO: Some hotels may charge for local calls, so you should ask before using the phone in your room. Your hotel concierge may be able to place most calls for you from the hotel's lobby (restaurant reservations, arranging a local tour, etc). Public phones take Ladatel cards for local as well as long-distance calls. For long-distance calls within Mexico dial 01 followed by the area code and the number.

TIPPING

In Mexico it is customary to tip waiters, maids, porters, and guides (make sure that a service charge has not already been added to your restaurant bill). Percentages for hotel and restaurant staff are similar to those in the USA and Canada. Taxi drivers are not usually tipped, except if they have performed some special service. Unlike the United States and Canada, theater ushers and gas station, washroom, and parking attendants all expect to be tipped. In general, calculate $1.50 per person for baggage handlers/porters, $1 per day for chambermaids. Tour guides and drivers should be tipped based on the cost of the tour and the quality of the service. Parking lot attendants and valet parking persons should get about 5 pesos.

TRANSPORTATION

AIR TRANSPORTATION: Most visitors come to Mexico by plane. More than 25 of the world's major airlines service Mexico and there are direct flights from many large cities such as Los Angeles, London, Miami, New York, Madrid, Paris, and Frankfurt. There are 60 airports in Mexico, 15 of which operate international flights. Mexicana and

Aeromexico are Mexico's largest airlines. You can fly to many small towns in Mexico using domestic airlines. Although the distances might look short enough to drive, you may want to consider air travel because travel time by car or bus may be prohibitive.

BUSES: Mexico has the largest bus system in the world, with more than 840 bus companies operating over 44,000 buses. Many Mexicans do not own a car, so buses are widely used and are available to take you to the tiniest town on the map. Every bus company labels their class of service differently so you need to ask what amenities are offered. We recommend that you use only the two top-category buses: *executive/deluxe/lujo* (the highest class of service offering fully air-conditioned buses with larger reclining seats and leg rests comfortable enough for overnight trips) or *first/plus/primera* (a high-quality bus with restrooms, air conditioning, cassette music). A few tips: Be sure to ask for a direct bus (*directo*), which makes only a few stops, or no stops (*sin escalas*)—avoid ones with lots of stops (*con escalas*). Bus tickets (*biletos*) are always sold one-way and you will usually not be refunded if you miss the bus. Your departure gate (*sala*) should be listed on your ticket along with your seat assignment if you are traveling on a first- or deluxe-class bus. Buying your bus ticket can be quite bewildering since you have to find the correct bus station (there may be more than one in town) and then need to know which bus company you want since often more than one offers service to your destination. We suggest that you ask the concierge at your hotel to help you with your reservations. Tickets need to be purchased in advance.

There is an international bus terminal in McAllen, Texas that makes traveling to Mexico by bus from the United States a breeze. At other crossing points, one has to get off the bus at the Mexican border, cross the border by foot, taxi, or local bus, and purchase a new ticket at the Mexican bus station on the other side.

CRUISE SHIPS: Mexico offers three basic cruise experiences. The short three- to four-day northern Baja cruises that usually depart from Los Angeles or Ensenada; the seven- to ten-day west coast "Mexican Riviera" cruises, which usually depart from Los Angeles and visit the port towns of Cabo San Lucas, Puerto Vallarta, Mazatlán, and Acapulco;

and cruises to the beautiful Yucatán Peninsula with ports of call including Cancún, Cozumel, and Playa del Carmen. Cruise ship companies serving Mexico include Carnival, Celebrity, Princess, Royal Caribbean, Cruise West, Lindblad Expeditions, and Voyager Cruise Line.

FERRIES: Passenger and car ferries leaving from Santa Rosalia and La Paz connect Baja California to Guaymas, Topolobampo, and Mazatlán on the Pacific mainland. On the Caribbean coast ferries leave from Puerto Morelos (car ferry) and Playa del Carmen (passenger only) to the island of Cozumel. Ferries from Puerto Juárez (passenger only) and Punta Sam (car ferry), both north of Cancún, travel to Isla Mujeres. Another, more expensive ferry leaves for Isla Mujeres from Playa Linda in Cancún four times a day.

TAXIS: Taxis are readily available in most towns and moderately priced. There are only a few things to remember: agree on the fare before getting into the car; if there is a meter, make sure the last fare was cleared; and avoid the green VW bug taxis. If you are in Mexico City, ask your hotel to order a cab for you, as there are many unauthorized cab drivers. If you are looking for a cab from the airport, look for a taxi counter where you prepay your fare and get a ticket before going outside to the taxi station. You do not need to tip taxi drivers unless they provide extra service for you.

TRAINS: The rail service in Mexico has deteriorated in the last few years and as a means of transportation we recommend bus over train travel. One delightful exception is the Chihuahua al Pacifico Railroad, which runs through the Copper Canyon (see our itinerary *The Copper Canyon, A Train Adventure to Hidden Mexico*). This train, although frequently off schedule, is definitely first class. Some tour operators, such as Tauck Tours, also offer train trips through the Copper Canyon using deluxe rail cars.

In addition to the Chihuahua al Pacifico Railroad, another exception is the Expreso Maya, a privately owned and operated train that began service in March, 2002, and runs between Mérida and Palenque. There are from one- to four-night deluxe tours offered that include archaeological sites in the Yucatán Peninsula. The Expreso Maya is expensive, but for train buffs, a great way to see the ruins.

VOCABULARY

Most travelers have had a bit of Spanish somewhere along the road of their schooling. If this holds true for you, you will be surprised at how words will pop back into your memory. It is fun to try your hand at speaking, even if only a few phrases. Below we have a few common words and phrases that might be useful. Before your trip, please do practice a few key phrases that are needed for common courtesy. If nothing else, learn to say "good morning," "good night," "thank you," and "please." A smile and a *please* and *thank you* will work wonders. The Mexicans are exceptionally gracious and you do not need to be fluent in Spanish to be warmly welcomed everywhere.

COMMON WORDS

Aeropuerto, airport
Almohada, pillow
Autobus, bus
Banco, bank
Centro, center of town
Cuchillo, knife
Correo, post office
Cuchara, spoon
Gasolineria, gas station (Pemex)
Jabón, soap
Malecón, boardwalk on waterfront
Mercado, market
Parada de autobus, bus stop
Plato, plate
Playa, beach
Restaurante, restaurant
Sanitarios, toilet
Servilleta, napkin

Tenedor, fork
Terminal de autobuses, bus terminal
Toalla, towel
Vaso, glass
Zócalo, central square or plaza

PHRASES

Adiós, goodbye
Buenas noches, good night
Buenos días, good morning
Buenos tardes, good afternoon
Cuánto cuesta? how much does it cost?
De nada, you're welcome
Dónde está __? where is __?
Gracias, thank you
Hasta luego, goodbye, see you later
La cuenta por favor, the bill please
Por favor, please
Tiene usted __? do you have __?

FOOD & DRINK

Agua, water
Jugo de Frutas, fruit juices
Almendrado, almond sauce spiced with tomatoes, herbs
Antojitos, snacks
Arroz, rice—staple in diet, served many ways, often with beans
Barbacoa, goat roasted in pit
Burrito, soft flour tortilla, rolled with beans and either meat, seafood, or poultry
Café, coffee
Café con leche, coffee with milk or, often, a glass of hot milk and a jar of Nescafé
Cajeta, carmelized goat milk
Carne, meat
Flautas, small corn tortilla stuffed with beef or chicken, then deep fried
Frijoles, beans—staple of Mexican diet
Cerveza, beer
Ceviche, cocktail of marinated raw fish, with lemon juice, chopped tomato, and onion
Chapulines, tiny grasshoppers fried in oil
Chiles rellenos, poblano peppers stuffed with cheese and/or ground meat then deep fried
Enchiladas, rolled tortillas filled with chicken or cheese, served with green or red sauce
Escamoles, ant eggs, often served with tortillas and guacamole
Flan, baked custard
Fruta, fruit
Guacamole, avocados mashed with onions and tomatoes
Gusanos de maguey, crisp-fried maguey worms
Huevos revueltos, scrambled eggs
Huevos a la Mexicana, scrambled eggs with onions, tomato and chile
Huevos rancheros, fried eggs on corn tortilla topped with red Mexican sauce
Jugo, juice
Licuado, fruit shake

Machaca, dried beef, similar to beef jerky

Machaca con huevo, dried beef scrambled with eggs, onions, tomato

Malteada, milk shake

Mantequilla, butter

Margarita, popular drink made of Tequila and lime juice, served in salt-rimmed glass

Masa, ground corn soaked in lime juice—basis of tortillas, staple of diet

Michelada, beer over ice with lime juice

Mixiote, piquant orange-colored sauce used to marinate meat

Mole negro, rich traditional sauce blending chili peppers, peanuts, garlic, and chocolate

Pan, bread

Papa, potato

Pescado, fish

Picadillo, minced meat mixed with tomato and onion

Pimienta, pepper

Pollo, chicken

Postre, dessert

Pozole, thick corn-based soup with variations throughout Mexico

Quesadilla, tortilla folded in half and stuffed with cheese, meat,or chicken

Refrescos, soft drinks or soda

Sal, salt

Salsa, sauce, most frequently a hot sauce either green or red

Sincronizadas, ham and cheese between two grilled flour tortillas

Sopa de limon: chicken-based soup with wonderful lime flavor

Sopa de frijol, black-bean soup with chunks of fresh cheese and tortilla chips

Sopa tarasca, bean-and-tomato soup with garlic, chilies, fried tortilla strips, and cream

Taco, corn tortilla wrapped around choice of ingredients and eaten by hand

Tamales, meat or chicken covered with corn meal, wrapped and cooked in a cornhusk

Té caliente, hot tea

Tequila, alcoholic beverage made from cactus

Torta, sandwich, usually made with a Mexican roll

Tortilla, thin pancake made of corn or wheat, served in many ways and staple of diet
Tostada, fried corn tortilla topped with chicken or beef, cheese, lettuce, and thick cream
Verdura, vegetable
Vino, wine

WATER

When traveling in remote areas we recommend having an ample supply of bottled water. This is absolutely essential when touring the aracheological sites where the weather is often hot and dry and places to buy water are not always available.

WEBSITE

Please supplement this book by looking at the information provided on our Karen Brown website (*www.karenbrown.com*), which serves as an added dimension to our guides. Most of our favorite hotels are featured on the site (web participation is a hotel's choice) and on their web pages you can usually link to their own websites for even more detailed information and directions. You can also link to their e-mail, so that making reservations is a breeze. Also featured on our site are comments, feedback, and discoveries from you, our readers; information on our latest finds; post-press updates; contest drawings for free books; special offers; unique features such as recipes and favorite destinations; and special savings offered by certain properties.

WHEN TO TRAVEL

Spring and fall are lovely times to travel throughout Mexico, but each season has its advantages. At the beach resorts, both on the east and west coasts, the hottest months are September and October. Although the thermometer doesn't read significantly higher than the rest of the year, the days seem muggier since this is the tail end of the rainy season and the humidity has had time to build up. If you want to miss the crowds (and frequently higher hotel costs), avoid traveling during Mexican holidays: Christmas, Easter, and school vacation (mid-July to mid-August). During these periods hotel space is at a premium and the resort areas crowded. November through June is usually lovely at the beach resorts and summer is very nice there also—although you might have some tropical showers, which commonly happen in the late afternoon. The east coast faces the Caribbean where hurricanes occasionally occur between mid-August through October. If your target is one of the major cities, really any time is a great time to travel, but in central Mexico, remember to bring warm clothes since the evenings are often chilly due to the high altitude.

Colonial Gems
Charming Towns by Car or Bus

Guadalajara, Cathedral

The following itinerary covers the trail of the Spaniards who built a necklace of beautiful towns as they spread their influence throughout the country. There is no better way to experience the romance and history of Mexico than following the path of these conquistadors. When Cortés arrived in Veracruz, he made a bravado gesture, burning the small ships that brought him and his soldiers to the New World. The message was clear—his men were supposed to stay, and stay they did. After the fall of the Aztec capital of Tenochtitlán, the conquistadors spread throughout Mexico, hoping to make their fortunes in the New World. Because precious metals presented the quickest path to wealth, these adventurous men, young and old, fanned out across the country looking for gold and silver. They were quickly followed over the years by newcomers from Spain, almost all looking for fortunes, which is why the majority of Colonial towns you see today had their roots in mining. What makes following the footsteps of these conquistadors especially intriguing is that some of the most beautiful of these early mansions, convents, and haciendas have come to life again as outstanding small hotels that simply ooze with charm.

Mexico abounds with these historic Colonial cities, which strongly reflect the architecture and layout of the towns where the conquistadors were born. As you travel in some of these lovely Colonial towns, you will think you are in Spain. However, the towns possess an extra richness, since when you look closely, a subtle Indian influence is always there—such as an Indian god discreetly worked in amongst the Christian images. Visiting these cities, you are magically transported back three hundred years. You can almost hear the clatter of horses' hooves on the cobbled streets and smell the fragrance of romance in the air.

These towns founded by the Spaniards look much as they did when built hundreds of years ago. The sturdy, handsome buildings, usually made of stone, look a bit stern from the outside and it is not until you enter through the massive wooden doors that their beauty is revealed, for the Spaniards secreted their delights within. Almost all homes have a central, enclosed courtyard with a lush garden enhanced by fragrant flowers, fountains, and trees. On the ground level is the family living area with dining room, parlors, and kitchen, and a wide, open stone staircase leading to the floors above. Galleried walkways (with bedrooms opening onto them) wrap around the upper floors and look down into the garden below. Small balconies adorned with black wrought iron embellish the upper windows overlooking the street, while intricate black wrought-iron lamps embrace each side of the entrance, adding both decoration and light. A huge, thick wooden door with iron braces is typically framed by an arched doorway, which is often surmounted by a carved-stone plaque displaying the original owner's family crest (escutcheon).

Not only the architecture of the buildings looks like "Old Spain," but also the design of the towns. Every town founded by the Spanish, even the tiniest, has a central square (*zócalo*) where the most important buildings and the homes of the wealthy were found. These squares generally have arcaded walkways on four sides and are like parks with trees, gardens, benches, and paths radiating from a central fountain or bandstand. The larger towns have a series of squares, but there is always a central one that is the most important, usually with a church on one side. Note: Although usually called a *zócalo,* this central square is sometimes called a *plaza* or *jardín* (garden).

Throughout all of Mexico many cities retain some hint of their Spanish heritage. Some have totally lost their appeal due to the intrusion of modern buildings, but others remain absolute jewels. At first encounter, some of the places we recommend appear to be huge modern cities (which they are), but have absolutely charming historic centers. Listed below are some of our favorite Colonial cities, many of which are described in this itinerary (others are featured in other itineraries and are so marked). The towns that have an asterisk (*) in front of them are exceptionally romantic jewels with very little from the modern world to spoil their charm.

COLONIAL TOWNS

Alamos (*Copper Canyon)*
Guadalajara
* Guanajuato
Mérida (*Mayan Mysteries)*
Mexico City
Morelia
* Oaxaca (*Oaxaca Valley)*

PERSONAL FAVORITES

Querétaro
* Pátzcuaro
* Puebla (*Mexico City & Beyond)*
* San Miguel de Allende
* Taxco (*Mexico City & Beyond)*
* Tlaxcala (*Mexico City & Beyond)*
Zacatecas

CHOICE OF TRANSPORTATION

Because these Colonial cities are highlights of Mexico, we designed this itinerary so that it could be used by everyone, including those who prefer not to drive. Therefore, we purposely planned this routing with stopovers in towns that are linked by good bus service and we explain with each destination how to use public transportation. We give times just as an indication to give you an idea of departure times and length of trip. Please be sure to verify current departure times.

A car offers greater flexibility, but bus transportation also works just fine. If you choose a deluxe line, the buses are excellent. Trains, with a few exceptions, are dreary, rarely on schedule, and much slower than direct bus service. Our introduction has in-depth information on Mexican buses, but here we'll repeat a few of the key factors in planning. Always choose the most deluxe bus company and take only a direct bus. Unless you are fluent in Spanish, ask the concierge at your hotel to arrange a taxi with instructions that you will pay the extra cost for the driver to go into the bus station with you and help you buy your ticket and show you where to board your bus. Some of the bus stations are pretty well organized, but others are quite confusing—so many people milling about and so many ticket counters, many of them seeming to sell tickets to the same destination.

It's really hard to know just where to go and which ticket to purchase. Once you have your ticket and know where to board the bus, the only hard part is over. The first-class buses and deluxe and premium buses are very clean, have reclining seats, toilets, reading lights, and often a snack served en route. Frequently there is a television, but this is no great attribute since the program being shown (often quite loudly) is usually nothing that will interest you. The whole scene, though, is fun. When you arrive at your destination, you really do not need much assistance since there are always taxis available outside the station to take you to your hotel. All you need to do is to tell the taxi driver where you want to go. If you don't speak Spanish, you might want to write down in advance the name and address of your hotel to show the driver.

RECOMMENDED PACING: We suggest eleven nights to follow this itinerary, more if you want to savor each destination in a leisurely fashion. With optimum bus connections in mind, we planned this itinerary as a loop, beginning and ending in Mexico City (or if you prefer, beginning and ending in Guadalajara). If you are driving, you could zigzag this itinerary, making it a one-way trip between the two cities. We recommend three nights in Mexico City, three nights in San Miguel de Allende, two nights in Guadalajara, and three nights in Morelia or Pátzcuaro. If you want to shorten the trip, you could skip one of the stops.

ORIGINATING CITY   MEXICO CITY

When you arrive at the Mexico City airport, don't pick up a cab at the curb or barter with hustlers in the lobby trying to entice you to use their cars. These are unregulated vehicles. Instead, go directly to the transportation booth and buy your ticket for your ride into the city. There is a set price for taxis and mini-vans so you won't need to haggle over the fee. Just tell the ticket agent your destination and you will be charged accordingly and issued a ticket to give to the driver who will take you to your hotel. Mexico City has a great selection of delightful places to stay in every price range. Study the hotels in the back of the guide to see which appeals to you. Note: Because driving is a hassle within the city, wait to rent a car until the day of your departure and use taxis or public transportation until then.

Mexico City with its 22 million inhabitants is the second-largest city in the world, and growing every day. Its importance as a cultural and political center is not new—with its fabulous location on a high, fertile plateau, the site has hosted a great city since long before the Spaniards arrived. The Aztecs had the seat of their flourishing empire here in a magical city they called Tenochtitlán. Set in the middle of a lake and connected to the mainland by causeways, laced with canals, and embellished with palaces and splendid temples, this city was indeed a sight to behold. Even Hernán Cortés, who had seen the wonders of Europe, was overwhelmed by its grandeur.

Three nights will give you two full days to visit some of the city's museums, which depict so richly the heritage of the Mexican people, setting the stage for what you will be seeing on your trip. We cover sightseeing for Mexico City in greater depth in the itinerary *Mexico City & Beyond*, but even through it will be duplicating information, we want to mention a few places you must not miss. Depending upon which hotel you choose, you can either walk or take a cab. Your hotel can arrange a guide or order one of their secure taxis to take you wherever you want to go.

First, head for the Museo Nacional de Antropología, one of the world's most outstanding museums. We first saw it when it opened in 1964 and now, almost 40 years later, it is even more fabulous, with tremendous improvements made in a massive renovation in 2001. The museum has a stunning architectural style with a spacious, partially enclosed central courtyard. Wrapping around the courtyard is a two-story building with 23 rooms displaying with artful elegance artifacts giving the history of the Mexican nation. Don't miss a single room. Visit them all and read the description in English of what you are viewing. Linger at the dioramas that show the glorious city as it was before Cortés's arrival. Enjoy the rooms that show the everyday life of the Indian people. Study carefully the information on the many archaeological sites and peek below the glass floor to see a royal tomb. Push all the buttons on the computerized televisions to watch videos of rituals and customs. You could spend an entire day here, which isn't a problem as there is a very good restaurant for lunch.

The second place you must include is a visit to Mexico City's fabulous zócalo (main square). This in an incredible, huge plaza capturing the magic of Mexico's past and present. It is surrounded by handsome Colonial buildings and dominated on one side by a superb cathedral, all built upon, and with the stones from, the mighty Aztec city that previously occupied the site. Wander through the square admiring its majesty and, of course, visit the breathtaking cathedral. Be sure not to miss the incredible Templo Mayor and Museo del Templo Mayor, which are situated on the northeast corner of the square. Scholars knew that a great Aztec city was the foundation for the one built by the Spaniards, but it wasn't until 1978, when workmen accidentally came upon a fabulous statue of the Moon Goddess, that the archaeologists knew where to dig. They excavated in the plaza to the right of the cathedral and unearthed the Templo Mayor, the most important pyramid in the Aztec world. Today you can explore the ruins by a series of rampways and bridges that crisscross above the excavations. To display the wealth of artifacts that were uncovered, the museum was built next door. Within are over 6,000 artifacts taken from the site, superbly displayed, showing the sophisticated culture that flourished here before the arrival of Cortés. Do not miss the model of Tenochtitlán, the Aztec city that was the predecessor of the one you see today.

DESTINATION I   SAN MIGUEL DE ALLENDE

Your destination today is San Miguel de Allende, one of our favorite Colonial towns, which radiates charm and old-world ambiance. Below is a suggested bus schedule in case you opt for public transportation.

BUS OPTION: We offer you two choices here since, if you take the bus, you might prefer to skip the suggested stop in Querétaro (as sightseeing is more complicated when you have luggage) and go directly on to San Miguel de Allende. The bus station for Querétaro is located south of town, not within walking distance of the historic center.

| 10:05 am | Leave Mexico City, Norte Terminal, ETN bus |
| 2:05 pm | Arrive San Miguel de Allende |

or if you want to make a stopover in Querétaro:

| 9:00 am | Leave Mexico City, Norte Terminal, ETN bus |
| 11:45 am | Arrive Querétaro |

| 3:30 pm | Leave Querétaro, La Central station, ETN bus |
| 4:30 pm | Arrive San Miguel de Allende |

Note: If you prefer more time in Querétaro, you can take a later bus at 7:30 pm, arriving in San Miguel de Allende at 8:30 pm.

CAR OPTION: If you are driving, before leaving Mexico City, purchase a detailed map and ask the concierge at your hotel (or the car rental agent) to highlight the best route out of the city heading north to highway 57. You will need all the help you can get because the confusion and congestion getting in or out of the city is staggering.

En route to San Miguel de Allende, stop at Querétaro, a city dating back to the 16th century. In the mid-1700s Franciscan missionaries founded a church here, but its real growth evolved from its strategic position as a stopping point on the main road between Mexico City and the flourishing silver and gold mines farther north.

You come to the Querétaro exit from 57 about 130 kilometers after leaving Mexico City. Follow signs to the center of the town. As you drive through its outskirts, Querétaro doesn't look too promising, but persevere since its Colonial heart holds much allure. Once you arrive in the historic center, find a parking lot or garage to leave your car and set out on foot. The center is small and has many pedestrian-only areas that are especially inviting for strolling. As you wander the non-touristy historical center you discover tree-lined lanes, baroque churches, intimate plazas enhanced by fountains, pretty gardens, benches set to enjoy the ambiance, small street-side restaurants, jewelry shops selling semi-precious opals and amethysts that are mined in the nearby hills, and ornate 18th-century mansions. If you want to overnight in Querétaro, we recommend two mansions, Mesón de Santa Rosa and La Casa de la Marquesa, which have been turned into outstanding small hotels (their descriptions are in the back of the book).

Before leaving Querétaro, if the timing is right, have lunch in the courtyard of La Casa de la Marquesa—the food is excellent and the ambiance is charming.

San Miguel de Allende

Return to highway 57 and continue north in the direction of San Luis Potosi. After about 38 kilometers, turn left and follow signs to San Miguel de Allende. Without a doubt, this is one of the most enchanting of Mexico's Colonial towns, so perfect that it has been designated as a national monument, which adds to its appeal since modern buildings are prohibited and all renovations must strictly adhere to the purity of the original design. If you want to gently immerse yourself in the delights of Mexico without too much of a cultural jolt, nothing is better suited to your first experience of Colonial Mexico than San Miguel de Allende. The town is a delight to the eye, with winding cobblestone streets, splendid 17th-century mansions, fine craft shops, gorgeous courtyards hidden behind thick wooden doorways, lush gardens, beautiful churches, beckoning art galleries, chic boutiques, and a wealth of appealing small restaurants.

San Miguel de Allende is a favorite of retired Americans and Canadians who are lured here by the beauty of the small town, the warmth of acceptance by the locals, and the delightful weather. Many of them have bought splendid old mansions and restored them to their original beauty. The expatriate element is one of the reasons the town is so appealing: without them there probably wouldn't be such a wealth of cute restaurants or so many lovely shops. Many who have discovered San Miguel are artists and writers, and the town has become known as an artists' colony with the added bonus that boutiques and galleries feature many fine works of original art. The town is also well known for its many language schools, the best known being the Instituto Allende, housed in a once-abandoned, 18th-century hacienda. This has grown into one of the most important schools for fine arts in Latin America, with not only language courses offered, but also year-round classes in fine arts, crafts, and culture.

For the tourist, there is another huge bonus. San Miguel has an abundance of truly outstanding places to stay in every price range that ooze with charm—from intimate bed and breakfasts to exquisite, world-class hotels within 18th-century mansions. Take your choice from the many places we recommend in the back of the book, all of which are either in the center of town or within walking distance. Many have pretty swimming pools nestled in their gardens, making your stay even more enchanting.

The heart of the town is the central plaza, the Jardín Principal (Main Garden). Indeed, it is a garden with a festive bandstand in the center, laurel trees, fanciful fountains, and pathways accented by ornate wrought-iron benches. On Sundays and holidays and in the evenings the square is often closed to traffic and it becomes the scene of what seems like a huge party, with everyone greeting friends, stopping to chat, children buying balloons from vendors, young lovers strolling hand-in-hand, and everyone eating snacks. Although there are many tourists, that doesn't in the least diminish the ambiance. It is real. It is unspoiled. By all means join in the fun—find a spot on one of the benches, buy an ice cream cone or a coffee, perhaps have your shoes shined, smile at the children romping about, and just enjoy watching the festivities around you.

Clustered around the square are many handsome stone buildings fronted by 17th-century archways. One side of the plaza is dominated by the town's landmark, La Parroquia, the parish church. This fanciful creation is not acclaimed as a masterpiece of design, however it is a pure delight with a personality of its own. It was built in 1683 by a local stonemason, an Indian named Ceferino Gutierrez who didn't really know what a proper church was supposed to look like—but that didn't stop him. He was enchanted by a postcard he had seen of a European Gothic church and decided to use it as his inspiration. The story goes that he sketched his plans in the sand with a stick. Since the postcard showed only the front of the church, he had no idea of how to

San Miguel de Allende, La Parroquia

design the back so improvised with a Mexican style. The result is a fanciful creation enhanced by pink spires that stretch into the blue sky.

Of the many churches tucked within the town my favorite is the Oratorio de San Felipe Neri, an extremely appealing church built of pink stone in 1712 by the local Indians. In addition to its many churches, San Miguel de Allende has six patron saints, a delightful excuse for many festivals to honor them. Lining the narrow cobblestone lanes are splendid mansions built by the wealthy aristocracy of the New World, many of which are still private homes. As you meander, if the thick wooden doors are open, discreetly take a peek inside to see the many gorgeous inner courtyards secreted within. On Sundays many of these splendid homes are open to the public. Ask at the tourist office about times.

There is much to see as you stroll the streets including the Teatro Angela Peralta, built in 1873, where many famous artists have performed; the Biblioteca Publica, a library in a beautiful Colonial building that houses Mexico's second-largest English library; the Centro Cultural Ignacio Ramirez, an art institute built within a former convent which has one of the largest interior courtyards found anywhere in the New World; the Santa Casa de Loreto, a chapel built to duplicate its namesake in Loreto, Italy; and Casa de Ignacio Allende, a mid-18th-century home which was the birthplace of Captain Ignacio Allende, famed hero of the War of Independence.

DESTINATION II   GUADALAJARA

Your destination today is Guadalajara, often called the City of Roses. Below is the bus schedule for those using public transportation.

BUS OPTION: If you are taking the bus, we recommend that instead of stopping en route at Guanajuato (as suggested with the car option), you visit it as a side bus trip from San Miguel de Allende. Ask at the tourist office or at your hotel for the schedules—there is frequent service.

4:15 pm   Leave San Miguel de Allende, La Central station, ETN bus
9:15 pm   Arrive Guadalajara, La Central station

CAR OPTION: When planning your drive to Guadalajara, allow enough time to stop en route to have lunch and visit the historic mining town of Guanajuato. From San Miguel de Allende take highway 51 north toward Dolores Hidalgo. About 14 kilometers after leaving San Miguel, turn left and go 3 kilometers farther along an unpaved road to the Santuario de Atotonilco, a lovely 18th-century church built by Father Luis Felipe Neri de Alfaro as a place of spiritual retreat. Inside are many sculptures, canvases, and frescoes painted by Indian artists. It was from this sanctuary that Father Miguel Hidalgo took off to join the Revolution in 1810, taking with him the standard bearing the image of the

Virgin of Guadalupe, which became the flag and symbol for the fight for independence. People from all over Mexico continue to flock to worship at this shrine.

After visiting the Santuario de Atotonilco, continue on highway 51 to Dolores Hidalgo, the town that is considered the cradle of Mexican independence. It was here that Father Hidalgo sounded the church bells on the morning of September 16, 1810, calling the townspeople to take up arms against the Spanish king. This was the beginning of the bloody war that would last for 11 years. Unfortunately for Hidalgo, he was soon captured, then executed, and his head was hung in nearby Guanajuato as a deterrent to liberals wanting freedom. Miguel Hidalgo left his mark in other ways in Dolores Hidalgo. In an effort to help the impoverished parish, he taught them the craft of making colorful ceramics and opened the first shop selling Talavera tiles and pottery. The industry thrives and today Dolores Hidalgo, along with Puebla near Mexico City, is one of the major producers of Talavera pottery in Mexico. Connoisseurs consider the pottery made in Puebla to be finer, but what you see in Dolores Hidalgo is beautiful and usually cheaper—the prices for beautiful lamps, dinnerware, vanities, vases, and colorful tiles are incredibly low. Many of the vendors make their own pottery in factories behind their shops and, if you are interested, will show you how the pottery is made and painted, every step done by hand. There are many shops selling the colorful ware in the center of town and the highway that wraps around town is lined with factories and boutiques. If you want to drive into the center of town, you will find it is not particularly picturesque, but if you are a history buff, you might want to take a look at the statue of Hidalgo in the central plaza and his simple home nearby, now the Museo Casa Hidalgo.

From Dolores Hidalgo take highway 110 for about 50 kilometers to Guanajuato. The road twists through the countryside, dropping down into the town, which nestles in a narrow canyon at base of the hills. In 1559 silver was discovered in the surrounding mountains and Guanajuato soon became one of the richest cities in Mexico, mining an astonishing one third of all the silver produced in the world. You mustn't miss this perfectly preserved city, which has been designated by UNESCO as a World Heritage Site. That being said, be aware that the town is almost impossible to drive into. Even detailed maps won't help you much. The town is largely pedestrian-only and those few streets that allow cars are narrow, poorly marked, and usually one-way. Below the city is a maze of underground tunnels that handle most of the traffic but the problem is that it is hard to know when or where to pop out of the tunnel, and when you do, how to find a place to park. As you drive toward town, there are frequently guides along the road offering to direct you to the center. This is a good idea. Otherwise, park on the outskirts of town and take a taxi. If you are brave, you can give the underground tunnel system a try. Good luck!

Guanajuato, Teatro Juárez

Guanajuato is a photographers' delight, with narrow cobblestone streets, inviting shaded plazas, ornate 18th-century mansions, spectacular churches, and pretty fountains. You can walk everywhere. The town's main plaza, which is in the heart of town, is quite unusual.

Instead of being designed as a square, it is a wedge-shaped plaza called Jardín Union, affectionately nicknamed Pedazo de Queso (Slice of Cheese). This tiny square is delightfully alluring, featuring an old-fashioned bandstand and pretty tiled walkways shaded by centuries-old trees that form an overhead canopy. In the evening strolling musicians add to the festivity of the scene. Located nearby is my favorite building in town, the Teatro Juárez, an ornate theater dating back to 1873 which is fronted by Greek columns adorned by statues of eight muses. Overlooking the plaza is the 17th-century Church of San Diego, a splendid church with an ornate doorway. Originally part of a Jesuit seminary, the Templo de la Compañia de Jesus is quite impressive, with a dramatic dome that looks like that of St. Peter's in Rome. Guanajuato was the birthplace of Diego Rivera, whose home is open as a museum displaying typical furnishings of the period including the brass bed in which he was born in 1886. Within the house is a collection of his paintings and preliminary sketches for his murals. Also visit the 17th-century Basilica of Our Lady of Guanajuato, located on the Plaza de la Paz. Here you find a wooden statue of the Virgin Mary, covered with jewels, that supposedly dates back to 714. King Philip II of Spain sent it to the church as a gift in 1557.

In the village of Valenciana, about ten minutes north of Guanajuato, you can get a glimpse into how vast the mining industry was. Here you find the Hacienda de San Gabriel de la Barrera, the home of a wealthy mine baron which has been restored and furnished with antiques and is now open as a museum. On the property are an outdoor restaurant and gift shop. You can also visit the Valenciana Silver Mine, dating back to 1558, which is still operational and open to the public. The enormously wealthy Count of Valenciana, owner of the mine that bears his name, spared no expense when he built the dazzling Church of San Cayetano, lavishly embellished with gold. Also in Valenciana is one of Guanajuato's most popular restaurants, the Casa del Conde de la Valenciana, which also houses an arts and crafts gallery.

If you want to stay overnight, we recommend two hotels in Guanajuato, the Hotel Posada Santa Fe in the heart of town and the Quinta Las Acacias, tucked in a residential area on a hill just outside the city center. Both are described in the hotel section of our book. If traveling in October or November, you need to reserve rooms far in advance since this is the time of one of the town's major events, the Festival Cervantino.

From Guanajuato, take the toll road in the direction of Leon. About 42 kilometers after the road bypasses Leon, turn west on highway 80, which takes you directly to Guadalajara. Buy a detailed city map in advance so that you can find your way to the hotel of your choice. In the hotel section we recommend several hotels in the city plus a bed and breakfast in the nearby handicraft-shopping mecca, Tlaquepaque.

Guadalajara is a huge, modern, cosmopolitan city with over 5 million inhabitants. It is studded with shady parks, statues highlighting small plazas, tree-lined boulevards, fine museums, world-class restaurants, handsome residential areas, large department stores, and fancy boutiques. However, at first encounter, especially as you drive into the city and experience its horrific traffic, uninspired apartment complexes, and swarm of humanity, you might be a bit less than enthusiastic about what the city has to offer. But hidden within its very heart is the 16th-century Guadalajara, which abounds with historic character. This core of old Guadalajara stretches for seven blocks and is laid out like a cross. At its western end is the Plaza Guadalajara, dominated by a stunning cathedral; at the southern end of the cross is the Plaza de Armas, enhanced by a park with a lacy wrought-iron bandstand where concerts are performed on Thursday and Sunday evenings; at the eastern arm of the cross is Plaza de la Liberacion, named in honor of the heroes of the Revolution for Independence; at the northern arm is Plaza de la Rotonda, enhanced by a ring of Greek columns in the center of its park. The majority of Guadalajara's Colonial architectural gems face onto this seven-block stretch of plazas.

If you are driving, you can park your car in the underground garage before setting out on foot to explore. Stop first at the tourist office located in an 18th-century mansion at Morelos 102 for general information and a map showing suggested walking tours. You must not miss the 15th-century cathedral, which is marked by two towers that soar 200 feet into the sky. Its interior is beautiful, with rows of columns, eleven altars, and fabulous paintings, some of which were donated by King Ferdinand in thanks for the financial help given during the Napoleonic Wars. Another precious work of art, a beautiful sculpture of Our Lady of the Roses, was also given as a gift; this one by King Carlos V. Across from the cathedral is another impressive edifice, the Palacio de Gobierno, which dates back to 1643. It has great historic importance since it was here in 1810 that Father Miguel Hidalgo, leader of the Revolution for Independence, announced the end of slavery. Within you can see a series of murals by one of Mexico's most famous artists, José Clemente Orozco, whose paintings depict the struggle for independence. A stroll down the block from the palace, in a building enhanced by interior courtyards, you find the Museo Regional de Guadalajara, which displays a wealth of exhibits including religious art, paintings, Colonial furniture, portraits, pre-Columbian artifacts, fanciful carriages, pottery, and Indian handicrafts. On Plaza de la Liberación is the stunning Degollado Theater. With its rich red and gold ornate interior and rows of balconies, it is compared by many to Milan's jewel, La Scala. All forms of art are presented here including opera, jazz, classical concerts, and ballet. This theater is also home to the internationally famous dance group, the spectacularly colorful Ballet Folklórico. Ask what is playing while you are in town and try to attend a performance to experience the plush amenities at first hand. Also in the historic center is the Mercado Libertad, a huge indoor marketplace, said to be the largest in the western hemisphere, where vendors sell everything imaginable. For local color, it can't be beat.

In addition to its historic center, Guadalajara has many other attractions for the visitor including many parks. Its largest and oldest, the Parque Agua Azul, not only has gardens, an orchid house, an aviary, and a butterfly sanctuary, but is also home to the Casa de las Artesanias where some of the best handicraft items made in the state are displayed and sold. There is always something going on here—concerts, outdoor theater, festivals, etc.—and it's a great place for strolling and soaking in the spirit of the city at play.

Mariachi music originated in the state of Jalisco, in which Guadalajara is located, so it is no wonder that you hear so much of it here. "Mariachi" derives from the French word for marriage, and its origin is that during the brief period when the French controlled Mexico, they often hired local musicians to play at their weddings. This jolly kind of band usually had at least a guitar, a trumpet, and a violin. Today, mariachis, smartly dressed in spiffy ruffled shirts, fancy jeans, jackets studded with silver, shiny boots, and large sombreros are called upon to celebrate not only weddings, but almost every festive occasion with their happy, exuberant music. If you want a sound dose of entertainment, go on a Sunday to the Plaza de los Mariachis, where roaming musicians perform (it is customary to tip).

If you want to shop for handicrafts, you can drive or take a taxi out to Tlaquepaque, an artists' town located in the suburbs about 9 kilometers from the center of Guadalajara. This once-small crafts village is now all but smothered within the growing sprawl of the city, but at its center Tlaquepaque still retains its charm of yore with cobbled streets, colorfully painted houses, and picturesque Colonial architecture. The heart of town is El Parian, which has at its core a series of restaurants, cafés, and bars—a favorite place to enjoy a cold beer and watch the activities while strolling musicians entertain. Surrounding El Parian, streets stretch out in every direction, lined with cute restaurants, stunning galleries, fine antique shops, and boutiques selling all kinds of crafts including hand-blown glass, articles made of leather, cheerful pottery, hand-loomed fabrics, embroidered clothing, painted furniture, wrought-iron fixtures, and original art. Usually the wares are artistically displayed and with over 300 stores, you are bound to find a treasure. The popular El Palomar pottery, known for its classic, simple design often featuring a dove, is made here. Their shop sells a large variety of items, including bargain "seconds."

OPTIONAL SIDE TRIP FROM GUADALAJARA TO ZACATECAS

If you are captivated by Colonial towns, you might want to take a round trip from Guadalajara to Zacatecas, which was declared a World Heritage Site in 1993. Squeezed in a narrow valley, high in the barren mountains, this once-famous and thriving mining town was one of the largest producers of silver in Mexico.

Since it is off the beaten path and doesn't fit neatly into any other of our other itineraries, this is your best opportunity for a visit if you are so inclined.

BUS OPTION: It is a long, six-hour bus ride from Guadalajara to Zacatecas and we don't really recommend the trip since it is so time-consuming. However, for your information, if you want to try it, the bus company that serves this route is Camions de los Altos: (tel: 333.679.04.55).

CAR OPTION: If you drive to Zacatecas, we suggest making the trip as a loop. Take highway 80 northeast to Lagos de Moreno, then north on highway 45 to Zacatecas, a total drive of about 390 kilometers. On your return, take highway 54 (a two-lane road) south to Guadalajara, about a 320-kilometer drive. En route, stop in La Quemada, mentioned in sightseeing below. Another option would be to drive to Zacatecas after leaving San Miguel de Allende, as a stop before Guadalajara.

Be sure to book ahead at the Quinta Real Zacatecas, a superb, deluxe hotel built within one of Mexico's oldest bullrings. Just across from the hotel, you can see arches of the city's old aqueduct.

The dazzling wealth of this once-prosperous mining town is displayed everywhere you look: opulent mansions, superb churches, ornate theaters, and many museums displaying fine art. You will not want to miss the ornate, pink-stone cathedral, considered by many to be the finest example of baroque architecture in the country. It was built from 1729 to 1752 from the riches of the local mines and its façade, with rows of intricately carved columns framing carved stone statues, is quite unbelievable. Zacatecas had its share of artists, two of whom, brothers Rafael Coronel and Pedro Coronel, donated fabulous museums to the city. One of the most unique museums in town is the Rafael Coronel Museum, in the beautiful Monastery of San Francisco, which displays a staggering private collection of over 5,000 masks and 19th-century marionettes donated by Rafael Coronel.

Not to be outdone, Rafael's brother Pedro gave his extensive collection of art to the city and this is housed in the Pedro Coronel Museum, an old Jesuit monastery. The museum features not only sculptures and paintings by Pedro, but also works of art by Picasso, Dalí, and Chagall. Adjacent is the fabulous Elias Amador Library where an incredible collection of over 25,000 antique books is magnificently displayed.

While in Zacatecas take the *teleférico* (cable car), which glides over the city to the Cerro de la Bufa, the hilltop that was the site of Pancho Villa's most famous battle. There are monuments on the hill commemorating this event. Also on the summit is a beautiful church. When the cable car returns you to town, ask directions for the short walk to La Mina Eden, just a few blocks away. At the entrance to the mine you buy a ticket and a guide leads you through the vast, dimly lit tunnels, hand-hewn by Indian slaves. Along the way you cross suspension bridges over cavernous dropoffs where water has collected. You cannot help being saddened when you see the horrific conditions in which the slaves—men and young boys—worked and died. We were told that not a day ever passed without a fatal accident. At the bottom of the tunnel, your guide leaves you and you board a little train that slowly returns you to a world of light.

About 57 kilometers southwest of Zacatecas on highway 54 there is the interesting pre-Columbian site of La Quemada. A visit here can be made as an excursion by car from Zacatecas or as a stop en route from or back to Guadalajara. La Quemada is a fortress-like pre-Columbian site situated on a hilltop overlooking the valley and the route of the ancient traders. The ruins of its massive buildings and stone walls attest to its ancient purpose of protection for traders and the valuable goods they carried. In addition, it probably also served as a warehouse for collection and storage of goods awaiting transfer by Mesoamerica's long trains of porters. Porters were a vital commodity in pre-Columbian Mexico as beasts of burden were not available and most goods moved on the backs of men. Somewhere around A.D. 1000–1200 the site was destroyed, probably by Chichimec tribes from the northern desert.

DESTINATION III   MORELIA OR PÁTZCUARO

Your destination for the next few days is in the heart of the state of Michoacán. This beautiful state, abounding with lush volcanic hills, dense pine forests, rivers, and lakes, is the homeland of the Tarascan Indians. This group of indigenous people had a number of characteristics that set them apart from the rest of the natives of Mexico. First of all, they spoke a language unrelated to any other in Mesoamerica; secondly, their architecture differed from the style used elsewhere; thirdly, their design and type of clothing was unique; fourthly, while, like the rest of Mesoamerica, they used gold, silver, and copper for items of jewelry, they also learned to make bronze from which they crafted tools and weapons; and finally, their independent kingdom centered at Lake Pátzcuaro was never conquered by the Aztecs. In fact, these two contemporaneous kingdoms, Aztec and Tarascan, were constantly at war with each other, skirmishing along an extensive shared border. It may be that the use of superior bronze weapons by the Tarascans prevented them from being overrun by the aggressive Aztec state.

To explore this region, we suggest you stay in either Morelia or Pátzcuaro, two of our favorite gems in Colonial Mexico. Since they are only 55 kilometers apart, choose one or the other to use as your hub while in the area. Each has its individual personality and great appeal. Morelia, a sophisticated, polished city, displays a rich Colonial charm highlighted by splendid buildings; Pátzcuaro, a simple, picturesque Indian village on a lake, has one of the most gorgeous squares in all of Mexico and abounds with authentic charm. In the hotel section of the book are suggestions for outstanding places to stay in whichever town you decide upon.

BUS OPTION: There is faster service on a better bus from Guadalajara to Morelia than there is from Guadalajara to Pátzcuaro, so if you are staying in Pátzcuaro, consider changing buses in Morelia rather than taking the direct service. Whichever town you choose to use as your base of operations, you will certainly want to visit the other, which is no problem as buses run between the two about every 15 minutes.

9:30 am	Leave Guadalajara, La Central station, ETN bus
1:00 pm	Arrive Morelia (buses leave for Pátzcuaro about every 20 minutes)
or	
11:00 am	Leave Guadalajara, La Central station, Pegasso bus
5:00 pm	Arrive Pátzcuaro

CAR OPTION: From Guadalajara take highway 15 heading southeast toward Mexico City. About 245 kilometers after leaving Guadalajara, turn right when you come to the turnoff for Morelia and continue on for another 24 kilometers to the city. If you are staying in Pátzcuaro, when you come to Morelia, don't go into the center of town but follow signs instead on to Pátzcuaro.

MORELIA

Morelia, the capital of the state of Michoacán, is an attractive, tidy, modern city with many classy stores and well-dressed men and women bustling to and fro. If you circumvent the center of town, you totally miss the best part: its fabulous historic center where you step instantly back to the 16th century when Morelia (whose original name was Old Valladolid) was founded by the Spanish. Its heritage, however, goes back to much earlier times for this rich plateau was the ancestral home of the proud Tarascan Indians and their influence is strongly felt in their native handiwork, which makes this area today one of the richest handicraft areas in Mexico.

Before you begin your sightseeing in Morelia ask at the tourist office or get a map from the concierge at your hotel and mark the places you want to see.

If you are driving, follow signs to the center of town, leave your car in one of the parking garages, and continue on by foot. Wear comfortable shoes because you will be doing a lot of walking. You will be in the vicinity of the main boulevard, Avenida Francisco Madero, which stretches through the center of town and is highlighted by pretty plazas, churches, sculpted gardens, and handsome Spanish-style buildings made of a pastel pinkish-colored stone. It is immediately obvious that Morelia was a prosperous city for its buildings are all grand and the boulevards wide. There aren't many tourists in Morelia, so you get the authentic feel of a *real* city.

A convenient spot to start your explorations of Morelia is on the above-mentioned Avenida Francisco Madero at the Plaza de Armas, nicknamed Plaza de los Mártires (Square of the Martyrs) in honor of two leaders of the Revolution of Independence who were executed here. This is an especially pretty square accented by a fanciful wrought-iron bandstand. This main plaza is easy to find since it is dominated by Morelia's exquisite cathedral, one of the most beautiful in Mexico. Designed and built by Indian artisans, it has a stunning dome embellished with brilliant blue-and-white tile and twin spires that soar over 60 meters into the sky—easily spotted from afar. When you see the immensity of the church, you understand why it took over 80 years to complete. You enter through massive doors covered with intricately tooled leather. Inside there is a central nave with a freestanding altar where an ornate 18th-century silver holder for the Holy Sacrament is displayed. Treasures are also to be found in the side chapels and the baptistery, both of which contain many antiques. If you happen to be in the cathedral when someone is playing the organ, you are in for a special treat since the music from this 4,600-pipe organ is astounding. Also noteworthy is the statue of la Señora de la Sacristía, made from a claylike paste of dried maize and wearing a gold crown, which was donated in the 16th century by the Spanish king, Felipe II.

Clustered within a few blocks of the cathedral are the following recommended sights:

Palacio de Gobierno (Government Palace): Facing onto Avenida Francisco Madero, catty-corner across from the cathedral, is the 18th-century Palacio de Gobierno. Formerly a seminary that educated many of Mexico's most important statesmen, it has been used as the government building since 1867. Step inside to view the sweeping murals depicting the history of Mexico, painted by Alfredo Zalce, one of Mexico's well-known artists.

Museo Regional Michoacán (Regional Museum of Michoacán), corner of Allende and Abasolo: Originally a private mansion where Emperor Maxmillian stayed during his visits to Morelia, this museum displays many pre-Columbian ceramics, Colonial arms, and paintings. Of special interest are Indian codices (most of these rare Indian manuscripts were destroyed by the Spanish). Also of interest is a mural by Alfredo Zalce.

Museo Casa Natal de Morelos (Museum of Morelos's Birthplace), Corregidora 113: The home where Morelia's native hero, José María Morelos, was born in 1765. It is now a library and a museum showing mementos of his life. A torch burns eternally in memory of Morelos.

Museo Casa de Morelos (Museum of Morelos's Later Home), Avenida Morelos Sur 323: This is the home where José María Morelos lived in his later life. This museum shows furniture, personal objects from his life, a wonderful old kitchen, and many displays about the War of Independence, in which Morelos was a hero.

Palacio Clavijero, Nigromante 75: This handsome baroque building, formerly a 17th-century Jesuit college, is now the tourist office. Stop in here for maps and information on places to see and events going on during the time of your visit.

Museo del Estado (State Museum), Guillermo Prieto 176: This tiny museum was the home of Ana Huarte, wife of Agustín Iturbide who was briefly Emperor of Mexico after the execution of Maxmillian. The museum displays archaeological artifacts representing pre-Colombian history and jewelry made by Tarascan Indians. You can see didactic displays showing Indian life in the eight regions of Michoacán. The museum also houses a complete pharmacy with a great exhibit of antique apothecary jars.

Templo y Exconvento de San Francisco (Church and Convent of Saint Francis), Fray Juan de San Miguel 129: This church and convent, built in dramatic Spanish-Moorish style, are some of the oldest buildings in Morelia, dating back to 1525. Today the convent houses the Casa de las Artesania, a museum displaying and selling handicrafts from around the state. As you enter, to your right is a museum with some of Michoacán's finest handmade items on display. A few are for display only, others are for sale. On a galleried upper floor, facing onto the cloister below, is a series of small shops, each representing crafts from Indian villages throughout the state. Sometimes the Indians are working on their crafts as you watch. These shops sell guitars, hand-loomed fabrics, brightly painted lacquer ware, copperware, embroidered clothing, and pottery.

Templo y Exconvento de las Rosas (Church and Convent of the Roses), Santiago Tapia, between Galeana Nigromante and Guillermo Prieto: Facing a small park called Jardín de las Rosas, the Convent of the Roses was built in the 16th century for Dominican nuns then later became a school to house and educate poor children. In 1785 it was converted to a music school which has become internationally famous for its Morelia Boys' Choir. If you are lucky, you might be in Morelia when a concert is being performed; otherwise, you might be able to quietly slip in on a weekday afternoon when they practice.

In addition to the above sightseeing there are a few recommendations that are not clustered around the cathedral. The following sights are still within walking distance, but be prepared for a bit more of a walk—about 4 kilometers round trip from the cathedral to the Santuario de Nuestra Señora de Guadalupe. All can be reached by walking east on Avenida Francisco Madero.

Plaza Villabongin: From the cathedral, turn right onto Avenida Francisco Madero and continue walking for about nine blocks. You will come to a triangular plaza with park, the Plaza Villabongin, which has a fountain featuring a handsome sculpture of three bare-breasted Indian women holding baskets of fruit and vegetables.

Aqueduct: Just beyond the Plaza Villabongin you see one of the symbols of Morelia, its aqueduct, built in the late 1700s to supply water from nearby springs for the growing city. It stretches for an impressive 2 kilometers and has over 250 dramatic high arches in excellent condition, which, when softly illuminated at night, are an impressive sight.

La Calzada Frey Antonio de San Miguel: Go under the aqueduct and continue ahead on La Calzada Frey Antonio de San Miguel. The street was named by Father Antonio de San Miguel who commissioned the aqueduct to be built. This pedestrian esplanade is lined by beautiful 18th-century mansions, which during its heyday housed Morelia's elite. This pretty street, which has a parklike causeway running down the middle, adorned with ash trees and ornate benches, is very tranquil except during the celebration of the Virgin of Guadalupe (early to mid-December), at which time it is very lively and its every inch lined with vendors.

Santuario de Nuestra Señora de Guadalupe (also called Church of San Diego): Continue walking down La Calzada Frey Antonio de San Miguel. The street dead-ends at the Santuario de Nuestra Señora de Guadalupe (Church of San Diego), an 18th-century church that is my favorite in Morelia. The exterior is rather staid and totally belies the treasure within. Step inside and you are surrounded by an interior façade that is awesome. Brilliantly colored plaster rosettes and endless gold totally cover the walls, the ceiling, and the domes. It seems as if you are surrounded by an exquisitely jeweled porcelain egg by Fabergé.

PÁTZCUARO

Pátzcuaro, a small Colonial gem with a strong Indian heritage, is one of our favorite destinations. For the first-time traveler to Mexico wanting to visit just one charming Colonial town, San Miguel de Allende might be a better choice since it is more sophisticated with chic boutiques and upscale restaurants. However, Pátzcuaro gives you the true feeling of being in Mexico, in an authentic Indian village that hasn't been prettied up yet for tourists—it is the real thing. Whereas magnificent 17th- and 18th-century stone mansions embrace the squares, simple one-story whitewashed adobe houses with rustic red-tiled roofs line the surrounding jumble of narrow cobbled streets.

You cannot visit Pátzcuaro without becoming familiar with, and quite a fan of, Don Vasco de Quiroga, a 16th-century bishop who is the heart and soul of the town. He not only dreamed of Pátzcuaro becoming one of the most important towns in the New World, but also influenced the lives of the Indians in all the surrounding villages. This gentle yet dynamic priest was sent by the Spanish king to try to make amends for the cruelty rained upon the Indians by one of the most hated of the Spanish conquistadors, Nuño Beltran de Guzman, a lieutenant of Cortés, whose brutality was so extreme and atrocities so profound that finally the Mexican governor ordered him back to Spain to stand trial for his deeds. Don Vasco de Quiroga was a genius with compassion, great organizational abilities, and profound wisdom. He was beloved by all and even today the local Indians affectionately speak of him as "Tata Vasco" (Uncle Vasco) and remember the years he dedicated to preserving their indigenous culture and improving the lot of their people.

What is especially remarkable is how much Don Vasco was able to accomplish in just a few short years. He was already 60 years old (an age most people think of retiring) when he made the tortuous voyage from Spain to the New World and then, upon his arrival, climbed upon a horse to complete his long journey overland to Pátzcuaro. By the time he died in his 90s, he had accomplished more after the age of 60 than most people could even dream of doing in their lifetime.

Below are suggestions for sightseeing:

Plaza Don Vasco de Quiroga: If for no other reason, Pátzcuaro would be worth a detour to see its stunning Plaza Don Vasco de Quiroga, in our estimation one of the two most beautiful squares in Mexico (our other favorite is the plaza in Tlaxcala—see *Mexico & Beyond* itinerary). This parklike plaza (also called Plaza Grande) it is a real jewel with huge, centuries-old ash trees shading paths radiating from the center, where a large circular fountain highlights a big bronze statue of Don Vasco de Quiroga standing on a pedestal. Stone benches are set along the paths so that you can enjoy the beauty of the plaza. Surrounding the square are handsome stone mansions fronted by arcaded walkways, some of which have been converted into restaurants and hotels. Try to visit this plaza at dawn. It is almost mystical at that time of day with the gentle illumination of the morning light filtering through the trees and tiny Indian women wrapped in striped, handwoven woolen *rebozos* (shawls) scurrying through the park on their way to work.

Plaza Gertrudis Bocanegra: A block north of the Plaza Don Vasco de Quiroga is another plaza that goes by several names: Plaza Chica, Plaza de San Agustín, or Plaza Gertrudis Bocanegra. This is a bustling square with many shops and commercial buildings around it. The activity really picks up on Friday morning, the big market day when Indians come from far and near to set up their stalls. In the center of the square is a statue of one of the heroines of the Revolution, Gertrudis Bocanegra.

Museo de Artes Populares: Don Vasco wanted to make Pátzcuaro an important religious, cultural, and political center. He decided the town needed a university and so, in 1540, chose a site a block from the main square and founded the Colegio de San Nicolás, which claims to be the second-oldest university in the New World. In 1580 the university was moved to Morelia, which began to surpass Pátzcuaro in political importance. The school now houses the Museo de Artes Populares, a lovely museum with nine rooms opening onto an open courtyard, displaying regional arts and crafts.

Pátzcuaro, Plaza Don Vasco de Quiroga

Also in the museum is a *troje* with typical furnishings. A troje is the type of wooden log home used by the Tarascan Indians, with a porch in front supported by carved columns. Note: As you stand at the entrance to the museum, look to your right to see a water tank with a niche holding the Virgin Mary. According to legend, Don Vasco de Quiroga struck his staff on the ground here and a spring miraculously appeared to supply water for the town.

Basilica de Nuestra Señora de la Salud: Another of Don Vasco's dreams was to build an extraordinary cathedral, which he designed to be three times larger than the Cathedral of Notre Dame in Paris. With that in mind, he built the Basilica de Nuestra Señora de la Salud on a gentle hill about two blocks from the plaza. Only one nave of the original plan was ever completed, but the simple basilica is appealing. One of its principal attractions is the Virgin de la Salud, a small statue encased in glass on the altar, made by the Indians in 1547 from wild orchids and corn paste. Indians come from afar, especially on feast days, to pay homage and ask miracles from their Virgin de la Salud (Virgin of Health).

Casa de los Once Patios: Not attributed to Don Vasco, but certainly a place you won't want to miss, especially if you are into shopping for crafts, is the Casa de los Once Patios (House of the Eleven Patios), a 17th-century Dominican monastery just a half block off the Don Vasco de Quiroga Plaza. The original building had eleven interior patios but today only five remain, each of which is lined by small craft shops selling all kinds of native handmade goods such as loomed fabrics, masks, wooden sculptures, embroidered linens, copper, lacquer ware, carved furniture, and colorful paper flowers. It is fun to wander from patio to patio to see what new delights await. You will be reminded that this was indeed a living convent when you notice in one of the patios an arch, supported by richly embellished columns, that shelters a small niche where the novices came to bathe.

AROUND PÁTZCUARO

Santa Clara de Cobre: It is great fun to explore the town of Pátzcuaro, but the outlying region holds many places of interest, including towns that blossomed under the tutelage of Don Vasco de Quiroga. To help the Indians make a transition from their pre-Columbian world to the Spanish culture brought by the conquistadors, Don Vasco established special crafts for each small village, based upon the skills they already knew. Each of these villages, even today, continues to thrive on what Don Vasco taught them. These handicrafts included weaving, woodworking, furniture making, pottery, lacquer ware, guitar making, and embroidery work. Perhaps the most successful venture occurred in the village of Santa Clara de Cobre (the official name of the town is Villa Escalante, but you will rarely hear it called that) where the people were trained in the working of copper. Today this small, out-of-the way village has become a hub for copper craftsmen throughout Mexico—fine artists come to learn the "old ways" of their craft and many stay on to continue working among their peers. You can see the artists and craftsmen at work here and buy wonderful copper objects directly from them. There is a competition each mid-August when all the artisans vie for the finest works of art; the winners' pieces are featured in Santa Clara's National Copper Museum. This is a village that should not be missed on a trip to Pátzcuaro.

Lake Pátzcuaro: This lake is located about 5 kilometers from the center of town. Tourist photos show it as an idyllic expanse of water with a cone-shaped island jutting up in the middle and fishermen out in rustic wooden boats fishing with butterfly nets. In our estimation, the beauty of the lake is overrated since the water is polluted, the fishermen rarely fish with butterfly nets (except for the tourists), and Janítzio (the town on the picturesque-looking island in the middle of the lake) is a bit dirty and scruffy-looking once you get up close. That being said, we still think a boat trip on the lake is fun and a very "non-touristy" outing since most of your companions will be Mexicans out for a day of fun. To visit the island in the lake, take a taxi to the wharf (called Melon Grande or embarcadero) where you will see many boats lined up at the dock.

It is confusing to know quite what to do, but just go to the ticket booth and ask for a round-trip ticket to Janítzio (which costs about 30 pesos). Go down the ramp to the boats and show one of the "officials" your ticket and he will point out which boat to board. The boats seem to leave whenever enough people appear. You shouldn't have to wait too long and in the meantime it's entertaining just to watch the action. On weekends and holidays the boats are full of tourists going to the island to have a meal at one of the many restaurants. During the week, most of the boat passengers seem to be locals, schoolchildren returning home and women returning from the market. When the boat arrives at the island, disembark and walk the many steps lined by vendors to the top of the hill, which is topped by a 70-meter statue of José María Morelos (about a 15-minute walk).

Butterfly-Net Fishermen at Lake Pátzcuaro

Within the statue is a museum with galleries on five floors joined by a rampway, each level covered with huge murals with titles in Spanish. Even if you can't read Spanish, it is pretty obvious that the tale being told is of the cruelty of the Spanish Conquest and the sad plight of the Indians. Walk back down the hill to the village to wait for the next boat back. There are many colorful restaurants on a terrace above the pier.

Tzintzuntzan: If you are interested in archaeological sites, you must not miss Tzintzuntzan (translated as "The Place of the Hummingbird"), located on the east side of the lake about 17 kilometers from Pátzcuaro. When the Spanish arrived in the 16th century, more than 40,000 Tarascan Indians lived in this town, which was the capital of their state. This unusual site sits on a rise just above Lake Pátzcuaro with a splendid view across the water to the islands and fertile fields of this lovely valley in the mountains. Five large *yacatas*, round keyhole-shaped stone structures, stand in a row along a great man-made platform on a ridge facing the lake. Behind the *yacatas* steps lead down into a plaza with remains of a palace, living quarters, and storehouses. While some archaeological excavations have been carried out at the site, very little information has ever been published. It is generally assumed, however, that these finely made round cut-stone bases were once topped with perishable temples dedicated to the major Tarascan gods. In addition, the *yacatas* were used as the burial places of the Tarascan kings. Rich finds from the tombs include magnificent examples of the metalwork for which the Tarascans were renowned as well as skeletons of retainers who were interred with their royal masters in order to serve them after death. Tzintzuntzan is also well known for its intricate straw weavings and there are numerous shops where handicrafts are sold. Note: On the road from Pátzcuaro to Tzintzuntzan you will see factories selling wrought-iron garden furniture, mostly tables and chairs and handsome tall, old-fashioned wrought-iron lamps, at excellent prices. Our choice of these shops, which makes the furniture in a factory behind, is Fundidora Los Fresnos, on the left side of the road as you go toward Tzintzuntzan.

Tocuaro: If you are interested in buying one of the region's popular carved wooden masks, drive along the western edge of the lake to the tiny village of Tocuaro, just a little distance beyond the town of Eroncuariquero. Here you will find a master craftsman, Señor Horta, who creates and sells his pieces of art in his home. His work and skill are so well known that he is frequently invited to the United States to lecture. Once you arrive in the village, anyone you meet should be able to point the way to his home (it has his name on the door).

Cuanajo & Tupátaro: Another skill of the Tarascan Indians is the making of intricately carved furniture. If you are interested in buying some furniture or just want to see how it is made, go to the tiny, nondescript town of Cuanajo. This is an interesting excursion because along the way there is an outstanding tiny church to visit. From Pátzcuaro, take the highway toward Morelia and about 10 kilometers after leaving town, turn right on a small road at a small sign marked to Cuanajo. Soon after leaving the highway you come to the postage-stamp-sized sized town of Tupátaro, which is not much more that a tiny, beautifully kept plaza enhanced with old-fashioned wrought-iron lamps and bordered on three sides by one-story whitewashed buildings with rustic tiled roofs. Across from the tiny park is an adobe wall enclosing a very old church. Although not in the least ostentatious, this tiny church is truly a gem. Aged shade trees dot the grounds and a rugged stone marks the entrance. Notice as you enter that adorning one side of the doorway is a moon, on the other, the sun—surely not Christian motifs but undoubtedly reflecting the culture of the Indian craftsmen who built the church. The exterior is very simple, making it all the more amazing when you step inside and see the breathtaking gold altar. Be sure also to look up—the ceiling too is quite amazing. Its beams are totally covered with intricate paintings of angels and scenes from the life of Christ, clearly reflecting the style of the early Indian artistic tradition. After seeing the church, continue on to Cuanajo where it is fun to stroll along the streets to see the vast array of furniture being made of pine wood. Most of the shops (often home fronts) offer intricately carved furniture at incredibly low prices. My favorites are the delicately carved headboards, but these are a bit large to tote home. You might want to consider one of the lovely small carved pine chests, which can be packed up to take on the plane.

Lake Zirahuen: Whereas Lake Pátzcuaro is polluted, Lake Zirahuen, located in the pine-studded hills 22 kilometers southwest of Pátzcuaro next to a town of the same name, is crystal-clear without a hint of pollution. Many Mexicans come here for family outings. If you want to combine sightseeing, dining, and lots of local color, go to Le Troje de Ala restaurant (open on weekends), which is built within a Tarascan-style wooden home called a *troje*. The restaurant faces the lake and has a long wooden pier stretching out into the water. It is possible to drive to the restaurant, but much more of an adventure to take a boat. Ask at your hotel for details on how to get there.

Paricutín Volcano: A truly off-the-beaten-path adventure, and one you would probably want to undertake only if you are making an extensive stay in the area, is to the remote village of San Juan Parangaricútiro, which lies covered in ash from the Paricutín Volcano. The volcano erupted in 1943 and for nine years rained ash upon the valley below. What you see today is a field of black lava punctuated by the steeple of the village's 16th-century church, which lies buried below. What makes this trip special is not so much what you see, or don't see, of the buried village, but the jaunt itself, which takes you into a beautiful, lush area of pine-covered hills and tiny villages in a remote area of Michoacán rarely seen by tourists. Here Indians are still living as they have done for countless generations in picturesque *trojes* (log homes with carved columns). Allow a full day for this adventure. From Pátzcuaro take the toll road west for 60 kilometers to Uruapan, a bustling commercial town that would win no beauty contests but is very important as it lies at the heart of Mexico's vast avocado plantations. Eduardo Ruiz National Park, on the outskirts of town, is a real beauty, with lovely streams, springs, waterfalls, and lush, almost tropical foliage. From Uruapan go north for about 13 kilometers on highway 37, turn left and continue for another 20 kilometers to Angahuan. Here you will find plenty of guides eager to rent you horses and guide you to see the covered town (a 6-kilometer round trip). Arrangements can be made also to take you up the volcano, but I think just the round trip to the buried village is enough.

When it is time to end this itinerary, you can return to Mexico City for your trip home, take a flight to one of the beach areas for a few days in the sun, or, if you want to continue your explorations of the countryside, link with one of the other itineraries featured in the guide. If you are traveling between mid-November and the end of March, an excellent "add on" would be a visit to see the Monarch butterflies since the site of this adventure lies between Morelia or Pátzcuaro and Mexico City. See our itinerary *Miracle of the Monarch Butterfly*.

BUS OPTION: Below we indicate some possibilities for public transportation back to Mexico City.

11:15 am	Leave Morelia, La Central station, ETN bus
3:15 pm	Arrive Mexico City, Observatorio station
or	
9:00 am	Leave Pátzcuaro, La Central station, Autovíos bus
2:15 pm	Arrive Mexico City, Observatorio station

CAR OPTION: If you are driving, return to highway 15 from Pátzcuaro or Morelia and follow signs into Mexico City, a total distance of just a little over 300 kilometers. Note that the highway changes numbers en route from 15 to 55.

Mexico City & Beyond

Taxco

This itinerary covers Mexico City (referred to by those who live here as "Mexico") and the high fertile valley that surrounds it. In this valley remains have been found of hunters and the mammoths they pursued, of early village farmers who cultivated the fertile volcanic soil, and of the amazing urban-centered warrior empires that followed them. All of these cultures and empires have left their mark upon the valley itself and their influence is reflected in many other cultures throughout pre-Hispanic Mesoamerica. The empire builders in this heartland region of Mexico left impressive art and amazing architectural monuments scattered throughout the valley and its environs. Their achievements are monumental yet, like all New World pre-Columbian cultures, these civilizations lacked draft animals such as horses and oxen, knowledge of the wheel, and effective metal weapons and tools. However, in their own way they were as sophisticated as their European counterparts. Isolated from the Old World, the civilizations of the Americas developed their own architectural styles, political and social structures, agricultural techniques, and religious beliefs. Their accomplishments and their magnificent cities astonished the Spanish invaders of 1519 and continue to amaze visitors in the 21st century.

One cannot fully appreciate a visit to this area without a bit of Aztec history, for the Aztecs built a mighty empire here, long before the Spaniards arrived. The Aztecs were not the first to be lured to this rich valley, but they were the ones that greeted the conquistadors and whose amazing culture impressed these men from Spain. So, to add more depth of understanding to what you will be seeing, we start this itinerary with some historical background.

THE AZTECS (c. A.D. 1200–1521)

The powerful Aztecs were the last indigenous group to control the Valley of Mexico. They had brought their kingdom to its height when the Spanish arrived in 1519, and they controlled vast territories from their island city of Tenochtitlán, now known as Mexico City. This city was the urban center of an enormous empire that stretched through the Valley of Mexico to both coasts and as far south as Guatemala. The Mexica, as they called themselves, were latecomers to the central Mexican plateau. They were descendents of the Chichimecs, members of barbarian hunting tribes who inhabited the desert frontiers of northern Mexico. Legend relates that they left their mythic homeland of Aztlan (hence the name Aztec) in A.D. 1111 and, led by their fierce tribal god, Huitzilopochtli, wandered for many years searching for a promised homeland. When they finally arrived in the Valley of Mexico (about A.D. 1200) the fertile inland basin was already heavily populated and lack of good agricultural land forced the Aztecs to occupy the undesirable swamps at the edge of Lake Texcoco. For over 100 years the Aztecs served as mercenary soldiers and servants for their more powerful neighbors and it was not until 1325 that they founded their own capital city. According to legend, this settlement was established at a place where they found an eagle with a serpent in its mouth sitting on a cactus, an image still seen today on the Mexican flag. At this sacred spot the Aztecs built a temple to their god and began to construct the city of Tenochtitlán.

Eventually, through political alliances, ruthless warfare, and intermarriages with important families, the Aztecs began their rise to power. Fierce warrior kings eventually extended the empire far beyond the boundaries of the Valley of Mexico and rich spoils of war poured in from conquered regions. The increasingly powerful military state enforced a tribute system that assured a constant flow of valuable goods such as jade, gold, rubber, food, and slaves into Tenochtitlán. These great riches supplied the Aztec nobility with wealth and the city itself with power and beauty. Tenochtitlán became the urban center of a vast empire but its roots remained entwined in knowledge and traditions derived from earlier civilizations. The Aztecs were cultural heirs of the past and the final powerful flowering of ancient Mesoamerica.

Much of what we know about the Aztecs and the city of Tenochtitlán comes from documents written by Spanish soldiers and priests who were eyewitnesses to the conquest of Mexico (1519–1521). The Spaniards, including their captain Hernán Cortés, were overwhelmed by the beauty and sophistication of Tenochtitlán. They describe this amazing urban center as a city built on islands in the waters of a large lake. Great causeways connected the city with the mainland and aqueducts brought fresh water for its fountains and gardens from the hill of Chapultepec. Edged with beaten-dirt pathways, canals with drawbridges formed the streets of the city. Thousands of canoes plied the lakes and canals daily, carrying people and supplies from one place to another. The city seemed like another Venice to the weary Spaniards.

At the heart of the capital was a walled sacred precinct. Here stood the Templo Mayor, a magnificent double pyramid which held temples dedicated to Tlaloc, the ancient Mesoamerican god of rain, and to Huitzilopochtli, the god of war. Pyramids dedicated to other gods, schools, a ball court, priests' quarters, and great royal palaces were also located there. This was the heart of the empire and the religious focus of the city. Here elaborate ceremonies took place and human sacrifices were offered to the demanding, ever-greedy Aztec gods.

Around the central precinct the Aztec elite dwelt in great palaces with gardens, flowers, and exotic birds. This rich noble class was composed of the relatives of the current ruler and of the many descendents of previous rulers, and was larger than might be supposed as noblemen were allowed to have as many wives and concubines as they could support. Thus elite households contained numerous offspring; reportedly the Emperor Montezuma himself had 150 children.

Beyond this sacred and wealthy center, the rest of Tenochtitlán stretched out into the lake on artificial islands connected by canals and bridges. Here were the *barrios* or neighborhoods where free commoners lived and where most of the daily functions of the city took place. Each *barrio* provided the essentials of life for its members: land, schools, markets, local priests and temples, and military training for all men and boys. Farmers, the backbone of Aztec society, lived on the outskirts of the great city on fabricated plots of land called *chinampas*, the basic agricultural unit of the Valley of Mexico. Their carefully planned cycle of crops (often as many as five a year) provided food for the thriving Aztec capital. Unlike the extensive plowed agricultural fields of Europe, *chinampas* provided one of the most intensive systems of horticulture ever developed. As the empire expanded and the population increased, more and more of these islands were created for cultivation by cutting drainage canals through the swampy areas around the lake. Many of these artificial islands, known popularly today as "floating gardens," are still in use and can be visited by small, colorful boats that carry visitors along the ancient canal system. (Excursions to these floating gardens will be described in more detail further on.)

In 1519 over a million people inhabited the Valley of Mexico; at least 250,000 of them lived in Tenochtitlán, making it then, as it still is today, one of the largest metropolises in the world. The stimulation and excitement of the great urban center drew a diverse population from all over the empire into itself like a magnet. Artists came to employ their skills in the service of the king and his nobles. Warriors came to win fame and fortune in battles of conquest. Traders with their burden-laden human caravans carried exotic treasures to the market. Foreign dignitaries paid state visits to the court of Montezuma. Priests and pilgrims visited the sacred shrines and thieves, performers, tourists, and prostitutes all flocked to the city. People came in search of common, everyday necessities or of the rich goods that filled the great marketplace. They listened to the orations of the priests, sought the services of soothsayers and healers, dined on food prepared at market stalls, and visited with friends. As directed by the gods, they participated in the city's rich ceremonial life and watched with awe as human sacrifices were offered on top of the majestic pyramids. This was Tenochtitlán, heart of the Aztec empire.

In the early days of November 1519, Hernán Cortés, with a handful of Spanish soldiers and a multitude of Indian allies from the town of Tlaxcala, wound over a high mountain pass and down into the verdant Valley of Mexico. The seasoned Spanish soldiers who accompanied Cortés were overwhelmed by the beauty and size of Tenochtitlán. Built of stone, adobe and wood, the city had whitewashed stucco walls that shone in the sun like silver; its streets were canals of water, and thousands of canoes could be seen on the lake. The soldiers gazed in wonder at the gardens, palaces, temples, and pyramids rising from the water. With their captain they waited on the causeway watching with excitement and fear as the elaborate royal litter carrying the Emperor Montezuma approached. The momentous encounter of two different worlds was at hand—this was the beginning of the end for the mighty Aztec empire and the birth of a new nation.

This itinerary covers not only Mexico City but also the valley that surrounds it. The first section, *Mexico City*, gives suggestions for what to do and see within the city. The second section, *Short Day Excursions from Mexico City*, highlights some of our favorite archaeological sites that are within a short radius and best seen on a day's outing. *Longer Excursions East of Mexico City* highlights Puebla and Tlaxcala and what to see nearby, while *Longer Excursions South of Mexico City* highlights Cuernavaca and Taxco and what to see nearby.

RECOMMENDED PACING: We suggest a week to cover this itinerary: three nights in Mexico City to give you time to savor its many wonders, then another four days for excursions into the countryside. These side excursions could be done as day trips or else you could spend one or more nights along the way.

Note: If you are apprehensive about driving, you really do not need a car for this itinerary. You *definitely* do *not* want a car while you are in the city since parking is expensive and traffic awful, but you will find that even when you take excursions to the suggested sights outside the city, a car is not necessary. Convenient, deluxe bus service is available to all of the towns mentioned, plus there are excellent tours available that have the added benefit of a guide to add richness to what you see. If this "carless" option appeals to you, the concierge at your hotel can assist you with bus schedules, tour options, and prices for a private car and driver.

MEXICO CITY

We begin our sightseeing in Mexico City, which has always been the heartland of an empire. It lies at an elevation of 2,340 meters and with its population of 22 million is the largest city in the western hemisphere. Today, this immense capital serves as the center and hub of modern Mexico. It has a dramatic setting on a verdant plateau surrounded by mountains, including two colossal volcanoes, Popocatépetl and Iztacchíhuatl, whose snowcapped peaks can be seen on clear days.

Be prepared that Mexico City is not a place of pristine perfection. Due to its size and uncontrollable growth, it has many problems, including pollution, crime, ugly buildings, congestion, lack of a good highway network around the city, and mind-boggling traffic within. However, the government is well aware of these troubles and is making great strides in dealing with them. These less-than-perfect aspects of the city should not deter you from visiting it. Here you find at its core not only a magnificent Colonial city, but also some of the world's finest museums, beautiful parks, fabulous restaurants, grand boulevards, splendid modern architecture, chic boutiques, lovely residential areas, and excellent universities. To top it off, there is a wealth of excellent hotels in all price ranges. Please check the hotel section in the back of the book for our favorites.

SIGHTSEEING SUGGESTIONS

Bosque de Chapultepec (Chapultepec Park): Although Emperor Maximilian ruled Mexico for only a brief period, he left a French influence upon the city, including wide, tree-lined boulevards. One of the finest of these is the Paseo de la Reforma, a 12-kilometer-long thoroughfare, which remains as one of the most important and beautiful boulevards in the city. It crosses through another one of the city's highlights, the Bosque de Chapultepec, which dates back to the 16th century. The park is host to many museums (including the Museo Nacional de Antropología described below), lakes, fountains, amusement parks, statues, theaters, and shaded walkways.

It is great fun to stroll through the park, which is the playground for the city. Here you soak in the local color with parents buying cotton candy and balloons for their children; vendors selling fresh produce; shoe-shine men looking for customers; lovers snuggled on park benches; electric trains; grandmothers pushing baby carriages; and stalls throughout for snacks. On a summit of the highest hill in the park you find the Castillo de Chapultepec (Chapultepec Castle) whose story is rarely elaborated upon in American history books. After the Revolution, the castle became a military academy for young men. In 1847, during the American-Mexican War, the American army assaulted the castle, which was bravely defended by the young cadets, most of whom died: one gallant youth leapt to his death wrapped in the Mexican flag to avoid capture. These young men were later to become known as the *Niños Héros*, or Young Heros.

Cathedral: This superb structure is the largest cathedral in Latin America and certainly one of its most beautiful. Sadly, today this Colonial monument is slowly sinking into the soft floor of the ancient lake bed that still lies under modern Mexico City, and there seems little can be done to maintain it. The cathedral took almost 300 years to complete and during that time architectural styles from many periods, from classical to baroque, were incorporated into it. Its façade is glorious, enhanced by 67-meter-high twin bell towers with a series of bells on various levels. Between the bell towers is a clock tower, adorned with statues of Faith, Hope, and Charity. In the center of the building there is a huge gold dome, reminiscent of St. Peter's in Rome. Inside, the magnificence of the richly embellished church continues, with beautiful oil paintings, exquisitely decorated statues, magnificently carved choir stalls, and the Altar de los Reyes, which is an ornate baroque masterpiece.

Museo Franz Meyer: Many visitors to Mexico are unaware of one of our favorite spots in Mexico City, the Franz Meyer Museum, located in the heart of the city. This jewel of a museum beautifully displays magnificent Spanish Colonial collections of paintings, furniture, silver, sculptures etc. Many of the splendid objects reflect the early Conquest Period and form an artistic bridge between Aztec and Spanish artistic traditions.

Museo Frida Kahlo: The Frida Kahlo Museum, located at the corner of Londres and Allende in the suburb of Coyoacan, is of special interest to those who want to know more about Diego Rivera and also gain an insight into the fascinating Frida Kahlo. This small, intriguing museum was the home of the dark-haired, tempestuous, talented beauty, Frida Kahlo, who was born and died here. Frida, who endured great pain resulting from childhood polio and later spinal injuries resulting from a bus/streetcar accident, had a 25-year turbulent marriage to Rivera. They must have been quite a pair, the diminutive Frida and the 300-pound Rivera. She was a talented artist in her own right, and her surrealistic paintings and free-spirited approach to life have gained great fame. When Frida died at the age of 47, Rivera left the house, along with the paintings inside, as a museum. The furnishings and personal items are much as they were when she and Rivera shared the home. In August 2002 *Frida*, a movie depicting her life, was premiered at the Venice Film Festival and is bound to gain her even greater recognition.

Museo Nacional de Antropología: The National Museum of Anthropology, located in Chapultepec Park, is housed in a spectacular modern building containing collections of archaeological objects from all the pre-Columbian cultures of Mexico. There is a large inner courtyard almost totally shaded by a long concrete canopy which protects against the hot sun. The courtyard is embraced by the two-story museum, which displays chronologically and geographically the history of Mexico. These collections provide an excellent introduction to the archaeology of Mexico in an environment that is most pleasing. When the museum opened in 1964 it was considered a masterpiece, displaying a whole new concept of how to make archaeology come alive. Instead of becoming outdated, the museum is more remarkable than ever following extensive renovations in 2001. You move from room to room in an organized way to follow the exhibits in a chronological order and you see many special effects and video displays that explain what you are seeing. Not to be missed are a few highlights such as an incredible funerary mask of jade, which is one of the museum's treasures. In the Aztec exhibit, you cannot miss the Sun Stone with its intricate design showing the sun god in the center surrounded by the Aztec calendar. The mother-of-pearl Toltec Coyote Headed Warrior is another gem. These are but appetizers of the many fabulous pieces you will see—plan to spend many hours here. (There is a very good restaurant on the premises for lunch).

Palacio Nacional: The enormous National Palace dominates one side of the Plaza of the Constitution. This is the site where Montezuma had his palace, which was later replaced by the residence of Hernán Cortés. Continuing its heritage, the magnificent structure is today the president's residence. Much of the building is used for government business, but you must go in to view Diego Rivera's stunning murals depicting the history of Mexico. Obviously Rivera had his personal opinion of the struggle of the Indians against the conquistadors, for throughout his murals the cruelty of the Spaniards is clearly embellished. The fact that long before Cortés arrived, human sacrifice, slavery, and brutality were prevalent is lightly downplayed. However, the paintings are even more intriguing because of Diego Rivera's prejudices and his sense of humor in depicting them. You are apt to miss a lot if you don't know what you are seeing, so try to have a guide or do a little reading in advance. Diego's murals depict the faces of real people and those he didn't like received their due at the end of his paintbrush. It is almost like a puzzle to figure out who everyone is. Look carefully and you will see Cortés's mistress, La Malinche, who is often at his side, sometimes holding their son.

Plaza de la Constitución: This main plaza, or *zócalo*, is at the very heart of the city. It was built upon the ruins of the Templo Mayor, described below. It is massive in size and incredibly impressive. This is one of the biggest public squares in the world and one of the most interesting, with handsome Colonial buildings facing onto it. Two of the most dramatic of these are the magnificent cathedral and the Palacio National (see above): One of the best times to visit the plaza to truly capture its magic is in the early morning. At dawn the colorful Mexican flag is raised on the towering pole in the center of the square, accompanied by music and lots of pomp and ceremony. At this time of the day the square is at its most beautiful, with soft light and few tourists. Later on, the square becomes far more congested with many vendors, lots of tourists, and the noise and bustle of the throng of the city going about its daily activities. This too is a fun time to be here and to feel the pulse of the giant square, which was probably as busy during Aztec times as it is today.

Templo Mayor & Museo del Templo Mayor: The Templo Mayor was the heart of the Aztec empire and must not be missed. The site consists of two parts: the outdoor section, encompassing the excavated, stabilized ruins of the great temple complex, which you can view from a series of elevated walkways, and the wonderful Museum of the Templo Mayor, next to the ruins, where the amazing treasures recovered from the temple are stored and displayed. This beautiful museum tells the story of the temple complex through artifacts and clear interpretive text.

In Aztec times, the great Templo Mayor stood in the sacred walled precinct in the middle of Tenochtitlán. Today this sacred area is the central plaza of modern Mexico City, but before the arrival of the Spanish invaders this was the actual and symbolic center of the ancient capital city and heart of the Aztec world. The immense pyramid, topped with two important temples, dominated the skyline of the metropolis. The elaborate temples were dedicated to the worship of the two gods who represented the power sources of the Aztec empire: Huitzilopochtli and Tlaloc—gods of war and rain, of tribute and sustenance.

Archaeologists knew there was a temple located somewhere near the modern plaza in Mexico City, but buildings constructed in Colonial times covered the structures of ancient Tenochtitlán and for centuries the Templo Mayor lay buried. In February of 1978, two electrical workers digging in the central plaza of the city discovered an immense round carved stone (over 3 meters in diameter) and notified the National Institute of Anthropology and History of Mexico. It was soon determined that the stone was carved with a depiction of the dismembered body of Coyolxauhqui, moon goddess and sister of Huitzilopochtli. It had once been situated at the foot of the pyramid steps below the temple dedicated to Huitzilopochtli. This serendipitous discovery of the spectacular carved stone concretely located the position of the great temple and initiated one of the most impressive archaeological excavations ever to take place in Mexico.

The Templo Mayor project focused on the excavation of the magnificent double pyramid complex and the interpretation of its objects. From the excavations it was clear that the great temple had been constructed in seven stages. The first stage related to the earliest temple built in A.D. 1325 when Tenochtitlán was founded and the last to the final reconstruction or building period that produced the temple seen and recorded by the Spanish in 1519. This last temple was almost completely destroyed by the invading Spaniards, both in defiance of the ancient gods and to provide building stones for the Colonial city. The various rebuildings and embellishments of the original small pyramid into the final massive structure were done by a succession of Aztec kings to honor the gods and to enhance their own power and status in the empire. Archaeologists found many precious offerings buried within the walls of the various construction periods of the pyramid. These offerings were dedicated to Tlaloc, the god of rain, earth, and fertility, who was responsible for the success of the crops that fed Tenochtitlán, and Huitzilopochtli, god of war and the sun, who was responsible for the fruits of warfare that sustained the Aztec state. Items representing water, such as green-jade beads, shells, mother-of-pearl ornaments, and bones of aquatic animals, reflect the role of Tlaloc as provider of sustenance for humans. Items such as sacrificial knives, weapons, and skulls relate to Huitzilopochtli as provider of sustenance for the empire itself in the form of sacrificial blood and the wealth of conquest.

The iconography of the tall pyramid of Huitzilopochtli and the magnificent carved stone found at its foot refer to an ancient Aztec legend that tells of the birth of the great god Huitzilopochtli on top of the hill of Coatepec and his defeat of his sister, the moon, and his brothers, the stars. The pyramid represents the hill of Coatepec, and the carved stone found at its base is the image of Coyolxauhqui's dismembered body. The defeat of the stars and moon, symbols of darkness and the night sky, by Huitzilopochtli, warrior of the sun, was the epic act that assured the place of the sun in the daytime sky. This legendary drama was re-enacted in special ceremonies on top of the pyramid. A victim was sacrificed, his heart torn from his chest, his blood offered as sustenance to the sun, and his body was thrown down the steep "hill" of the pyramid onto the surface of the stone of Coyolxauhqui, thus re-creating the symbolic battle between the sun and moon.

Tlatelolco: Tlatelolco is a section of the ancient city of Tenochtitlán that was once the center of the Aztec market system. In this great plaza the last battle for Tenochtitlán was fought between Aztec warriors and the troops of Cortés. In 1965 a plaque was installed in the ruins of Tlatelolco to commemorate the momentous events of the first encounters of the Spanish and the Aztecs. Its inscription that addresses the fatal outcome reads:

On the 13th of August in 1521,
heroically defended by Cuauhtemoc,
Tlatelolco fell to Hernán Cortés.
This was neither a triumph nor a defeat,
it was a painful birth
of the mestizo people
who are the Mexico of today.

This site, now known as the Plaza of the Three Cultures, has the excavated ruins of Tlatelolco's main temple in the foreground and a large, very early, Colonial church and convent behind the temple ruins, with the tall buildings of modern Mexico rising in the background. The Plaza of the Three Cultures symbolizes the three cultures that make up Mexico today.

Xochimilco (Floating Gardens): Before the Spaniards arrived, the Aztec city of Tenochtitlán was an island in the center of a lake, connected to the mainland by causeways. Around the periphery of the city was a maze of floating islands laced by drainage canals that were laid out in an orderly fashion. These weren't really "floating" islands, but began as rafts piled with rich lake mud and then anchored to the bottom of the lake by fast-growing trees with a deep root system. This is where fresh produce and flowers were grown.

Floating Gardens of Xochimilco

Mexico City & Beyond

Today most of these islands are gone, but a few still exist and continue to produce vegetables and flowers for the city, just as they have for hundreds of years. These floating gardens are located in the outlying suburb of Xochimilco, about an hour's drive from the center. There are tours that go here, or you can hire a guide. The way is quite confusing, so we don't recommend you driving yourself. We delayed going to these gardens for many years, both because they were off the beaten path and also because we expected them to be overly touristy. How wrong we were! Yes, the islands are touristy, but they are also real—actual remnants of an ancient civilization that remain in use today. The tourists are basically Mexicans who have come for a family outing.

You climb aboard a brilliantly decorated, flat wooden boat with a Venetian-style "gondolier" who steers the craft through the narrow canals. The waterways are jammed with boats with all sorts of passengers: children having birthday parties; school kids on outings; young lovers who snuggle in a boat by themselves; mariachis serenading; women selling flowers; photographers who want to snap your picture; vendors selling postcards; entrepreneurs with cold drinks; even boats with kitchens aboard where women in colorful costumes cook up a hot meal. What a jolly experience, especially on a sunny day—the local color just can't be beat.

The sightseeing suggested above is just a taste of what the city has to offer, but should keep you occupied for several days. If you extend your stay, there is a wealth of other places to visit. The tourist office (corner of Amberes and Londres in the Zona Rosa) or the concierge at your hotel can provide you with more suggestions, plus information on special events being featured during your stay.

SHORT DAY EXCURSIONS FROM MEXICO CITY

The sightseeing excursions below usually involve a day trip from Mexico City. You can take a bus tour from the city or hire a car and driver. Check the difference in price because if you have several people in your group, a car with an English-speaking driver/guide might be almost the same price and is definitely more efficient. The concierge at your hotel should be able to assist you with either.

TEOTIHUACÁN (100 B.C.–A.D.750)

Only 40 kilometers northeast of Mexico City is the spectacular site of Teotihuacán, the enormous ruins of the great city that was pre-Hispanic Mexico's most important ancient metropolis. Its immense stone pyramids, temples, palaces, streets, and apartment complexes cover over 20 square kilometers and are best seen and enjoyed by walking through the huge abandoned city. Either before or after a walking tour, make a stop at the new Teotihuacán Museum, which highlights and displays the most recent excavation and research at the site.

Begun about 100 B.C., the magnificent city reached the height of its importance around A.D. 500. It consisted of approximately 600 pyramids and stretched for 4 kilometers. At that time, with an estimated 200,000 inhabitants, it was the sixth-largest city in the world. Unlike in other ancient Mesoamerican cities, these Teotihuacán city dwellers lived in apartment compounds, some built and decorated with great luxury for the royalty and elite of the city, others obviously tenements constructed for the lower classes. These communal dwellings were laid out in *barrios* or blocks according to a well-thought-out city plan with streets, plazas, plumbing, and cisterns for collection of rainwater installed before the construction began. The massive stone pyramids of the sun and moon dominate the Avenue of the Dead (main roadway of the city), their awesome size replicating in cut stone the great mountain peaks of the city's skyline. Their powerful architecture, based on the stepped pyramid style of construction, influenced the ceremonial architecture of almost all the cultures that followed. Cities and cultures as far away as the Maya region to the southeast, Tajin on the Gulf Coast, and Monte Albán in the Valley of Oaxaca reflect contact with Teotihuacán. Much of this influence may have traveled along pre-Hispanic Mexico's great trade routes which brought valuable raw materials such as jade, feathers, and cotton into the city's workshops and carried finished products, including tools made of the local obsidian, to the hinterlands. However, strong new evidence now exists that indicates that Teotihuacán rulers were also powerful warriors and thus military conquest may also have been responsible for the spread of Teotihuacán influence into other regions of Mesoamerica. Walking through the site, one sees everywhere traces of the white stucco and painted fresco murals that once covered both the exterior and interior walls of the buildings with imagery of the gods and rituals. Some of these brightly colored frescos still survive and give us a glimpse of the brilliance of the city at its height.

Around A.D. 600 Teotihuacán began to decline and in the early 700s it was sacked and burned. People gradually abandoned the ancient city but the memory of its power and glory and many of its massive buildings survived. Over the years, other empires arose and seats of power shifted in the valley. The Toltec empire flourished from about A.D. 1000 to 1250, its demise leaving a power vacuum, which was eventually filled by fierce Aztec warriors from the north. However, rulers and priests of these later city-states remained in awe of the massive ruins of the ancient city of Teotihuacán. Over many centuries pilgrimages were made to the abandoned site and legend and memory continued to associate it with past glory. It remained as one of the most sacred places in the Aztec world where it was known as the place where the gods were born.

TULA (c. A.D. 1000–1250)

The site of Tula, located about 70 kilometers north of Mexico City, was the legendary home of the Toltecs, who were credited by the cultures that succeeded them with being the greatest warriors and artists of ancient Mexico. Whether this was actually the case is uncertain. The site today is considerably smaller and less impressive than one might expect for such a powerful state. However, warrior themes and iconography depicting death, sacrifice, and war dominate the art that remains and the architecture with its step-style pyramids, stone sculptures, platforms, and temples, and a massive central plaza continue traditions established at the earlier site of Teotihuacán.

LONGER EXCURSIONS EAST OF MEXICO CITY

PUEBLA

Puebla is a delight: a very special town that is another of our favorite Colonial destinations. Although it has grown into a sophisticated city, the fourth largest in Mexico, it still maintains the rich cultural traditions of its past and the charm of a small town. Located 123 kilometers southeast of Mexico City, it can be easily reached by taking an excellent toll road, highway 150, or by public transportation. There are convenient buses from Mexico City plus frequent bus service directly from the Mexico City airport. If you want to overnight in Puebla, we describe several of our recommendations in the hotel section, all within walking distance of the sightseeing suggestions below.

For several thousand years before the Spanish Conquest, Puebla was the center of worship of the great god Quetzalcoatl and one of the most important pilgrimage sites in Mesoamerica. Legend has it that when the Spanish arrived in 1519 they found 365 functioning temples in the city, one for every day of the year. After the Conquest it continued as a religious center, with the growing wealth of its leading Catholic citizens supporting rich monasteries and convents as well as numbers of magnificent churches. Until recently many of the beautiful churches were closed as a result of the bitter Revolution. Under the laws of 1857, church lands were sold and convents closed, although many of them continued to function as meeting places for underground religious orders. Today the churches and convents are being refurbished by wealthy patrons to their original richness and beauty. There are over 60 churches in town, many of them centuries old.

Puebla's downtown area, clustered around the central plaza, just oozes old-world ambiance, with nothing unsightly or modern to mar its purity. Some suggestions for places to visit are given below. All are within walking distance of the main plaza and you will find strolling a delight since many of the streets are closed to cars.

SIGHTSEEING IN PUEBLA

Barrio de los Artistas: If you like to shop, visit the Barrio de los Artistas at 5 Oriente & 6 Norte. This is an upscale, fun place to browse and poke around small shops laden with crafts and art. There are also many small stalls selling really nice-quality goods. Many artists have studios here and there are several antique shops nearby.

Catedral de Nuestra Señora de la Asunción: Located a block away from the Plaza Principal, this former Franciscan monastery was the first building erected by the Catholic fathers in the New World.

Catedral de Nuestra Señora de la Immaculada Concepción: Dating back to 1562 and considered by some to be one of Mexico's most splendid cathedrals, the Cathedral of the Immaculate Conception is tremendously imposing with its twin bell towers, massive doorway, and intricately carved façade. The interior is opulent, with soaring vaulted ceilings, elaborately gilded chapels, baroque altarpieces, and fine oil paintings.

Museo Emparo: Don't miss one our favorite museums, the Emparo, housed in an elegant Colonial mansion. The fine pre-Columbian objects displayed here were once part of a magnificent private collection but now are on view to the public. Don't miss seeing the beautiful pieces once carefully selected by some of Mexico's true connoisseurs of pre-Hispanic art.

Museo Regional de Puebla & Casa del Alfeñique: Puebla's Regional Museum is housed in an 18th-century baroque mansion which derives its name from the intricate white plasterwork around the windows and roof that resembles an almond paste called *alfeñique*. On the ground floor is an archaeological museum while the second floor exhibits the furnishings of a Colonial home.

Palacio de Gobierno: Standing on the north side of the central plaza you find the 16th-century Government Palace, which features inside colorful murals depicting the history of Puebla.

Palacio de Justicia: This handsome 16th-century building with an ornate crest above the doorway dominates the northwest side of the Plaza Principal.

Plaza Principal (Zócalo): As in most Mexican cities, the central plaza is an ideal place to capture the ambiance of the town. The impressively large one in Puebla is a real beauty with fountains, gardens, shade trees, wrought-iron benches, and a lace of paths. At its center is a statue of the Archangel San Miguel, the patron saint of Puebla. The square is faced on three sides by an arcade that stretches in front of handsome Colonial buildings, and on the fourth side is dominated by the Cathedral of the Immaculate Conception.

Santo Domingo Church: Located two blocks from the plaza, this church is famous for its intimate, 17th-century Rosary Chapel, whose ornate plaster walls, ceilings, and altar are covered with gold leaf.

Talavera Tile: Puebla was the first city in the New World to produce the beautiful, Spanish-style Talavera ceramics which included dinnerware, all kinds of pottery, and, of course, colorful tile. The production was closely controlled by the king and only certain families were granted permission to make the pottery. Many buildings in Puebla reflect the importance of the craft, with façades covered by tile. If you are interested in buying some of this beautiful ceramic ware or would just like to see how it is made, visit the Uriarte Factory (Avenida 4 Poniente 911), a stunning building totally faced with colorful tiles, where the same family has been making the pottery since 1827.

TLAXCALA

Tlaxcala, located 33 kilometers directly north of Puebla, is a treasure. If you are spending time in the area, either Puebla or Tlaxcala would make a superb base of operations but, whichever you choose, be sure to visit the other. There is a frequent bus service between them, or it is just a short drive if you have your own car. Many travelers have never heard of Tlaxcala, perhaps because Puebla is so well known and so close. However, it is one of Mexico's jewels—a stunning small village that retains its Colonial ambiance without any intrusion of modern buildings. Its central plaza is one of the most beautiful in Mexico. If you want to spend the night, or several nights, you can stay in an excellent hotel facing the square, the Posada San Francisco, which is described in the hotel section.

Within months after his ships landed in Veracruz, Cortés continued on to Tlaxcala, making this one of the oldest Colonial towns in Mexico. The Tlaxcalans were deadly enemies of the Aztecs, a hatred Cortés played upon in persuading them to join forces with him as he marched forth in pursuit of Montezuma. (Of course, the fact that the choice he offered was either to join him or be killed might have influenced their decision!) Thus Tlaxcala has special significance in the history of Mexico: without the assistance of their warriors, Cortés might never have defeated Montezuma.

Not only is Tlaxcala brimming with charm, but also there is much to see. Following are some of the places to visit.

Bullfighting: There are over 40 haciendas nearby that specialize in the raising of fine fighting bulls. There is a very old, picturesque bullring in town that you can see to the right as you climb the path up to the Nuestra Señora de la Asunción Cathedral. Built in the early 1800s, this is one of Mexico's oldest bullrings and although it is now used only during certain festivals, you can take a tour of it.

Catedral de Nuestra Señora de la Asunción: Our Lady of the Assumption Cathedral, perched on a hill just a short walk from the Plaza de la Constitución, was the first permanent Catholic church in America. Leaving the southeast corner of the plaza, go through the small square and take the pretty, cobblestone pathway lined by trees that leads steeply uphill to the cathedral. As you walk up the path, look down the hill to your right and you can catch a glimpse of one of Mexico's oldest bullrings. When you enter the cathedral be sure to look up at the splendid ceiling studded with gilded stars, a Moorish style very popular in Spain at the time of the Conquest. It was here that Cortés had king Xicoténcatl, who had joined forces with him, baptized before he and his Tlaxcalan allies set off to conquer Mexico City. In the cloisters of the church there is a museum of pre-Columbian artifacts.

Museo de Artisanías: The simple Museum of Handicrafts is just a few blocks west of the central plaza. Here you can see how some of the local handicrafts are made plus visit a small shop where you can buy handmade items.

Museo de la Memoria: The Museum of Memory displays fascinating, rare codices (books) that tell the history of the Tlaxcalan Indians.

Palacio de Gobierno: The Government Palace is a handsome brick building with ornate stone trim that dominates the north side of the plaza. On the ground floor and along the walls of the staircase to the upper level is an impressive series of brilliantly colored murals painted by a local artist, Desiderio Hernándes, depicting the early history of the Indians and the story of the conquest of Mexico by Hernán Cortés. These strong, vibrant, 20th-century paintings were done by a local artist, Desiderio Hermández Xochitiotzin.

Parroquia de San José: The Parish Church of San José, facing a small square just off the northwest side of the Plaza de la Constitución, dates back to the 17th century. This is a real beauty with an ornate entrance, a single spire, and a splendid tiled dome. Be sure to go inside—the cheerful yellow-and-green interior is quite unusual. Look carefully for a 17th-century painting of the baptism of a Tarascan chief and see if you can find Cortés standing nearby with La Malinche, his mistress, at his side.

Plaza de la Constitución: Located in the center of Tlaxcala, this enormous plaza is one of the most stunning in all of Mexico. Surrounded on four sides by handsome Colonial buildings fronted by arcades, the park has majestic, centuries-old shade trees, gurgling fountains, trimmed shrubs, wrought-iron benches, beds of flowers, and, center stage, a bandstand given to the city by King Philip III of Spain.

Santuario de la Virgen de Ocotlán: The Sanctuary of the Virgin of Ocotlán is another "must see" and is an easy 20-minute walk from the heart of town. Wear good walking shoes since you must climb a long flight of steps to visit this very holy shrine, built on the site where, so the story goes, the Virgin appeared in 1541 to a very poor Indian, Juan Diego Bernardino, and told him to take water from a stream that had miraculously appeared to cure his people who were ill. She asked him to send monks into the forest and when they split open one of the pine trees, they found secreted within a wooden statue of the Virgin Mary, which is now in the church. Since then, many miracles have been attributed to the Virgin of Ocotlán. Within the sanctuary, which was built in the 18ᵗʰ century in an ornate, baroque style that resembles a wedding cake, are scenes depicting the sequence of the events following the appearance of the Virgin.

Shopping: In addition to sightseeing, Tlaxcala is a handicraft town. There is much to buy here including beautiful Talavera pottery, woolen goods, hand-woven rugs, woven baskets, onyx figurines, and woodcarvings.

SIGHTSEEING OUTSIDE OF PUEBLA OR TLAXCALA

Cacaxtla: Another outstanding archaeological site highly recommended as a side trip from either Puebla or Tlaxcala is the city of Cacaxtla (A.D. 600–900.) If you are the least interested in delving into the rich accomplishments of the Indians prior to the arrival of the Spanish, this site should not be missed. Wear comfortable shoes because there is a lot of walking involved in this adventure. You can hire a taxi to take you to the ruins or, if you do it on your own, there is a place to leave your car. First visit the museum, which displays many of the original artifacts found in the site plus reproductions of some of the paintings you will see. From the museum it is about a 1-kilometer walk on a well-defined path to the site of the ancient city perched on top of the nearby hill. The site is covered by a gigantic corrugated-steel roof to protect it from the destructive elements of sun and rain. What make this ruin so exceptional are the murals, which rank among some of the best-preserved frescos in Mexico. You can still see huge paintings on some of the walls showing life-sized warriors vividly dressed in jaguar costumes and fancy feather headgear. These amazing works of art, probably dating back to A.D. 700–900, decorate numerous walls of the ancient city and, to varying degrees, reflect Mayan influence since similarities are seen between these and the magnificent murals at the site of Bonampak. It is astonishing that the colors are in such excellent condition. This site is truly a treasure.

Cholula: While in Puebla or Tlaxcala you will certainly want to visit the nearby archaeological site of Cholula, lying just on the outskirts of the town. This great pyramid of ancient Cholula (1500 B.C.–A.D. 1521) was the largest in the New World. Originally dedicated to the god Quetzalcoatl, it looks like an immense hill but is really a massive man-made edifice built and rebuilt over many centuries during the pre-Hispanic Period, and today has a Colonial church, the Santuario de los Remedios, sitting on top. This massive pyramid and most of the ancient site of Cholula are, like Mexico City, covered by Colonial buildings. However, the ancient pyramid is well worth a visit and while there is little remaining of the site itself, a guide will take you through dark tunnels deep into the bowels of the pyramid where you will be able to see the evidence of the various building stages and cultural levels connected with this vast structure.

LONGER EXCURSIONS SOUTH OF MEXICO CITY

CUERNAVACA

Cuernavaca, located 90 kilometers southwest of Mexico, is a popular weekend getaway for many wealthy Mexicans, some of who have sumptuous second homes here. Due to its excellent climate, Cuernavaca is called "The City of Eternal Spring" and has been a favorite retreat since the time of the Aztec emperors—even Hernán Cortés and Emperor Maxmillian had homes here. The city has a strong Colonial heritage, but traffic congestion and crowded, unkempt streets detract a bit from its ambiance. You will find that most of the mansions and lovely hotels hide away behind high walls, displaying a lush beauty with gardens and inner courtyards once you enter through the thick wooden doorways. If you want to stay overnight, or indulge in a delicious meal in an exquisite garden setting, one of our favorite hotels, Las Mananitas, is highly recommended.

SIGHTSEEING IN CUERNAVACA

Plaza de Armas: Cuernavaca's main plaza is faced by several Colonial buildings including the Palacio de Cortés and the Palacio de Gobierno, but the Colonial style in the area of the plaza is not pristine since modern buildings managed to slip in before architectural controls were put in place.

Cathedral: Cuernavaca's cathedral is within a walled complex of churches that includes not only the 16th-century cathedral, but also the 18th-century Templo de la Tercera Orden de San Francisco and the 19th-century Capilla del Carmen.

Palacio de Cortés: The Spanish king bequeathed 30 cities to Cortés, including Cuernavaca, which was supposedly his favorite, and here he built a mansion known as the Palace of Cortés just off the main square. This is now a fine museum displaying many photos of the Revolution, costumes, arms, and splendid murals by Diego Rivera. The exhibitions are well displayed and many have explanations in both English and Spanish.

Museo Robert Brady: This museum, housed in a lovely Colonial home that was owned by Robert Brady, contains over 1,300 diverse pieces of his art. Brady, born in the backwaters of Fort Dodge, Iowa, settled in Cuernavaca in 1960. He was a decorator who loved antiques, sculptures, and paintings and had a fabulous, eclectic collection of art and handicrafts from all over the world. The home is just as he left it. It is on a pretty side street between the cathedral and the Palace of Cortés.

TAXCO

Taxco, which is designated as a national monument, is one of Mexico's quaintest Colonial towns. Being close to Mexico City and on the route to Acapulco, it has many tourists and is a bit more commercial than some other silver towns that are more off the beaten path. Nevertheless, the charm of this small town, squeezed in amongst barren hills, still prevails. The setting is picture-perfect, with narrow, cobbled streets twisting up and down the hill, lined by whitewashed buildings topped by rustic tiled roofs. The colorful plaza in the center hugs one of the few level pieces of ground in town. The church is a masterpiece.

One would never expect to find a town in such a precarious setting, but the reason is obvious: silver. Hernán Cortés was constantly on the alert for rumors of gold and silver, hoping to discover mines so that he could please his king by enriching the coffers of Spain. When he learned that the Aztecs traded in silver from the Taxco area, he sent his engineers to investigate and soon mining was under way.

SIGHTSEEING IN TAXCO

Museum of William Spratling: This museum, located two blocks from the Plaza Bora on Calle Porfirio A. Delgado, features William Spratling's collection of silver and pre-Hispanic art. (Read more about Spratling below.)

Plaza Borda: This small plaza in the center of town is a photographers' delight—the epitome of what one imagines the perfect Mexican square should look like. It is tiny (there isn't much room to spare in Taxco), but as pretty as can be with shade trees, the typical bandstand, and whitewashed buildings with tiled roofs and wrought-iron balconies everywhere you look.

Santa Prisca Church: One would never dream of finding such an incredibly beautiful church as Santa Prisca tucked away in a small mining town, but then most towns didn't have such a wealthy benefactor as José de la Borda. When the word trickled to Europe that silver had been found in the New World, a Frenchman by the name of José de la Borda packed his bags and rushed (as fast as you could rush in the 18th century) to Mexico to make his fortune. Finding nothing, he was about to give up and head for home, when his horse slipped and exposed a rich vein of silver. To thank God for this miracle, Borda built the Santa Prisca church, where his son Manuel became priest. No expense was spared and the church is a jewel. Its twin bell towers and ornate dome have become a landmark of Taxco, repeatedly seen on postcards and posters.

Shopping: It seems every building has its silver shop. You cannot go more than a few steps before finding another one (at last count there were more than 200). Many sell silver items at the same price and in similar style to those found in resort shops throughout Mexico, but what is special, and can't be found elsewhere, are the shops where individual pieces are designed. Many of these are exquisite, and not inexpensive. The reason for the prolific number of skilled craftsmen here is partly due to the American ambassador to Mexico in the 1920s, Dwight Morrow (father of Anne Morrow, wife of Charles Lindberg). He was a dedicated statesman who went far beyond the line of duty in trying to improve the lot of the local people. Morrow had a friend, William Spratling, a young professor from New Orleans, who fell in love with Mexico. Morrow persuaded him to stay and set up workshops to teach jewelry design to the artisans in Taxco. This he did, and Taxco is now known worldwide for the skill of its designers.

Silver Museum: Just across from Santa Prisca is a silver museum run by a local silversmith. At first glance it seems more like a shop, but what is interesting is that on exhibit are award-winning pieces of jewelry. It is fascinating to see the superb designs and craftsmanship in these lovely pieces of art.

SIGHTSEEING OUTSIDE OF CUERNAVACA OR TAXCO

Malinalco: Located west of Cuernavaca, the impressive hilltop site of Malinalco (A.D. 500–1521) was inhabited over the years by various groups of people but reached its peak during the final years of the Aztec Period (c. A.D. 1475–1521). The ruins are reached by climbing almost a mile up a winding, well-maintained pathway that offers beautiful views of the valley and the modern town of Malinalco. The location of the site at the top of a defensible hill suggests that over time one of its roles must have been as a military fortress; however, after its capture by the Aztecs in 1476, it seems to have become a sanctuary or ritual home for the Eagle and Jaguar warriors, the elite fighting units of the Aztec military.

There are only a few buildings at the site, the most impressive being an amazing pyramid/temple cut out of the solid rock face. One climbs the pyramid steps and enters the temple through the open mouth of a massive serpent that serves as the entryway to a round, inner chamber. This dark inner room may have been used for secret initiation ceremonies or military rites. Its central altar and semicircular bench are decorated with sculptured stone images of eagles and jaguars. Other buildings in this hilltop complex are thought to have been meeting halls, chambers for ritual events, and storage facilities.

In the modern village below the fortress-like site is an early (1537) Augustinian monastery and church built of cut stone carried down from the archaeological site of Malinalco. This early fortress-church has an interesting open chapel with the Stations of the Cross placed around its large enclosed courtyard.

Xochicalco: To the south of Cuernavaca you find the site of the pre-Hispanic city of Xochicalco (c. A.D. 650–900), one of several that rose to power after the fall of the great metropolis of Teotihuacán. The disintegration of that immense city left a power vacuum throughout the region and various smaller city-states, Xochicalco among them, challenging each other for power. The city was situated on a hilltop overlooking the approaches of the ancient trade routes that ran west towards present-day Acapulco, south to the Valley of Puebla, and east to the vast Valley of Mexico. At its height the city held perhaps 10,000 to 15,000 people and its major function must have been the control of access along the long-distance routes that carried precious goods throughout pre-Columbian Mexico.

The elite precinct built on top of the hill is one of the most recently excavated parts of the site. In this section of the city are found the large storage rooms, ball courts, palaces, and temples of the rulers of Xochicalco. This well-protected precinct was situated to take advantage of the beautiful views across the valley and the cooling breezes during the hot summer months. It was heavily fortified with thick fortress-like walls, ramps, and defendable staircases. These massive fortifications can be seen from far across the valley and clearly controlled access to the site.

The commoners lived in the lower sections of the city where a number of large temple complexes, pyramids, and buildings are found. Here, on an artificially leveled hill, one of the largest ball courts in Mesoamerica is located. In addition, around the site and in the surrounding valley, terraced hillsides indicate the use of intensive agricultural techniques.

The site, like several others of the same time period, appears to have been inhabited or at least strongly influenced by several different contemporary cultures. Most obvious is the Mayan influence, which is clearly seen in the elaborate decoration of the Temple of the Feathered Serpent. This unusual stepped pyramid is carved with a series of Mayan dignitaries each seated within the coils of a great feathered serpent that stretches around the pyramid base. An underground chamber at the site is now recognized as a solar observatory marking the sun's zenith in May and July, dates that were also important in the Mayan calendar and may reflect further Mayan influence at Xochicalco. A new museum has recently been built at the site and is well worth a visit. It not only exhibits artifacts recovered from the excavations but also presents the results of the recent research.

Oaxaca Valley & Archaeological Treasures

Monte Albán, Grand Plaza

Oaxaca, tucked high in a fertile valley 485 kilometers southeast of Mexico City, is one of our favorite places in Mexico. Without a doubt it is one of the most colorful, best-preserved Colonial cities in the country, with the added bonus of a lovely climate year round. It also offers visitors a glimpse of a city and region that truly exhibit three distinct faces of Mexican culture—the ancient archaeological ruins; the wonderful Spanish Colonial art and architecture; and the skilled craftsmen and artists in the surrounding villages. Like the valleys of Puebla and Mexico City, the history and pre-history of the Oaxaca Valley extends far back in time to the end of the last Ice Age when hunters roamed the area in search of game. In fact, Oaxaca is one of the longest continually inhabited regions in Mexico. Archaeological evidence demonstrates that the ancestors of the modern Zapotec people were contemporaries of the early Olmecs (1500 B.C.–A.D. 400) whose cultural influence spread from the Gulf Coast of Mexico throughout much of Mesoamerica. Today villages in the valley and its surrounding mountains remain the home of the Zapotecs and later arriving Mixtec peoples whose languages, costumes, and traditions are still a significant factor in modern Oaxaca. Amazingly, over half of the population still speaks their own dialect.

An added bonus of Oaxaca is that its wealth lies not only in archaeological sites and fabulous Colonial buildings, but also in the rich selection of places to stay: some of the loveliest hotels and bed and breakfasts in Mexico are found here. Look in the hotel section of the book for our many suggestions.

There are direct flights from Mexico City to Oaxaca as well as deluxe bus service (which takes about six hours). If you are driving, it is about five hours via the toll road. Unless you have your own car, don't bother with a rental car when you arrive. Instead, take a taxi to your hotel and from there, walk to see the sights. One of the joys of Oaxaca is just wandering its quaint streets. The places we highlight within town are close enough to walk to from all of the hotels we recommend, except for the Hacienda los Laureles, which is located nearby in San Felipe del Agua.

RECOMMENDED PACING: We suggest five days in Oaxaca, though a week would be preferable so that you could relax and enjoy the ambiance of this Colonial jewel at leisure. You need three days to explore the city and two more to take side trips to the nearby archaeological sites and local craft villages. There are truly many wonderful places to visit, both in the city and in the surrounding valley. Detailed below are some of our favorites.

COLONIAL OAXACA

Basilica de Nuestra Señora de la Soledad (Church of the Virgin of Solitude), Avenida Independencia 107: This beautiful 16th-century church, whose ornate façade is studded with statues, is most famous for its shrine containing Oaxaca's patron saint, the Virgin of

Solitude. This statue of the Virgin mysteriously appeared in the pack of a mule that died where the church now stands. The statue, which supposedly has special healing powers, is greatly revered and people come from afar to ask for miracles.

Casa de Juárez (Home of Juárez), Garcia Vigil 609: This is the home where one of Mexico's most famous leaders, Benito Juárez, lived as a servant during his youth and the furnishings reflect the style of that period (early 19th century). Benito Juárez, a Zapotec Indian born in the nearby village of San Pablo Guelato, was an outstanding man of great intelligence. Orphaned at the age of 3, he was educated by village priests, who must have done a remarkable job, for he went on to become a leader of Indian rights and, in 1858, Mexico's president.

Oaxaca, Santo Domingo

Oaxaca Valley & Archaeological Treasures

Museo de Arte Contemporáneo de Oaxaca (Contemporary Art Museum of Oaxaca), Macedonio Alcalá: This collection of contemporary art is housed in one of Oaxaca's most historic buildings, the 16th-century Casa de Cortés, supposedly commissioned by Cortés himself. Here you find paintings of some of Oaxaca's most famous artists including Rodolfo Morales, Francisco Toledo, Rodolfo Nieto, Rufino Tamayo, and Francisco Gutierrez.

Museo de las Culturas de Oaxaca (Museum of Culture of Oaxaca): This striking museum is connected to and part of the Santo Domingo Church, being housed on two floors of the former monastery attached to the church. (If you have visited Oaxaca previously, do not be confused—it used to be called the Museo Regional.) Here you find a breathtaking collection of artifacts gathered in excavations at nearby archaeological sites. The most spectacular display consists of more than 500 stunning pieces of silver, jade, gold, and turquoise that were found in Monte Albán in just one tomb, number 7. A rich collection of archaeological and ethnographical objects from all over the state of Oaxaca are also exhibited here. One room of special interest is that featuring a collection of pre-Hispanic musical instruments, attesting to the sophistication of the early Mixtec culture.

Plaza de Armas: This tree-studded main plaza in the heart of Oaxaca is truly a gem. For the price of a beer or a cup of coffee you can sit at a café table and watch the colorful world of Oaxaca—with Indian, *mestizo*, Spanish, and gringo faces—pass through the busy plaza. You could sit endlessly and time would slip by with never a boring moment. Totally closed to traffic, the square is always filled with people and is the social center of town. Here you find non-stop action: vendors selling everything imaginable, including huge bunches of brilliantly colored balloons; students on their way to school; tourists basking in the sun; men on their way to work; children splashing in the fountain; roaming mariachis; mothers nursing their babies; shoeshine men buffing shoes to a brilliance; old men snoozing on benches; pretty girls dressed in colorful native costumes; and, unfortunately, beggars asking for a few coins, reflecting the poverty that sadly underlies much of rural Mexico. If you are hungry, you can buy an ice cream from one of the many stalls or if you have a sense of adventure, try one of Oaxaca's specialties, *chapulines* (fried grasshoppers). This lively square is the perfect place to start your sightseeing or to take a break between museums. There are many excellent restaurants overlooking the square.

Rufino Tamayo Museo de Arte Prehispánico (Rufino Tamayo Museum of Pre-Hispanic Art), Avenida Morelos 503: Four blocks from the Plaza de Armas is a museum you must not miss—its stunning archaeological collection is outstanding, with over 1,000 pre-Hispanic works of art beautifully displayed in a handsome mansion. The collection was given to the town by Rufino Tamayo, a famous artist who was born in Oaxaca. Since his death, more pieces of art have been added.

Santo Domingo Church: Santo Domingo, built by the Dominicans in 1670, is a dazzling baroque church. The exterior is handsome with twin bell towers crowned with brightly colored tiles, but there is little hint on the outside of the opulence within. It was here that Pope John Paul II blessed a huge crowd when he visited the city. Like so many Catholic churches in Mexico, its sanctuary and its convent were partially destroyed and its treasures stolen during the days of the Revolution. The interior was particularly badly defaced and its gold leaf and rich decoration dismantled. However, the church has been restored to its original magnificence with an ornate façade, incredible golden interior, and splendid paintings and murals. The lovely small chapel dedicated to the Virgin is not to be missed.

SIDE TRIPS FROM OAXACA

When it's time to take your day trips, hire a car with an English-speaking driver who is qualified as a guide (ask your hotel to recommend a reliable person). The cost is not exorbitant—especially when considering you are saving the expense of a car rental—and well worth the convenience and greater appreciation of what you see. The sightseeing on the following pages is highly recommended.

MONTE ALBÁN

Because it is so close to Oaxaca (less than a 30-minute drive) and such a superb site, we suggest a visit to Monte Albán (500 B.C.–A.D. 700) as your first taste of the many archaeological sites around Oaxaca.

Monte Albán, Ball Court

Get up early and try to be the first ones there to enjoy the beautiful ruin in the early-morning sun before the busloads of tourists arrive. This imposing site is one of Mexico's most spectacular ancient cities and also one of its oldest. Monte Albán sits on top of a mountain, leveled off long ago by the indigenous Zapotecs to serve as a plateau setting for their great city. The view from the top is particularly lovely just after the rainy season when the foliage is green and the flowering trees begin to bloom. This impressive archaeological site has one of the largest plazas in pre-Columbian Mexico, stretching the whole length of the man-made plateau with massive pyramids, temples, and palaces at each end of the immense space and along the sides. In addition, the site has many underground tombs built beneath the patio floors of houses, an observatory, a particularly beautiful ball court, and a fine new museum. The city was founded about 500 B.C. when populations from various smaller sites in the region came together at this easily fortified high point overlooking the valley. Here they started construction of a city that by the early centuries A.D. had become a powerful state that was in contact, probably through trade, with the other civilizations of Mesoamerica.

By about A.D. 700 the site was abandoned and people moved from the mountaintop back to the farmlands in the valley, settling once again in smaller villages. The site itself, however, survived and the Mixtec peoples who followed the Zapotecs as a power in the Valley of Oaxaca used the terraced mountainsides of the older city as a place of burial for their important families. In fact, the richest tomb ever excavated in Mexico was found here in 1970. The golden necklaces, turquoise mosaic masks, crystal cups, and shell jewelry from tomb 7, now in the museum at the Church of Santo Domingo in Oaxaca, indicate that it may have been a royal tomb of the Mixtec kings.

MITLA

Reserve a full day to visit Mitla (A.D. 900–1521) since there are places to see along the way. Mitla is located 46 kilometers east of Oaxaca on highway 190 and your first (quick) stop en route is in Santa María del Tule, 9 kilometers outside Oaxaca. Here you find the famous El Tule Tree standing next to the church, just off the road—and what a tree it is! Over 2,000 years old, the cypress has a massive trunk and a sweeping canopy of leaves. Many of the redwoods in California are impressive, but El Tule supposedly has the widest girth of any tree in the world.

Mitla, Design Detail

After a brief stop, continue directly on to Mitla. At the ruins there are rows of stalls with vendors ardently selling all kinds of crafts and souvenirs. There is also a church here that is built from stones taken from the site. These ruins are totally different from those at Monte Albán—whereas Monte Albán has a glorious setting, in splendid isolation on the top of a hill, Mitla sits in the valley, embraced by the town. The site was built by the Mixtecs who succeeded the Zapotecs as the major power in the Oaxaca region. Mitla was still a flourishing religious and civil center when the Spanish arrived.

There are two main parts of the site to visit. The first is the Church Group, so named because the Spaniards built their church in the middle of the courtyard. This was a clever maneuver since they also pinched the stones from the temples to build the church you see today. Don't spend much time here since the Columns Group is far more interesting.

Here you find examples of the special feature of Mitla: its intricate geometric designs. There are 14 geometrical patterns in all, with each building embellished with its own artwork. To create these patterns, small pieces of stone were cut and set into the wall. The zigzag pattern in many of the designs is frequently duplicated in their woven designs.

YAGUL

After leaving Mitla, retrace your way back towards Oaxaca on the same road. After a short distance, at the sign, turn right for about a kilometer to Yagul, positioned on the slope of a gentle hill. This is a small site, but really worth seeing. One of its charms is that there are usually few tourists there. If you are lucky, you might be the only ones about. At the top of the ruins is a fortress, below which is a palace with six courtyards linked by intricate passages. Yagul is also noted for its superb ball court, one of the largest and best preserved in the Oaxaca Valley.

TEOTITLÁN DEL VALLE

After leaving Yagul, continue on towards Oaxaca. Watch for the turnoff to the right to Teotitlán, a craft town located about 4 kilometers from the main road. There are many craft villages in the area, but Teotitlán del Valle, which specializes in fine rugs, is one of our favorites. Here not only can you see the weavers at work and buy directly from them, but you can observe the entire process from gathering the wool then carding and spinning it, to making cochineal, the amazing red dye. This brilliant dye is made from crushing the bodies of thousand of tiny insects that live on nopal cactus leaves. Often you can see children gathering the bugs in containers for the use of the weavers. This process for making cochineal dates way back to the early pre-Columbian years. With the arrival of the Spanish in 1521, the dye remained popular and became in great demand by weavers in Europe. It is one of the continuities that so intriguingly still surround life in Mexico.

If you want to stop for lunch and are in no rush, you might enjoy the Restaurant Tlamanalli, located on the approach road into town. The service can be frustratingly slow, but the three sisters (dressed in local costume) who own it and prepare the food are extremely gracious. The fresh corn tortillas for your meal are patted out by hand and cooked on a *comal* (a round ceramic cooking platter placed over a charcoal fire) while you watch.

In addition to the above-mentioned places to see, there are many more if you have the time or inclination to continue your explorations around Oaxaca. There are small ruins tucked throughout the valley plus many towns where you can see and buy excellent crafts. When it is time to leave, you can return to Mexico City or perhaps link with another of the itineraries we suggest.

Oaxaca, Balloon Lady in the Park

Mayan Mysteries
A Loop of the Yucatán Peninsula

Tulum

In all of Mexico there is no place more enchanting than the Yucatán Peninsula, the country's southeast corner that swings up like the tail of a fish with one side facing the Gulf of Mexico and the other facing the Caribbean. Tucked onto this peninsula is a treasure chest of delights: splendid stretches of sugary-fine white-sand beaches; crystal-clear turquoise water; the second-largest coral reef in the world; superb snorkeling; incredible scuba diving; deep-sea fishing; expansive nature reserves including remarkable bird sanctuaries; vast jungles; appealing small islands nestled just offshore;

rich Mayan culture evident throughout; women still wearing typical white, gaily embroidered dresses; wonderful crafts including intricate handmade hammocks; charming Colonial towns; quaint fishing villages; splendid 17th-century haciendas (many converted to stunning small hotels that are featured in our guide); luxurious resorts; romantic, secluded hideaways. And, adding icing to the cake, the area is studded with breathtaking Mayan ruins—an archaeologist's dream.

This itinerary puts great emphasis on the wealth of Mayan sites, cloaked in the mysteries and glories of one of the world's great civilizations, which has faded into memory. It would be a pity to come to this niche of Mexico without visiting at least a few of these once-grand cities. Even if your idea of the perfect vacation is napping in a hammock on the beach (an option explored in our itinerary *Places to Play in the Sun: The Mexican Caribbean*), sneak away at least one day to visit a Mayan site.

There can a bit of confusion when one speaks of the Yucatán since Yucatán is both the name of the peninsula and also one of the states within it. In total there are three states that make up the peninsula: Campeche, Quintana Roo, and Yucatán. This itinerary makes a loop, passing through all three and slipping briefly into the adjacent state of Chiapas to visit Palenque, a remarkable Mayan ruin that can't be missed.

Following is some background information about the Mayan civilization and the Yucatán Peninsula to enrich what you will be experiencing en route.

THE MAYAN CIVILIZATION

One of the most advanced cultures of the pre-Columbian World was that of the Classic Maya. Technologically they were a Stone-Age people, lacking metal tools, draft animals or knowledge of the wheel but their artistic and intellectual achievements rank them with the other great civilizations of antiquity. The flowering of their culture encompassed a period from about A.D. 250–900. This span of years is defined for us by dates carved on large stone monuments known as *stele*. These stele are found at numerous Maya sites and their dates can be read and correlated with our modern calendar. The earliest known so far is A.D. 292 and the last is A.D. 889. These two dates mark the beginning and the end of the 600 years of the Classic Period.

The Maya people themselves neither begin nor end with this designation of time. For 2,000 years they lived in the jungles and mountain valleys of the region creating a base of art and cultural traditions from which the Classic Period developed. Today over 4,000,000 people of Maya descent still inhabit their original area, a geographical region that includes all the Yucatán Peninsula, Guatemala, and Belize, portions of Honduras and El Salvador, and parts of the Mexican states of Chiapas and Tabasco. While environment and climate vary widely, the culture itself was remarkably uniform, indicating close contacts and shared values during the Classic Period.

Maya Classic civilization has intrigued scholars and laymen alike since its rediscovery about 150 years ago, but only recently have archaeologists begun to uncover the reality rather than the myth of this ancient culture. For many years the Maya were thought to have been a peaceful group of talented farmers, devoted to religion and led by brilliant, intellectual priests whose primary concerns were astronomy and the recording of time. Recent discoveries now challenge these assumptions. The Maya elite may indeed have been the intellectual giants of their era and artistic and religious

Chacmool

activities were certainly intimately interwoven in the culture. Realistically, however, the Maya world was composed of small and large warlike states with constantly changing alliances based on military action and royal intermarriage. Their economic and demographic growth was built on secular activities such as trade and exchange, tribute payments, and military conquest. Even Maya religious practices were not peaceful, simple ceremonies as previously thought. Instead we now know that they were elaborate costumed rituals, which included blood letting, brutality, and human sacrifices—all dedicated to demanding gods and the rulers who were their earthly representatives.

As evidence of the bloody religious ceremonies practiced by the Maya and other cultures in Mesoamerica, archaeologists found at some Mayan sites an almost life-size sculpture called a *chacmool*. This is a finely carved stone figure reclining on its back with knees drawn up in front. It was here that the heart was cut from the sacrificial victim and probably placed on the stone disk on the chacmool's abdomen as an offering to the gods.

Like many other early civilizations, the Maya had an overwhelming concern with death and the afterlife and they buried their rulers and elite with elaborate gifts of pottery, jade, and stone. These artifacts, along with recent major advancements in reading the Maya hieroglyphic texts and meticulous archaeological excavations, have done much to expand our understanding of the ancient Maya and their way of life.

There are a number of specific traits and accomplishments of the Classic Period that set it apart from the Pre-Classic and Post-Classic Maya Periods. Among these are: a sophisticated calendrical system that can be correlated with our modern calendar; a hieroglyphic writing system; the erection of tall stone stele to commemorate actual events in time; the use and possibly the invention of the concept of zero; the development of an elaborate and complicated style of art; and the construction of monumental stone architecture using a corbel arch.

Architecture is probably the most important, and certainly the most visible, form of Maya art and creativity. While sites on the seacoasts, in the mountain valleys, and on the Yucatán Peninsula are fairly easily seen and visited, massive stone ruins of ancient cities still lie buried deep in the jungle. Structures at almost all Maya sites include palaces, pyramids, temples, roads, reservoirs, markets, and ball courts—all built of stone and covered originally with a coating of white stucco and bright paint.

Palenque, El Palacio

The magnificent high stepped pyramids that rise above the landscape were once surmounted by temples dedicated to the Maya gods and often hidden within their depths are the rich tombs of Maya kings. At large sites, these immense pyramids usually dominate both ends of central plazas with lower platforms supporting the palaces and public building associated with them. *Sacbes* (stucco-covered stone roadways) connect regional sites and were probably used for commerce and trading caravans, movements of troops, and for ritual processionals. A ritual ball game was played on stone courts found all over Mesoamerica. In the Maya area the game took on cosmic significance relating to the ongoing struggle between the forces of the day and night (the sun and moon, good and evil, etc.). In addition, the actual origin myth of the Maya was based on the outcome of a game of ball. In the Maya book, the *Popol Vuh*, two young twin ball players descend to the underworld to play a game of ball against the gods of pestilence, famine, and death. They eventually defeat these gods of darkness on the underworld ball court of Xibalba. Their hard-won game assures the victory of light and life over the forces of darkness and death. The ritual sport often ended with the decapitation of the captain of the losing team; numerous depictions of this event are seen on painted and carved pottery, colorful murals, and the carved friezes on the walls of the ball court at the site of Chichén Itzá.

Though architecture may be the most impressive of Maya achievements, other artifacts also offer concrete evidence of the skill of Maya craftsmen and artists. These highly trained professionals were probably attached to ruling families or ceremonial centers and held special status in Maya society. With a few recently discovered exceptions, artists and craftsmen remain anonymous. Most creations were unsigned by their makers and the artist was primarily important as an instrument through which the rulers and gods were honored. These talented artists used various media to create beautiful objects. Stonemasons carved tall limestone stele with figures of rulers wearing the elaborate feather headdresses and jade ornaments that were status symbols among Maya elite. Scribes carved or painted hieroglyphic texts and calendrical information on stone monuments, walls of buildings and the pages of *codices* (Maya books). Potters decorated the smoothed surfaces of ceramic vessels with scenes from the underworld, activities of gods and kings, and repetitive hieroglyphics texts. It has been suggested that the primary function of some artists may have been as scribes, craftsmen who painted the codices, which were once abundant in the Maya world. All but four of these books have been lost due to damp climate and to their intentional destruction by the invading Spanish conquerors. Nevertheless, enough evidence remains to indicate strong resemblances between these lost books and the scenes and hieroglyphs painted on Maya burial ceramics and on the walls of the ancient buildings.

The Maya were also highly skilled workers in jade, shell, flint, and bone. Jade was the most precious of all materials to the Maya. They were especially fond of the emerald-green or imperial jade and carved it into bead necklaces, masks, pendants, and ear-spools. Gold and other metals were not worked by the Classic Maya, but later when gold was known and used during the post-Classic Period, jade remained the more valued and preferred material. The Classic Maya used the same hieroglyphic symbols to mean jade, water, and precious—indicating the gemstone's supreme value in their life and religious activities.

Other artifacts made of perishable materials are now lost from the archaeological record but can be identified from depictions on ceramics and stone. Finely woven and decorated textiles, paper ornaments, bark-paper books, and many objects carved in wood were documented in this way, but have not survived the damp tropical climate.

After about A.D. 900, the Classic Maya cities located in the tropical jungle region collapsed. In other Maya regions, such as the Yucatán Peninsula, Maya traditions continued, but the magnificent sites of this lowland area were abandoned to the jungle and the great art of the period ceased. Rulers, dignitaries, and priests disappeared and the elaborate religious ceremonies were no longer performed in the temples and plazas created for them. The reasons for the collapse are still unclear. Possibly constant warfare, overpopulation, drought, epidemics, and military invasion may all have been contributing factors. Whatever the causes, the collapse was so complete that some of the lowland tropical areas once occupied by this civilization were only sparsely inhabited until about 50 years ago. Yet this vanished civilization is not truly "lost". Archaeologists continue to work and recover artifacts and information from the once-forgotten jungle sites and magnificent works of art still remain to speak to us across the centuries of the culture and people of the Classic Maya world.

THE YUCATÁN

The Maya cities of the Yucatán Peninsula survived for over 300 years after the fall of the heartland sites. While the Yucatán sites shared fully in the Classic Maya traditions, their location on important trade routes and an influx of population and new ideas (some no doubt from the collapsed jungle cities) apparently encouraged continuing prosperity.

The Yucatán Peninsula is a limestone shelf. At the base of the peninsula are Mexican jungles and the frontiers of Guatemala and Belize. Much of the Yucatán is devoid of ground water such as springs or rivers, and is dependent for its supply of water on *cenotes* (fallen limestone sink holes which reveal underground rivers) or catchment systems for preserving heavy seasonal rainfall. As might be expected, the major sites of this geographical area occur where fertile soils can be supplied with water by the use of *chultuns* (man-made cistern systems) or where cenotes occur naturally.

Chichén Itzá, El Caracol

During the pre-Classic Period (600 B.C.–A.D. 300) there were a number of important early cities in the Yucatán. These were sites with massive architecture and sophisticated water control systems, such as Calakmul, Edzná, and Dzibilchaltún. They were of major importance in establishing the artistic and intellectual traditions on which Classic Maya culture was built.

Throughout the following Classic Period (A.D. 300–900) some of these Yucatán sites faded but the area still remained a part of the amazing cultural development of such well-known Maya jungle cities as Tikal, Palenque, and Copan. Amazingly, the Yucatán region did not share in the collapse of the sites in the heartland area. Indeed, we now know that the rise of the great Puuc sites such as Uxmal, Kabah, Sayil, and Labná and the florescence of the magnificent city of Chichén Itzá occurred as sites to the south were declining. The emergence of the greatest period in the Yucatán began perhaps as late as A.D. 800 and continued until the fall of Chichén Itzá at around 1250. During these years new ideas and new populations became part of the Maya civilization, yet lifestyle and world view retained the Classic Maya concepts of culture.

Chichén Itzá was the most important Maya city on the Yucatán Peninsula until A.D. 1250. It exhibits clear influence from the valley of Mexico at this time. Contacts were probably established by ongoing trading interaction between Central Mexico and the Yucatán beginning at around A.D. 700. However, influence did not flow one way; Mayan influences can be seen at Cacaxtla and Xochicalco in Central Mexico and people and ideas must have moved freely in both directions. The mechanisms for these exchanges/contacts may not have been direct (e.g. migrations, conquests) but may have been mostly closely tied to the increasing role of merchants and traders toward the end of the Classic Period throughout Mesoamerica. Archaeological research indicates that the Yucatán was a prime source for the trade of salt, honey, slaves, cotton, and perhaps cacao as well—all major items of exchange in the pre-Columbian world.

Around A.D. 1250 Chichén Itzá fell to a group of competing Yucatán states led by Mayapan but it remained a center of religious pilgrimage and activity until the middle of the 16th century. By that time the Maya/Yucatán region was torn apart by small warring states participating in a complex trading system. This was the situation encountered by the Spanish when they first landed on the Mayan island of Cozumel.

The actual conquest of the Yucatán did not come until 1528 when Francisco de Montejo, under the auspices of the Spanish crown, invaded the region. However, the dispersed states of the peninsula did not succumb easily to the invaders and fought on until 1542 when a Spanish capital was finally established at Mérida.

Today descendants of the Maya live on in towns and villages of the peninsula. Customs from the pre-Hispanic era dominate much of rural life, and traditions in agriculture, religion, and language still reflect the ancient patterns of the Maya world.

RECOMMENDED PACING: We recommend 12 nights if you want to follow this itinerary in its entirety. More, if you are a real archaeology buff and want to linger at each site; less, if you want to just choose a section of the itinerary to tag on as a bonus to a holiday at one of the Yucatán's superb beach resorts. We suggest two nights in Chichén Itzá, three nights in the Mérida area, two nights in Palenque, three nights in Río Bec, and two nights along the Riviera Maya.

DESTINATION I   CHICHÉN ITZÁ

Cancún makes a convenient starting point since its international airport has numerous planes arriving daily from other Mexican cities, the United States, Canada, and Europe. It's hard to believe that only a few years ago there was practically nothing here except long stretches of deserted white-sand beaches studded with coconut palms. Only an adventuresome few found this hidden paradise until the government, wanting to lure more tourists to Mexico, developed Cancún into a planned resort. Since then, the government has created other tourist destinations, but none have come close to being such a tremendous success.

If your flight arrives late in the day, or if you prefer to relax on the beach before starting out, spend a few days in Cancún. The best hotels are not in the town but line a narrow, 22-kilometer spit of land that wraps around a large lagoon. Here you find an endless row of hotels stretching along the beach. Most of them offer an "all-inclusive package," which includes your airfare (usually a charter flight), your room, your meals, and sometimes even drinks. Most of the hotels are huge high-rises (several with over a thousand rooms) but, by and large, they are of attractive design and high-quality construction. Modern hotels, fast-food restaurants, golf courses, trendy bars, and shopping malls dull the cultural shock of leaving home. If you prefer a more intimate, Mexican ambiance yet want to be close to Cancún, consider staying at Isla Mujeres, a delightful small island about half-an-hour's boat ride off the coast. If this option interests you, ask about the boat schedule when making your hotel reservations. Check the hotel section for suggestions of hotels both in Cancún and Isla Mujeres.

After picking up your rental car, continue on to Chichén Itzá. It takes about two hours for the 200-kilometer drive via an excellent highway, the 180. The exit to Chichén Itzá is well marked and it is just a few minutes from the highway to the town. We highly recommend two hotels here, the Hotel Mayaland and the Hacienda Chichén. Each has its own personality; each is exceptional. Look in the hotel section to see which most appeals to you. Both are snuggled right next to the ruins, so you can walk from your hotel to the entrance in minutes.

If you arrive at your hotel in the afternoon, plan to attend the Sound and Light program that is performed each evening (go early to get a good seat). You can rent earphones that translate what you are hearing into English at the ticket counter. These frequently don't work very well but this is no great problem as the story is really self-explanatory. As dusk settles into darkness, the temples are gently illuminated, one by one, and the saga unfolds. One of the stories told is of the decline of this powerful city, which, according to legend, began when the city's emperor stole, on her wedding day, the beautiful bride-to-be of his greatest rival, who retaliated by laying siege to Chichén Itzá.

You will not only enjoy the ambiance of your hotel, but its convenience to the ruins. Chichén Itzá is one of the Yucatán's most popular archaeological sites and attracts hordes of tourists. Being so conveniently close, you can be the first one at the gate in the morning and be able to enjoy the site at its finest—before many people arrive and in the cool of the morning when the soft light is best for photography. We suggest you spend several hours exploring the site then, during the heat of the day, return to your hotel for lunch and perhaps a nap by the pool. Then, as the shadows lengthen, walk again through the site on your own for a final viewing and wonderful photographs. You will probably be lured to climb up and down many of the pyramids and, even if you don't, you will be walking a lot since the site stretches over almost 10 square kilometers, so wear comfortable shoes. To increase your enjoyment, we suggest you hire a guide. They are available at the gate as you enter, or else your hotel can arrange one for you. Below is a bit of history and information on what to see.

CHICHÉN ITZÁ (A.D. c.700–1250)

The places mentioned below just begin to touch on the rich selection of fascinating places to see within this once-mighty city. They are some of our favorites, and will get you started.

Cenote de los Sacrificios (Cenote of the Sacrifices): This natural well, reached by a path through the jungle from the central plaza, served not only as a water source for the city but also as a place where offerings were made to the gods. Over the years a number of archaeological expeditions have recovered artifacts from the bottom of this deep limestone sinkhole. Golden figurines and disks, jade objects, and ceramic bowls were found along with skeletons, primarily of adolescents and children. All had been offered as sacrifices or perhaps messengers to the gods.

El Caracol (The Snail): Located a bit away from the central plaza, reached by a ten-minute stroll, is a second set of buildings. Be sure not to miss the path, as here you find one of Chichén Itzá's highlights: a fascinating, very unusual domed structure that was obviously used as an observatory. The name "snail" comes from the inner staircase, which, if you stretch your imagination, looks a bit like a snail.

Chichén Itzá, Cenote

Grupo de las Mil Columnas (Complex of the Thousand Columns): Flanking two sides of the Temple of the Warriors are row upon row of stone columns, some carved, some plain. This awesome scene looks like something one would expect to find in Greece, not Mexico. It is surmised that these columns originally supported a thatched roof covering a huge open market. The temple and the columns make a wonderful photograph when taken in late afternoon from the top of the Pyramid of Kukulkán.

Juego de Pelota (Great Ball Court): This dramatic ball court is the largest in Mesoamerica and while there are 12 other ball courts at Chichén Itzá, this one is spectacular. The game was played as a ritual performance as well as a sport, and is one of the hallmarks of pre-Columbian Mesoamerican culture. At the end of the ball game the captain who lost was often sacrificed to the gods. This sacrificial scene is realistically carved in a long frieze along both side walls of the court. Look carefully and you will see two rows of ball players standing behind each captain. At the center, these captains face each other across a large rubber ball enclosing a skeletal head. One of the captains stands holding a knife in one hand and a severed head in the other; his opponent kneels and from his headless neck issue seven streams of blood. This graphic scene speaks clearly to the practice of human sacrifice and the offering of human blood to the gods to ensure fertility of crops and the continuity of life.

Pirámide de Kukulkán (Pyramid of Kukulkán): This impressive, 24-meter-high pyramid soars above the other buildings in the complex. Two of the four sides have been restored and this is a favorite target for schoolchildren who seem to zoom up the 91 steps to the top. You might want to join them for there is a terrific view up there. When you add up the steps on all four sides plus the platform above, the sum is 365, which clearly links its significance to the Mayan calendar, which had 365 days in its year.

SIDE TRIPS FROM CHICHÉN ITZÁ

If you want to extend your stay in Chichén Itzá, you can take a few side trips. Among the nearby places we suggest are Izamal, an early Spanish Colonial town with a church and convent built on top of one of the Yucatán's highest pyramids, and the Sacred Cave of Balankanche, which lies about 7 kilometers from Chichén Itzá. This cave contains numbers of chambers which were once filled with hundreds of ceramic incense burners and miniature *metates* (grinding stones) laid out on the cave floors as offerings to the rain god. Caves were seen by the Maya and most other Mesoamerican cultures as sacred places and as entrances to the underworld. The one is still used by local *shamans* (priests) who continue to regard it as sacred.

Excuse us for not giving an exact location for your next few nights' sojourn, and instead rather vaguely saying your destination is the "Mérida area"—after pondering where to suggest you stay, it was impossible to recommend just one place. You can, of course, choose a hotel in the heart of Mérida, but dotting the countryside that wraps around the city is a rich selection of hotels, including gorgeous 18th-century haciendas that have been converted into superb small inns. Here you find the centuries slip away and you feel like a guest in the home of a wealthy Spanish aristocrat, landlord of a vast sisal plantation. Some of these architectural treasures are so secluded that their addresses are listed under Mérida, followed by a name that will give you a clue to their location. Any one of the following properties (all described in detail in the hotel section) would make an outstanding choice to use as a base of operation: Hacienda Katanchel, Hacienda Santa Rosa, Hacienda Temozón, Hacienda San José, Hacienda Xcantún, and the Lodge at Uxmal. Another of our favorites, Hacienda Uayamón (which is closer to Campeche than to Mérida) would also work well as a hub.

Below are described some of the places to visit in this region of the peninsula.

MÉRIDA

Mérida, founded by the Spaniards in 1542 upon an earlier Mayan city, is worth a visit to enjoy its rich Colonial heritage. The city is laid out with all streets converging at a large, pretty, central plaza called the Plaza Grande or Plaza de la Independencia. Facing onto this parklike square is the imposing **cathedral**, the oldest in the Americas. Across the square from the cathedral is the **Palacio Municipal**, enhanced in front by a series of arches and topped by a tall clock tower. A few blocks away is the **Teatro José Peón Contereas**, an elaborate theater that attests to the wealth and sophistication generated by the prosperous sisal plantations nearby.

CAMPECHE

The small port city of Campeche, located on the Gulf of Mexico, 178 kilometers southwest of Mérida, makes a great outing. Be sure to include at the same time the nearby archaeological site of Edzná (see below). At the heart of Campeche is a colorful small Spanish Colonial town whose stone walls, battlements, watchtowers, and churches still stand. You can stroll through the cobbled streets of the old town and walk along the top of the massive walls that once kept out the English, French, and Dutch pirates who preyed on the rich port cities on the Gulf of Mexico during the 16th and 17th centuries. Few tourists know about Campeche, but it is a jewel, well worth a visit both for its intimate glimpse of the Spanish Colonial period and for its small museums that contain archaeological treasures from the surrounding region. At the south edge of town is a picture-perfect fort, the Fuerte de San Miguel, set on top of a hill with commanding views of the sea. Inside is a superb museum, renovated in 2001. Ceramic figurines from the Island of Jaina and steles with carved surfaces and hieroglyphic writing can be viewed here but, above all, don't miss the incredible jade pieces from rich burials at the ancient site of Calakmul. These astonishing items, consisting of bead necklaces, large ear spools (large round ear ornaments), and mosaic jade masks are some of the rarest and most beautiful objects remaining from the Classic Period of the Mayan culture.

RÍO CELESTÚN BIOSPHERE RESERVE

On the coast southwest of Mérida you find the small village of Celestún where fishermen still pull their boats up onto the wide sandy beach at night as they have done for generations and lining the waterfront are simple restaurants featuring the catch of the day. This is a very laid-back place with few tourists. The main attraction here is a wonderful wildlife sanctuary, an enticing spot for all naturalists, but especially for bird watchers as there are more than 200 species of birds to be seen here. As you drive into town, the road crosses over the estuary and at the far end of the bridge, as you look down to your left, you see many flat-bottomed boats docked with boatmen eager to be your guide. There is a cute little office with a tiny museum where you can buy your ticket (the price is set and varies only according to the length of tour). Most of the tours last about an hour and a half, during which time you go up the shallow waterway. Your guide will point out many birds along the way, but the highlight of the trip is seeing the flocks of pink flamingos that come to the shallow waters to feed. Although at some times of the year they are more abundant than others, you can almost always see them. To avoid frightening the birds away, the boats are not allowed to get close, so it is difficult to get good photographs. On the way back, the boatmen stop at some intriguing *cenotes* — freshwater pools formed by underground springs. These are especially fun because you get out of the boat and walk through the tangle of mangrove jungle on a raised pathway. For those so inclined, there is time to swim in the crystal-clear water. If you really want to get away from the world, we recommend the Hotel Eco Paraíso Xixim, located on the beach within the Biosphere Reserve, about 10 kilometers north of Celestún (see the hotel section for details).

ARCHAEOLOGICAL SITES

The history of this part of the Yucatán Peninsula dates far back in time. During the middle to late pre-Classic Period (600 B.C.–A.D. 300) a number of important early cities arose on the peninsula with massive architecture and sophisticated water-control systems. During the following Classic Period (A.D. 300–900) while the cities in the Yucatán shared the amazing cultural development of such astounding Mayan cities in the southern lowland jungles as Tikal, Palenque, and Copan, they remained somewhat on the periphery of the Maya heartland. It was during the late Classic and early post-Classic Period (A.D. 700–1050), at the time Tikal, Palenque, and Copan were declining, that the great cities of the Yucatán rose to their height of power and continued to flourish for another 300 years. Below are a few highlights of these sites. You can see any of them by driving yourself, but your experience will be enhanced if you splurge and hire a car with a driver/guide (the concierge at your hotel can help you with arrangements). Below are suggestions of what to see in each area.

UXMAL

Uxmal, 70 kilometers southwest of Mérida, is found in the Puuc Hills, a low range of hills in the southwest region of the Yucatán Peninsula. In this area the Maya developed a magnificent style of architecture named Puuc, after the hills, characterized by immense palaces, pyramids, and temples decorated with three-dimensional mosaic stone friezes. Cities here were connected by roads called *sacbes*, which cut through the jungle and entered the towns through beautiful vaulted archways, many of which can still be seen. The Puuc Hills are dotted with ruins (probably more than 200 are scattered in the area), with Uxmal being the largest and most impressive. Only a small portion of the massive site has been excavated and one wonders what is yet to come.

Cuadrángle de las Monjas (Quadrangle of the Nuns): Just beyond the Pyramid of the Soothsayer is a broad courtyard surrounded on four sides by large, richly embellished buildings. This large quadrangle reminded the Spaniards of the cloisters of a nunnery, hence its name.

Juego de Pelota (Ball Court): Like most Mayan cities, Uxmal had its ceremonial ball court. Spectators watched from two thick walls, one on each side. This is a particularly well-preserved ball court and shouldn't be missed.

Palacio del Gobernador (Palace of the Governor): This gigantic building (almost 100 meters long, 12 meters wide, and 9 meters high) is one of the finest masterpieces of Mayan architecture. Its exterior is richly embellished with intricate stonework geometric patterns and friezes.

Pirámide del Adivino (Pyramid of the Soothsayer): This is a most unusual, extremely dramatic building with rounded sides and steps leading up on two sides to a temple crowning the top. From the summit, which is nearly 28 meters high, there is a stunning view.

KABAH

At the height of its glory Kabah was one of the largest cities in northern Yucatán. At the entrance to the ceremonial city are the ruins of an arch that marked the start of the great Mayan road connecting Kabah to Uxmal, 23 kilometers to the northwest. Kabah's main attractions include:

Arco Monumental (Monumental Arch): This intricately decorated arch, which frames a high open gateway, is one of the most highly embellished, best-preserved arches in the Mayan world.

El Palacio (The Palace): This 30-room, two-story building standing on a hill was perhaps a palace housing the nobility of Kabah.

Palacio de los Mascarones (Temple of the Masks): Over 250 intricate stone mosaic masks depicting the rain god, Chac, adorn this entire structure. These grinning faces with trunk-like noses are quite extraordinary.

LABNÁ

Labná, 30 kilometers southeast of Uxmal, is not as large as its neighbor, but has several interesting structures including its magnificent archway, one of the most beautiful in the Maya World.

SAYIL

We like Sayil, which, although small, is a particularly appealing site. Its highlight, El Palacio, is a three-story stone palace with more than 90 rooms. The base structure is crumbling, but the two upper stories are in much better condition. The middle level, by far the most eye-catching, is enhanced by a double row of columns, the lower row alternating with porticoes leading into narrow passageways and the upper row enhanced with ornate carvings.

OXKINTOK

This extensive Mayan site has towering pyramids, palaces, ball courts, and numbers of elaborate causeways. While this Puuc-style city has been mapped and some of its great buildings have been uncovered and preserved, many of its structures are still unexcavated. The site lies somewhat off the beaten track so it attracts only a few tourists, but you can explore the city on your own, climbing the pyramids and walking through the abandoned plazas of this ancient Mayan center.

EDZNÁ

The first major flourishing of the magnificent Mayan city of Edzná occurred during the Late Pre-Classic Period (450 B.C.–A.D. 300). Long before the other Puuc sites were established, this city was home to a large population that tilled the fertile soils of the valley. Its resurgence in the Classic Period saw the construction of massive pyramids, public buildings, and palaces. The largest and most impressive of these is a five-story palace/pyramid structure that dominates the large main plaza. From its summit you can look out over this immense ancient center and see the outline of the causeways and canals that once ran through the site as well as earth-covered mounds that mark buildings yet to be uncovered. Here at Edzná the Maya built the most extensive hydraulic system in the region, with canals and ponds preserving water for irrigation and the city's needs. At this site the population also raised many steles to honor their kings and commemorate royal events; some are still standing in the plaza but a number of these can be seen beneath a modern thatched-roof structure at the entrance to the site.

DESTINATION III   PALENQUE

In order to include the stunning ruins at Palenque, this itinerary dips briefly away from the Yucatán Peninsula. Get an early start—this is a long drive, but the treasure at the end is well worth the effort. The amount of time it takes depends upon where you are staying in the Mérida area (to give you an idea, it is about 550 kilometers from Mérida to Palenque). Although the road is good (part of it four-lane) and there is usually not much traffic, expect the drive to take most of the day. From Mérida take highway 180 south toward Campeche, bypassing the town and continuing on to Champotón. Here the road splits and you continue on 261 to Escárcega, a scraggly town that you go through before joining highway 186 in the direction of Villahermosa. Before reaching Villahermosa, the road passes very briefly into the state of Tabasco and then into Chiapas. After crossing over the river that marks the border into Chiapas, it is about 35 kilometers to where you turn left on 199, continuing for 22 kilometers to Palenque. Remember, you will need to a minimum of two nights here.

PALENQUE

Palenque, Ball Court

Palenque, one of the most beautiful ancient cities discovered in the Americas, is tucked in the jungle where the Usumacinta River drainage meets the coastal plain of the Gulf of Mexico. Due to the interest and dedicated scholarship of a number of talented epigraphers and art historians, the history of Palenque is better known than that of any other Mayan site. The rich hieroglyphic texts carved on stone panels, buildings, and monuments have brought to life the story of the rulers of Palenque, their names, dates, and historic events.

There are many hotels here, but surprisingly few outstanding ones for such a major tourist destination. Our favorite, by far, is the Chan-kah Resort Village. Although a rather commercial hotel catering to tour groups, it offers intimacy and simple charm in small bungalows nestled in a jungle setting (see the hotel section for details). By the time you arrive in Palenque and get settled, it will probably be too late for sightseeing so relax by the hotel's large, lagoon-like swimming pool and have dinner in the open-air restaurant before turning in for a good night's sleep. Tomorrow is a big day.

You need at least one full day to explore this lovely Mayan ceremonial city. Get up early and be ready to buy your ticket as the gates open. Not only do you want to arrive before countless busloads of tourists pull into the parking lot, but morning is a magical time. The mists from the mountains hang over the ancient buildings, lending an air of mystery to the magnificent city. Stone structures of amazing beauty rise on every side as you walk among the ruins of the great *castillo*, the immense palace, temples, and ball court. The pyramids, crowned by temples, cluster around plazas, each temple decorated with inscribed panels and tall, soaring roof-combs of open-stone fretwork. There are guides available who will enhance your explorations, though all of the buildings have plaques describing them in Spanish, English, and Mayan. There is a treasure of wonders to see here and to get you started, we mention below a few of our favorites.

Templo de las Inscripciones (Temple of the Inscriptions): This towering pyramid that dominates the landscape is named for the stone hieroglyphic panels found within. In 1948 a Mexican archaeologist, Alberto Ruz, discovered a steep hidden stairway leading from the floor of the elevated temple deep into the heart of the tall pyramid. At the bottom of the stairway, under 400 tons of rubble which were removed by hand, he found a royal crypt occupied by Pacal, the most important ruler of Palenque. He had been buried with great splendor and was accompanied by magnificent jade jewelry and an elegant jade mosaic mask. His sarcophagus was topped by an elaborate lid carved with figures and a hieroglyphic text tracing his dynastic descent from the gods and assuring his royal presence and rebirth in the afterlife. The discovery of this tomb was of major importance to Mayan archaeology because it definitively established that many of the massive Mayan pyramids were the sites of royal burials. Note: To the right of the entrance you will see the tomb of Alberto Ruz, who wanted to be buried next to the temple where he made his remarkable discovery.

El Palacio (The Palace): This huge, imposing complex is quite unlike others in the Mayan world. It looks more like a structure one might expect to find in Europe, with a slender, tall watchtower, a labyrinth of intricate rooms, a series of inner courtyards, galleries faced by columns, and exquisite stucco designs. This building is thought to have been the dwelling of royalty since steam baths and bedrooms were found here. What is especially interesting about this building is that many of the rooms still have roofs, making it easier to visualize what life here might have been like. It is fun to explore this maze of rooms via dimly lit passageways. El Palacio is the building that the intrepid explorer John Lloyd Stephens and his talented artist colleague, Frederic Catherwood, chose to make their home when visiting Palenque. These two men explored this fascinating region between 1839 and 1841, laying the groundwork for later archaeological expeditions. Before heading off to Mexico, borrow Stephens's book, *Incidents of Travel in Yucatán*, *Volume II*, from your local library. It is enthralling to gaze at Catherwood's wonderful illustrations and see what Palenque looked like before being rescued from its slumber of many years within the jungle.

Templo del Conde (Temple of the Count): This temple is named for Jean Frederic Maximilien de Waldec, an eccentric German count who lived here for a year in 1832 in a small temple tucked at the top of this high pyramid The count brought along his mistress, who must have been quite madly in love with him to camp high atop a pyramid in the middle of a steaming jungle without running water or air conditioning—modern

Palenque, Temple of the Count

amenities that today might make such a romp quite fun. No doubt the views were romantic, but the steps up and down each day must have been quite arduous.

When visiting this gigantic complex, it is intriguing to realize that only about a third of this awesome city has been uncovered. It is interesting to walk along the paths lacing the dense jungle, watching teams of archaeologists going about their meticulous work.

To complete your day, before returning to the hotel, be sure to stop by the fine Museum of Palenque, which you passed on the right side of the road as you drove into the site. This museum contains many objects of jade, stone, and pottery excavated at the city. In addition, in a building next to the museum is an exceptionally attractive gift shop that handles not only books and replicas of objects but also wonderful ethnographic materials such as textiles and carvings made by modern Mayan artists.

SIDE TRIP FROM PALENQUE—AGUA AZUL

If you have the luxury of time and a personality that never wants to miss a thing, consider an off-the-beaten-path side trip from Palenque to Agua Azul. Although the distance is only about 65 kilometers, it takes over an hour to get there since the road is winding and there is usually a lot of traffic. To reach Agua Azul, from Palenque go south on highway 199. After about 10 kilometers the road splits and at the junction, keep to the right on 199 toward Ocosingo and San Cristobal de las Casas. As the road climbs into the lush mountains you need to watch the road markers—at about marker 87 turn to the right at a sign to Cascadas de Agua Azul. You pay at the entrance and find yourself in a favorite spot for Mexican families. If you are into "local color," this is it! A river rushes through the rich foliage, forming rapids and waterfalls that drop into tranquil pools of turquoise water. On holidays and weekends the place is positively packed with people: children splashing in the crystal-clear water; babies napping in the shade; women preparing tables laden with food; grandmothers asleep in hammocks stretched between the trees; men chatting while enjoying cold beers; lovers strolling hand in hand; youngsters climbing steep paths to the top of the waterfalls. There is an amazing number of open-air restaurants, sitting in a long line. Note: Don't even think about visiting Agua Azul during the rainy season, which turns the clear turquoise waters into a muddy river.

DESTINATION IV   RÍO BEC

When it's time to leave Palenque, retrace your way to highway 186 then turn right toward Escárcega. Go through Escárcega and continue east on 186, following signs to

Chetumal. Dotting this stretch of highway between Escárcega and Chetumal is a group of fabulous Mayan ruins in an area called Río Bec. These are some of our favorite archaeological sites in Mexico—not only because they have awesome structures, but also because you are frequently the only person about, a truly magical experience.

We suggest two hotels in the Río Bec area: the Chicanná Ecovillage across from the ruins of Chicanná and The Explorean Kohunlich near the ruins of Kohunlich. Although approximately 70 kilometers apart, either makes an excellent hub from which to visit the various sites. We highly recommend both hotels, although they are quite different. The Chicanná Ecovillage has simple rooms in attractive two-story thatched-roofed bungalows that look like something out of *Robinson Crusoe*. The super-deluxe Explorean Kohunlich has beautifully decorated rooms in cottages overlooking dense jungle as far as the eye can see. For details on both, check out the hotel section.

Río Bec, Becán

The Río Bec style occurs in a series of important archaeological sites that reached their zenith from A.D. 600 to 900. Some of these are incredibly well preserved. Until recently, access to these ruins was appalling, with four-wheel drive needed to maneuver the potholed roads. All that has changed—the government has improved all the roads and now access is easy. Some of the sites that tour books said even recently were five-hour drives from the highway are now within an easy hour's drive. However, news of these huge improvements has not yet leaked out, leaving a visit to the archaeological sites a sublime experience. Nowhere else can you visit such outstanding Mayan monuments in such blissful isolation. But don't wait too long because tourists will surely soon be flocking here. When we explored all of the ruins described below, we usually had the place to ourselves. Another bonus here is that the signs are excellent and each building is clearly labeled in English, Spanish, and Mayan so that you know what you are seeing. Below are descriptions of the various cities we suggest seeing, arranged according to their location along highway 186, starting with Calakmul as the most western site and Dzibanche as the most eastern site. There is no way that you can see all these in one day: you will definitely need two since Calakmul alone will take a day. Study the recommendations below. If your time is limited, you might like to know that our personal favorites are Calakmul, Becán, and Kohunlich.

CALAKMUL

If you have time to visit only one ruin, choose Calakmul. It is stupendous and although rarely visited, ranks in grandeur with its greatest rival, Tikal, which is somewhat alike in layout and architecture. It is not surprising that they share similarities, since although Tikal is in Guatemala, the border is only 30 kilometers away. This site is farther off the highway than any of the others that we mention in the Río Bec area. After leaving the main road, it takes about an hour to drive there, with most of the distance along a single-lane road. However, the road is straight and has little traffic. Best of all, you pass through the Calakmul Biosphere Reserve (established in 1989 to protect the natural rainforest) and you are likely to spot many species of exotic birds and some wild animals. In the spring, wild turkeys, resembling colorful peacocks, are common. The city spreads over a huge area of 25 square kilometers and it is estimated that at the height of its grandeur (A.D. 400–800) as many as 200,000 people lived here. It is fascinating to wander along the jungle paths, coming across grand structures rising from the tangle of trees, including the highest pyramid ever built by the Maya, which soars 53 meters into the sky and has a base of 5 acres. As found in other sophisticated Mayan sites, Calakmul had an observatory for charting the movements of the stars. Other places of interest include a huge market and ball courts. The site is still in the process of being renovated. (Plan to make Calakmul an all-day outing.)

CHICANNÁ

From Calakmul go back to highway 186, turn right, and continue for 44 kilometers to Chicanná, located on the right side of the highway, just across from the Chicanná Ecovillage Resort. This is the third-largest of the Río Bec cities and is known for its stunning architecture. Its special feature is Temple 2, called the Earth Monster. Its doorway is a giant mouth through which the high priests entered to communicate with the underworld. You can clearly see the eyes, the nose, and the menacing teeth, which hang down above the door.

BECÁN

Leaving Chicanná, it is only 2 kilometers on 186 to Becán, which is on the left side of the highway. Although intimate in size, this is a real gem. You find here a series of courtyards surrounded by huge pyramids, so steep that a rope is provided to give you leverage as you ascend. Some of the buildings have deep tunnel-like staircases that lead to nowhere. Fun to explore, but be aware that you need to back out the same way you entered. Also of interest is a giant mask on one of the temple walls, covered by glass to protect it against the elements. The ubiquitous ball court is here too, of course. The city was originally surrounded by a 2-kilometer moat crossed by seven bridges. The moat is now dry, but you can clearly see its remains.

XPUJIL

The next ruin is Xpujil, only 6 kilometers beyond Becán on 186 on the left side of the highway. This site isn't as impressive as the others you have visited, but worth a stop to see the three crumbling towers, which must have been quite splendid when originally built. Notice the picture that depicts what the towers probably looked like in their prime.

KOHUNLICH

Leaving Xpujil, it is 62 kilometers farther east on 186 until you see the turnoff to the right to Kohunlich, which is about a 15-minute drive off the main highway. The special features here are an impressive pyramid, the Temple of the Sun (also called Temple of the Masks), whose steps are flanked on each side with eight huge stone masks, some of which show traces of their original red paint. These quite fearsome faces have bulging eyes and protruding ears. Kohunlich covers a vast area and it is fun to wander the paths that wind through the jungle. You will come across a ball court and also a large plaza which was the market place.

DZIBANCHE & KINCHUA

From Kohunlich, return to highway 186 and continue east. In about 2 kilometers you come to a turnoff to the left marked to Dzibanche and Kinchua, located about half an hour's drive off the highway. These are two individual sites, but so close together that one entrance fee covers both. Don't bother going to Kinchua unless you have an interest in seeing what archaeological sites look like before restoration. Dzibanche, however, is beautiful, not so much for its structures as for its setting. You walk through a splendid forest with the path meandering through lovely glens when suddenly in a clearing before you, a giant pyramid appears. The setting is mystical.

DESTINATION V   RIVIERA MAYA

Your next destination is the Riviera Maya, a stunning coastal stretch of white-sand beach lying between Cancún and Tulum. This once-sleepy area is booming with huge hotels and condominium complexes secreted behind high walls with security guards at the gates. These developments aren't intrusive, however, because they are far apart and hidden from the road. In addition to these hotels, there is a rich selection of fabulous smaller places to stay in every price range, from luxurious hotels with every imaginable amenity to simple thatched-hut bungalows tucked on secluded beaches. Look in the hotel section under Riviera Maya and choose a property that appeals to you. Any one of the places we recommend would make a suitable hub to explore the archaeological sites featured below.

When it's time to leave the Río Bec area, drive east on 186 to Chetumal, the capital of the state of Quintana Roo, located on an estuary of the Río Hondo, which divides Mexico from Belize. Chetumal has little of historic architectural ambiance since in the 1950s most of the buildings were destroyed by a hurricane. At the entrance to the town is a powerful sculpture of Gonzalo Guerrero standing proudly next to his wife and children. Guerrero was one of the first two Spaniards to land in the Yucatán, as a result of being shipwrecked offshore in 1511. Guerrero married a Mayan princess and fathered the first *mestizos* (persons of mixed Spanish and Indian blood) to be born in Mexico. The other sailor who survived the shipwreck was Jerómimo de Aguilar, who played a key role in the conquest of Mexico. When Cortés landed in the Yucatán, he persuaded Jerómimo de Aguilar (who by then spoke fluent Mayan) to come along as an interpreter. A little bit later, when Cortés arrived in Tabasco, he was presented with a gift of 20 maidens, one of whom was La Malinche, who not only became Cortés's mistress and bore him a son, but also helped to make the conquest of Mexico successful. She quickly learned Spanish, and with the combined dialects of La Malinche and Jerómimo de Aguilar, Cortés was able to forge alliances with Indian groups against the Aztecs. La Malinche was of particular help, not only because of her interpretive skills, but also because of her knowledge of the ways of the people. When Cortés returned to Spain, he "gave" La Malinche to one of his captains.

The town of Chetumal is not special, but its Museo de la Cultura Maya (Museum of Mayan Culture) is stunning—small, but exquisite and tasteful, and no expense seems to have been spared to create a jewel. The floors are made of gleaming green marble and classical music plays softly in the background. The museum is designed around three floors (connected by ramps) representing the underworld, the human world, and the celestial world. Throughout the museum are excellent exhibits and video presentations enhancing what you see. The most dramatic visual display is along one wall where a huge screen features a constantly repeating movie that takes you flying over the great Mayan cities in a small plane.

Leaving Chetumal, head north on highway 307 in the direction of Cancún. The highway traces Lago Bacalar (Lake Bacalar), a narrow but very long lake, stretching for 104 kilometers. It is fed from underground *cenotes*, so its water is crystal-clean and quite remarkable in color, shading from dark blue to turquoise.

Chichén Itzá, El Castillo

Continue north on 307 to Tulum, which is about 260 kilometers north of Chetumal. Rather than doing more sightseeing, call it a day and settle in at the hotel of your choice along the Riviera Maya. All of the hotels we recommend are on the sea, so take a swim in the warm Caribbean water and perhaps a walk on the beach. The next day begin your sightseeing, for which we suggest the following:

TULUM (A.D. 1000–1521)

Tulum is one of the loveliest small Mayan sites on the Yucatán Peninsula and due to its convenient location, just off the main highway, it is heavily visited by tourists. The ruins open at 8 a.m. and it is best to go as early as possible to avoid the extremely hot sun and the flood of tour buses that visit the site each day. The ruins are on a lesser scale than in most other areas of the Mayan world and you will notice that the pyramids are smaller and the buildings somewhat sloppily constructed. However, this is one of Mexico's most picturesque spots, one captured endlessly on calendars and tourist brochures, and there is an incredible view from the site's magnificent headland overlooking the Caribbean. Originally Tulum was a port for long-distance trading canoes and its defensive walls can still be seen along with a fine watchtower looking out to sea. The beach at the foot of the cliffs was once used to pull large seagoing trading canoes from the sea and if you bring your swimming suit, you can enjoy a swim in the warm, clear, turquoise water. Tulum and the Island of Cozumel, just across from it, were the first Mayan sites visited by Cortés on his initial voyage to Mexico in 1519. Unlike most pre-Columbian sites, they continued to flourish into the Colonial Period.

COBÁ (A.D. 200–1000)

The large ruined city of Cobá lies about halfway between Tulum and Cancún and is situated 40 kilometers inland from the coast at the end of a good road. It is built around a group of five small lakes that once provided water for a region of perhaps 50,000 people. The presence of lakes and an abundance of water are rare in this area and sustained Cobá as a major Mayan center until its conquest in about A.D. 1000 by a group of militant Mayan traders known as the Itzá. It has immense pyramids, a ball court, and palaces but it is best known for its many *sacbes*, the raised causeways or roads that connected the site with other great Mayan centers of the Classic Period. These roads also run through the city itself, connecting various clusters of buildings, and where they have been cleared visitors can quite easily walk to the majestic, towering pyramids whose tops rise above the trees. If the idea of staying next to the ruins appeals to you, we recommend a very pleasant small hotel, Villas Arqueologicas Cobá. From here you can take an early-morning walk through the jungle to the ruins, a very special way to see this ancient city.

CENOTES

The surface of the land in this part of the Yucatán Peninsula that lies in the state of Quintana Roo is basically a limestone shelf, beneath which flows a network of underground rivers. Occasionally the limestone collapses, exposing the water below and forming natural wells, which the ancient Maya called *cenotes*. The location of these cenotes determined the location of many of the Mayan cities where they not only provided a source of pure water, but also served for religious ceremonies. Today these cenotes are popular places for the tourist to visit. Some people like to swim in the crystal-clear, turquoise water, while others don scuba gear and enter a cenote at one point, swim underground in the river, and pop up at another cenote. Large theme parks, such as Xel-Ha and Xcaret, have developed to highlight natural wonders in the area and include underground rivers in their list of attractions. These places are fun, especially if you are traveling with children, but extremely commercial, and we definitely prefer the secluded, lesser-known cenotes. Ask the concierge at your hotel to recommend one nearby—they are dotted throughout the landscape.

When it is time to return home, you can quickly travel from the Riviera Maya to Cancún airport, completing your loop of the Yucatán Peninsula.

Ladies in Typical Mayan Dresses

Whale Watching in Baja: The Gentle Giants

One of the world's most awesome adventures must surely be visiting the incredible gray whale (*la Ballena Grise*) in its natural habitat. These gentle giants, which can weigh up to 35 tons and can measure up to 80 meters, leave the cold Arctic waters off Alaska every fall to begin the long 9,000-kilometer, two-month journey south (one of the longest migrations of any mammal). The females enter into one of three bays (Bahía Magdalena, Laguna Ojo de Liebre, or Laguna San Ignacio) midway down the west coast of Baja California to give birth to their calves. Usually the males do not enter the lagoon, but linger in the deeper waters at its mouth. Most species of whales have their babies in the open ocean, but the gray whale chooses the warm, shallow water of these protected bays as its nursery. At birth the winsome calves weigh in at over a ton and are approximately 4 meters long, then in the space of a few months, thanks to their mothers' rich milk, they more than double their weight and by the time they are ready to start the long journey back north, they have grown to about 6 meters in length. Whales can live to be 30 to 40 years old and in a female's lifetime she will usually have about three babies with a span of three years between each pregnancy, which has a gestation period of 12 months. The calves stay with the mother for two years and are then sent off on their own.

In the course of researching and detailing our own trip, we struggled with conflicting information and recommendations of just what to see, where to go, and how to pace it. Based on our own travels and experiences, we now feel confident in sharing with you what to consider when planning your journey.

WHERE TO GO: You can spot many different types of whales all along the coast of Baja, but since the bays and lagoons have a defined space, they offer a superb opportunity to view a high concentration of gray whales up close. Plan to visit one or more of the three bays where the majority of gray whales migrate each winter. These three bays are Bahía Magdalena, Laguna Ojo de Liebre (nicknamed Scammon's Lagoon for the whaling captain who discovered the bay), and Laguna San Ignacio. The two most accessible of these are Bahía Magdalena and Laguna Ojo de Liebre. Laguna San Ignacio requires a difficult three-hour round-trip drive (best suited to a four-wheel drive vehicle) along a bumpy, ill-kept road from the town of San Ignacio. Very important: It is a bit confusing when you read advertisements for whale watching. Many companies offer whale watching tours or boat trips that leave from La Paz and explore the Sea of Cortez. Indeed, these are fun trips that enable you to see an incredible amount of wildlife (including whales), but, be aware, if you *really* want to see the whales, you must go to one of the three bays mentioned above where the gray whales come to have their babies.

LOCATION OF THE BAYS: Bahía Magdalena (closest town, San Carlos) is located on the west coast of Baja, about midway between La Paz and Loreto, and is the most easily accessible bay if you are flying into La Paz. It is about a two-and-a-half-hours' drive northwest of La Paz or about a two-hour drive southwest of Loreto (both La Paz and Loreto have international airports). Laguna Ojo de Liebre (Scammon's Lagoon) is located near the town of Guerrero Negro, on the main Highway 1, about a five-hour drive northwest of Loreto or about a ten-hour drive south of Tijuana, the border town with the

USA. Laguna San Ignacio is located approximately midway between Ojo de Liebre and Bahía Magdalena. The closest town is San Ignacio, on Highway 1, but it takes two hours to reach the lagoon from the highway because the coastal access road is very rough.

WHICH BAY TO CHOOSE: All three bays mentioned above provide wonderful whale-watching opportunities and no experience can ever be duplicated or guaranteed—so, which to choose? Laguna Ojo de Liebre and Laguna San Ignacio are considered to offer the best likelihood to see mothers and babies up close. It is a tossup which of the two is better—both are excellent. On the other hand, Bahía Magdalena has the advantage of being the closest destination to see the whales if you are staying in La Paz. Our advice is that if you have the luxury of unlimited time, visit all three bays. If time is limited, just include Bahía Magdalena and Laguna Ojo de Liebre since access to Laguna San Ignacio is so difficult. If you want to concentrate on just one bay, we recommend Laguna Ojo de Liebre because it has an abundance of whales (50% of all the babies are born here) and it is easily accessible by a good road.

WHEN TO SEE THE WHALES: The whales can be visited from late December through March. The optimum time to see them is in February and March.

HOW TO SEE THE WHALES: Although whales can be spotted from the shoreline, without a doubt the best way to see them is by boat. It would be a waste of money to go so far to see this marvel of nature and then not be able to enjoy the adventure to its fullest.

There are several ways to view the whales—we have listed below some of the options, information on closest towns to the whale-watching areas, and recommended pacing.

ESCORTED TOURS BY CHARTERED PLANE: There are companies that operate chartered flights in February and March from the USA. Some of these tours depart from San Diego, California, by bus and cross the border to Ensenada where they take a charter plane to an airstrip near Laguna San Ignacio. Other tour companies board a charter plane in San Diego and fly to Laguna San Ignacio with a stop en route for customs. Usually these tours spend four nights at a tent camp near the lagoon, returning on the fifth day to

San Diego. Days are spent whale watching, hiking, bird watching, and kayaking. (Two companies that operate whale tours are Baja Expeditions and Baja Discovery. See our website, *www.karenbrown.com*, for more information).

INDEPENDENT ARRANGEMENTS BY BUS: It is not difficult to make your own arrangements and you have several choices of transportation. If you are really on a tight budget, the least expensive option is to take a Greyhound bus from San Diego to Tijuana and then a first-class bus (ABC Bus Line, Tres Estrelles de Oro, or Transportes Aguila) from Tijuana to Guerrero Negro where you can visit the whales in the Laguna Ojo de Liebre. You can call the Tijuana Bus Terminal for schedules and rates (664-626-7101). Before arriving in Guerrero Negro, make a reservation at the Hotel Malarrimo (for details see the description of the hotel in the back of this guide). The Achoy family, who own the hotel, also operate whale-watching trips, so when you book your room, reserve a place on one of their tours, which leave the hotel by bus at 8 am or 11 am. After a few days in Guerrero Negro, you can either return home or continue on by bus to San Ignacio and then to Loreto.

INDEPENDENT ARRANGEMENTS BY CAR: Another choice of transportation is to drive your own car south from San Diego on Highway 1, but this is a long, arduous journey best suited to those with lots of time. Much easier than driving down the long Baja Peninsula is to take a commercial flight from Los Angeles to either Loreto or La Paz and then rent a car. Loreto is the most central place to fly to if you want to visit more than one bay. There are good hotels in both Loreto and La Paz, but no exceptional places to stay in any of the towns close to where the whales congregate. The town with the best accommodations is Guerrero Negro, near Laguna Ojo de Liebre. Once you arrive at any of the three lagoons, you can either join an organized tour to see the whales (these can be arranged from most of the hotels) or else drive or take a taxi to one of the coves and hire one of the licensed guides (often local fishermen) who linger nearby with their boats, called *pangas*, to take you out into the lagoon or bay. Note: There is no guarantee that there will always be someone available to take you out without a prior reservation.

TOURS ORIGINATING IN MEXICO: In Loreto, Posada de las Flores (recommended in the hotel section of our guide) has its own tour company called P.D.F., which offers packages to see the whales. These tours vary in length from three to eight days and one, their five-day "Kiss the Whales" tour, is very similar to the routing we suggest in our itinerary. What makes this tour so hassle-free is that one phone call can wrap everything up—when you book a room at the Posada de las Flores, you can also reserve a tour. If none of the packages offered are quite right for you, request a quote on what it would cost to have a tour designed to suit your needs.

CRUISE SHIP: During the whale-watching season, cruise lines sometimes offer whale-watching itineraries. Most of these ships have a naturalist aboard, adding greatly to the experience. However, before signing up, read the brochure carefully to be sure the ship offers side excursions on small boats that go into the bay because you can't see the whales up close from a cruise ship. Also, cruise ships are not allowed into the "nursery" during birthing season. Note: Some of the ships (especially those from La Paz) go only into the Sea of Cortez and this is not where you find the greatest concentration of whales.

INFORMATION ON GUERRERO NEGRO (LAGUNA OJO DE LIEBRE): Guerrero Negro, a salt-mining town, is the closest town to Laguna Ojo de Liebre (Scammon's Lagoon). There are two points of departure for whale watching in the lagoon. Area 1 is used by most of the tour operators in town and the cost of the tour includes round-trip transfers to the pier from which the boats depart. It is about half an hour's drive in each direction, passing through the salt mine production area. There are two tours a day: one leaves town at 8 am and the other at 11 am. The tour costs about $45 per person and includes lunch. One of the major tour operators in town is Malarrimo Eco Tours, a professional and very dependable tour company owned by the Achoy family, entrepreneurs who also operate a restaurant and a simple hotel, Hotel Malarrimo, described in the back of our guide. (Reservations and information: telephone and fax: 615-157-0100, e-mail: malarimo@telnor.net.) Enrique Achoy was the first tour operator licensed by the National Ecology Institute of Mexico to conduct guided excursions to Scammon's Lagoon. Area 2 (used mostly by people who have their own car or camper) is located at the end of a 27-kilometer dirt road that turns off the highway to the south of town. A cooperative called Ejido Benito Juárez has the concession, located right on the beach. Reservations can be made in advance (615-157-0025), though even if you specify an exact time of departure in advance, if your group is small, they might ask you to wait up to 45 minutes for more passengers. The cost of a boat ride from Area 2 is about $25 per person, which does not include transfers from town or lunch. The maximum time any boat can be out amongst the whales in Scammon's Lagoon is two and a half hours, a time limit set by the government to protect the whales. Private boats such as kayaks, sailboats, motorboats, or rafts are not allowed into the lagoon when the whales are in residence.

INFORMATION ON SAN CARLOS (BAHÍA MAGDALENA): Local tours are available from the town of San Carlos on the edge of Bahía Magdalena. One of these is Mar y Arena, owned by Fito Glez, who gives a short history of the area before taking you out into the shallow water of the bay. They have recently acquired a glass-bottom boat, which would be wonderful for when the whales swim underneath—which they often do! (Reservations and information: Mar y Arena, Zona Portuaria Int. API de B.C.S., Pto. San Carlos, B.C.S., Mexico; telephone and fax: 613-136-0076 or 613-136-0453, email: fitoglez@yahoo.com.mx, *www.bajamagbay.com*.)

INFORMATION ON SAN IGNACIO (LAGUNA SAN IGNACIO): Underground springs make San Ignacio one of the most verdant spots in Baja California. Date palms and flowering shrubs are a welcome sight after hours of driving through a beautiful but starkly barren desert whose vegetation consists mostly of towering cacti. This tiny town has a small central square dominated by the Misión San Ignacio, which was founded in 1728 by Jesuit priests. Local tour operators for Laguna San Ignacio are located in town, which is a two-hour drive away from the lagoon on a rough gravel road. Ecoturismo Kuyima, located downtown on the square opposite the church, offers single or multi-day whale-watching excursions (telephone: 615-154-0026, fax: 615-154-0070). One of the best choices for accommodations in San Ignacio is La Pinta, a simple, low-rise, white hotel built around an open courtyard, which also organizes tours to see the whales. La

Pinta belongs to the La Pinta affiliation, which features a chain of simple, clean, dependable hotels dotted up and down the Baja Peninsula (800-511-4848 from the US).

RECOMMENDED PACING: To follow this itinerary we recommend eight nights. For those traveling independently, we suggest flying into Loreto and spending two nights there, giving you time to explore the town and then travel south to view whales at Bahía Magdalena. From Loreto drive north to Guerrero Negro where we recommend a stay of three nights in order to have two full days to take several whale-viewing outings. We then suggest driving south and settling in at Punta Chivato for three nights so that you have an entire day to look for shells along the beach and enjoy the beauty of the setting, and another full day to travel to Mulegé to explore the prehistoric caves. Depending on your departure from Loreto, it might be possible to drive directly from Punta Chivato to the Loreto airport (approximately two hours), or you might want to consider an overnight in Loreto if you have a morning departure.

Note: If you have a tendency for seasickness, before your departure you might want to ask your doctor about the advisability of purchasing Transderm patches as the sea can be rough.

ORIGINATING TOWN   LORETO

The town of Loreto, the oldest town in Baja California, its first capital, and home to its first mission, enjoys a spectacular setting on the Sea of Cortez, looking out to the Coronado Islands, with a backdrop of the magnificent Sierra de la Giganta mountain range. It is an easy trip into town from the small airport, with taxis readily available. Tourism has developed to accommodate both seasonal whale watchers and fishermen who claim that Loreto has some of the best marlin fishing in the world. We recommend two hotels in Loreto: the Camino Real (opened in 2002), which is located on the bay to the south of town, and the Posada de las Flores, which sits at the heart of town next to the town square. (See the descriptions of these hotels later in the book.)

Misión Nuestra Señora de Loreto

The first mission in Baja California, Misión Nuestra Señora de Loreto, was founded in Loreto in 1697 by an Italian Jesuit Padre, Juan María Salvatierra. The first structure, a tent, was replaced by a permanent building and by 1752 the lovely church, as you see it today, was completed. This mission served as hub for the exploration of the entire Baja Peninsula and was the starting point for Padre Junipero Serra's expedition to establish a chain of missions northward into Alta California (he is well known as the priest who founded many missions in the San Francisco area).

Loreto was destroyed by a hurricane in 1829, although the mission church survived. Fear of another hurricane motivated the move of the capital from Loreto to La Paz. After this the town remained dormant for many years, until it gained life again in the mid-1800s when a small band of English settlers came to the area (evidence of this can still be seen in the many local British names). The town didn't really grow again until the 1950s when sports enthusiasts, looking for unspoilt waters, discovered this fishing paradise. In 1997 President Zedillo declared the 60 kilometers of coastal waters off Loreto as a marine park, forbidden to commercial fishing.

Loreto is a small town and easy to explore on foot. The town square is across from the Posada de las Flores, and it is an easy stroll up the cobbled street to the Misión Nuestra Señora de Loreto. Loreto also boasts an interesting museum, the Museo de las Misiónes, one block west of the plaza. The museum features paintings and displays showing the life of the early Jesuit priests who played such a large part in the development of not only Baja California but of "our" California (Alta California), which used to be part of Mexico. Loreto has a number of shops selling pottery, baskets, embroidered dresses, T-shirts, and blankets, and it also has the only bank in the region with an ATM machine (opposite the Posada de las Flores). We were surprised how few people accepted credit card payment, so we needed more cash than we normally travel with. However, it is not necessary to convert to pesos as everyone seems quite comfortable accepting U.S. dollars, giving you change in pesos or sometimes in dollars. It is always handy to have $1 bills ready for tipping.

We recommend two nights in Loreto. On the day of your arrival, explore the heart of the historic town and the waterfront promenade. On your second day, take a side trip to see the whales at Bahía Magdalena.

To reach Bahía Magdalena, leave Loreto traveling south on Highway 1, which hugs the coastline. The drive along the coastline from Loreto is spectacular, with Isla Coronado, Isla del Carmen, and the gorgeous blue waters of the bay on your left and dramatic jagged mountain peaks rising on your right. There is a turnout at Nopoló with a gorgeous view of water and mountains. Soon after the vista point the road travels inland, banded by desert, cacti, and high mountain peaks. The road then climbs to a plateau as it crosses over to the west coast of Baja and overlooks a river valley. It takes approximately two hours to reach the town of San Carlos, the departure point for tours of Bahía Magdalena. You will know when you've arrived as the terrain changes dramatically from rocky desert to sandy inlets on the approach to town.

In San Carlos, Mar y Arena Tours, situated next to the tourist office, offers whale-watching excursions. It is just a short drive from their office to the pier next to a thatched-hut complex that is home to an international whale-study foundation. The two-hour tour goes to the center of the bay where it is easy to see whales because of the shallow water and the white sandy bottom but we suggest taking the three-hour trip, which takes you closer to the mouth of the bay and deeper waters. The return includes a stop by the buoys to see the barking seals and a landing on a white stretch of beach backed by spectacular high drifts of sand dunes.

If you are hungry and want a bite to eat before the drive back to Loreto, ask Fito Glez, owner of Mar Y Arena Tours, for restaurant recommendations—this is a wonderful region for seafood such as lobsters, shrimp, and clams.

DESTINATION I   GUERRO NEGRO

Mulegé, Misión Santa Rosalia de Mulegé

Today's agenda is to travel the distance north from Loreto to Laguna Ojo de Liebre at Guerrero Negro, a journey that should take approximately five hours. Upon leaving Loreto, the road travels inland from the Sea of Cortez, cutting a path through desert forested by cacti and then a mountain canyon, which opens up on the other side to the gorgeous turquoise waters of Bahía Concepción, a huge bay protected by a long, jutting peninsula. You might want to ask the hotel to prepare a box lunch, as there are numerous white-sand crescent beaches where you can stop to picnic and enjoy the crystal-clear water with its backdrop of pink-hued mountains. During the winter, the beaches are lined with campers and trailers since this is a paradise for northerners escaping the cold. Bahía Concepción is designated as a nature reserve and you find here an amazing variety of marine life, birds, whales, dolphins, and shellfish.

As you continue, Highway 1 goes through the town of Mulegé (approximately two hours from Loreto), which is just up the coast from Bahía Concepción. It is worth a stop to visit Misión Santa Rosalía de Mulegé, a simple old stone mission crowning the hillside above a grove of palm trees. Note: Mulegé is also the departure point for visiting the prehistoric wall paintings and etchings, which we take you to later in this itinerary.

Santa Rosalía, a copper-mining town and the departure point for ferries across the bay to Guaymas, is located another twenty minutes north of Mulegé. Soon after Santa Rosalía, the road turns inland and cuts a path through volcanic mountains. Past the volcanic peaks the terrain levels and the road is banded on either side by a vast expanse of flat desert colored only by cacti and tumbleweed, with the dramatic peaks of the Sierra San Francisco in the distance. San Ignacio is located 3 kilometers off this road and it is perhaps worth the detour to see the small town square and its lovely old mission.

The drive between San Ignacio and Guerrero Negro is monotonous as you travel through dry, flat desert and the scenery becomes even more desolate as you approach Guerrero Negro. If you want to include a whale-watching expedition this afternoon, before you reach Guerrero Negro, turn left on a road marked with a sign "Laguna Ojo de Liebre and Whales." This dirt road goes for 27 kilometers through a 33,000-acre easement of land owned by the salt company and you have to stop for registration soon after leaving the highway. As you approach the bay, there is another entry point where you are required to pay a 30 peso or $3 entrance fee. The skeleton of a large whale is on display in front of the only restaurant, which is also where you sign up for a whale-watching excursion ($25 per person). It was here we learned the sad story behind the name "Laguna Ojo de Liebre" (Eye of the Jack Rabbit)—apparently the bay looked like the red eye of a jack rabbit when its waters were stained with blood during the whale slaughter of the 1800s.

Boats are tethered as close to the shore as possible, but how far you have to wade out depends on the tide. In any case, we recommend that you don waterproof shoes or go barefoot as the sand is very sticky and claylike and will destroy shoes. The boats (accommodating up to ten people) depart from 8 am to 4 pm and the trip lasts for about two hours.

After the tour return to the main road and complete the short journey farther north to the town of Guerrero Negro. Soon after entering town, turn right into the parking area for the Malarrimo family operation. This is the headquarters for Malarrimo Eco Tours and also the Malarrimo hotel, restaurant, and gift shop. Check in with Enrique Achoy Jr. in the tour office (on the right side of the parking area) to secure your reservations and tickets for tomorrow's whale-watching tour. Departures are at 8 am and 11 am. Although afternoon trips can provide an absolutely fantastic experience, in general, the mornings are considered the best for viewing whales as the winds and tides are calmer and afford easier sighting through the waters. Catty-corner from the Malarrimo Eco Tours office you find the hotel and restaurant (see our description of the hotel in the hotel section). Elena, Enrique's sister, is in charge of the gift shop and has a tempting selection of T-shirts, jewelry, and pottery. In addition to offering some of the best accommodations in Guererro Negro, the simple Hotel Malarrimo is very convenient since it is the starting point for your whale-watching tour. You can enjoy a leisurely breakfast knowing that you are just steps from the bus, whose departure is announced by the courtyard bell.

Your tour price for the whale-watching expedition includes a box lunch so there is no need to pack food or drink, but you most definitely want to wear sunscreen and dress in layers as the winds can affect the temperature dramatically. The bus ride through the salt factory property to the boat launch takes about half an hour, passing by the bird sanctuary where from the bus you can spot herons, sandpipers, seagulls, egrets, and the dramatic osprey guarding their enormous nests perched on man-made pillars constructed to facilitate their migration. It is quite fascinating to pass by piles of salt so huge that they look like mountains of snow.

At the boat launch you board a *panga* (motor boat), which then travels quickly for about 15 minutes, bouncing across the water to where the gray whales are most easily seen. There is no doubt that you will see whales—it is just a question of how many and how friendly they will be.

Every whale-watching outing is different and one never knows how many whales will be seen. Tides and winds impact the situation dramatically. On our first trip (the 11 am departure) the boat slowed and lingered in what seemed a quiet location and within minutes we were literally surrounded by whales that kept diving under and around our boat—they truly seemed as curious about us as we were about them. It was endearing to see the mothers and calves swimming and diving side by side, and while whales seemed to come and go, a few of them (we could recognize them by their markings) stayed with us for more than an hour. They would *spy hop* (poke their heads out of the water), seemingly to better study us. Then they would playfully whip their tails right at the side of the boat (without question trying to splash us in fun), and would breach and blow spray just a few feet from the boat. A few particularly friendly whales rose right at the boat's edge, lingering for us to touch them. It was an incredible, once-in-a-lifetime experience.

Our second excursion (the 8 am departure) was also exciting, and had we not had the experience of the day before, we would have been thrilled. Our boat captain motored to a number of locations and at each we would be visited by whales who would stay awhile and then move on—curious but seemingly not as friendly as the day before. One or two came right up to the boat to look us over, but did not stay long. Our captain explained the tides were strong and the whales were having trouble lingering at the boat's edge.

While our first experience was incredible, we saw lots of whales on both excursions, both at the boat and swimming in the distance and loved seeing them leap completely out of the water—but always a great distance away. Be sure to pack lots of film—it seemed everyone underestimated how many photos they would take. Whereas when viewing whales in U.S. waters, boats by law may not get up close to the whales, in Mexico no such rules prevail. However, there is absolutely no fear that you are intruding upon their privacy. When the boats stop in the water, these gentle giants take the initiative and they seem to come up to the boats just to say hello.

Other than the whale-watching tours and walking through the bird preserve, the town of Guererro Negro has very little to offer the tourist. It is basically a simple little town with one main street lined by basic, rather bland motels. The production of salt and whale watching during season is the means of its existence. But since this is the most accessible town to outstanding whale watching, and its lagoon, Laguna Ojo de Liebre, is considered one of the best two in Mexico for spotting these gentle giants, we recommend staying three nights in order to have two full days for whale watching.

Retrace the drive back from Guerrero Negro, past San Ignacio, to the coast at Santa Rosalia. About twenty minutes south of Santa Rosalia, at the town of Palo Verde, there is a sign for the Posada de las Flores (sister hotel to the one in Loreto) directing you to turn left and travel 18 kilometers down a rugged dirt road. You will be rewarded at its end as the hotel is gorgeous, sitting right on the water's edge in Punta Chivato. (See our description in the next section of the guide.) Because of its isolation and incredible setting it is not surprising to learn that this was once a getaway for movie stars. Recently renovated by its new owners, the hotel is more beautiful than ever. La Posada de las Flores serves as a base for whale-watching trips, and yet guests come here all through the year just for the beauty of the hotel and its remarkable setting (it is actually possible to watch the sun both rise and set over the bay)—it is truly an oasis and destination in its own right. After getting settled in your room, take a stroll along the expanse of white-sand beach with its incredible bounty of beautiful shells. If you enjoy beachcombing, this beach is paradise.

If you are interested in prehistoric drawings, we recommend taking a day trip from Punta Chivato to Mulegé to see the cave paintings. The paintings, located on a private ranch, Rancho La Trinidad, approximately half an hour's drive along a rugged dirt road, can be visited only with a private guide. Salvador Castro Drew, one of the two authorized tour guides, has as his base of operations (until he builds his own office) the Hotel Las Casitas in the center of Mulegé. The hotel is easy to find but, for an additional fee, Salvador will pick you up at the Posada de las Flores in Punta Chivato. Wherever you rendezvous with Salvador, you will have to stop in town at the government offices as they require that individuals register and show proof of identification before being allowed to access to the caves. You also have to pay a small fee per camera (30 pesos at the time of our visit). For this excursion you wear comfortable shoes and pack binoculars and bottled water.

Canyon at Rancho Trinidad

Salvador offers a variety of tours of different lengths. We recommend that you request the abbreviated version of his full-day trip—four hours should be ample. Your first stop is at an organic citrus farm, then you enter the boundaries of the Rancho La Trinidad, which encompasses 5,500 beautiful acres and produces goat and cattle for cheese, milk, beef, and leather products. The next stop is to explain and identify the various plants and cacti (some of which are incredibly 400 years old) before continuing on to where, seasonally (April through September), you can observe goat cheese production as well as the making of lassos and whips and the process of tanning leather. A final stop is at the caretaker's cottage where you must register once again. Then it is just a short distance to where you park and begin a hike on a trail that climbs up over boulders and the barriers of an old dam into the beauty of the red-rock canyon. In about 20 minutes you come to an

Whale Watching in Baja: The Gentle Giants

open cave where the paintings date back to the Neolithic period—some 1,500 to 4,500 years B.C. This area was later home to the Cochimies Indians.

Rancho La Trinidad, Cave Paintings

It is incredible that these prehistoric paintings are unprotected, left just as they were when first discovered—the only restriction is that one stand at least 3 meters from the paintings. Salvador provides an interesting narration of the history and explanation of the various paintings and their significance. You see fish, deer, children's handprints, and warriors painted in hues of red, black, and white. It is possible from here to journey farther up the canyon to view more cave drawings (although the first are considered the best) and even swim in a high mountain reservoir, but we suggest returning to the van and using the time to see some rock etchings. Salvador will point out to you the first of what turns out to be many etchings—fish, turtles, warriors, animals—carved in boulders above a dry riverbed.

Salvador Castro Drew can be reached directly at P.O. Box No. 9, 23900 Mulegé, B.C.S., Mexico; telephone: 615-153-0232. Price for a four-hour tour is about $40 per person.

Note: If you have a great interest in prehistoric drawings, there are other caves to visit, many of which are found in remote canyons through the sierras of Baja, and many of which were discovered by the famous naturalist, Harry Crosby. Said to rival the paintings of Lascaux in France and Altamira in Spain, one of the most stunning is the huge mural at Cueva La Pintada in the overhanging rocks in the Cañon de Santa Teresa. Ten meters high and stretching for over 160 meters, the mural is of mystic animals and stylized people with hands extended into the sky. You might also want to consider traveling to San Ignacio, which is central to the majority of the cave paintings. Pictographs are found in caves and arroyos north of San Ignacio. It is possible to arrange tours from Guerrero Negro to an area called the Sierra de San Francisco, named as a World Heritage Site by UNESCO in 1993. In each case the access is rugged—not for the casual archaeologist—and you must always have a guide and a permit, a government regulation designed to protect these precious relics of the past. The easiest site to reach is the Cueva del Ratón (Cave of the Rat). You park near the road, climb a stone staircase, travel across a wooden bridge and through a cleft in the ridge, and then come to the rock overhang where you can see deer, sheep, and other game depicted in the overhanging rock. The journey, the experience, and the setting cause one to wonder what inspired this artistic achievement in such a challenging place.

From Mulegé, we recommend returning to the luxury of Posada de las Flores in Punta Chivato and spending at least one more night enjoying its beauty and setting. From there it is an easy two-and-a-half-hour drive back to Loreto where, depending on your flight itinerary, you might opt to go directly to the airport or spend a last night in town.

Miracle of the Monarch Butterfly

It is not only the gray whale that embarks on an incredibly long journey each fall to enjoy the warmth of Mexico: the Monarch butterfly (*Mariposa Monarca*) makes a similar trip south. But what a difference! The gray whale weighs up to 35 tons, whereas the dainty Monarch is so light that it feels like a feather when it lands on your wrist. For years we read about the Monarch migration, and had heard from friends that it was quite an amazing sight. However, it wasn't until we saw it for ourselves that we could really appreciate this truly breathtaking event. This wonder of nature far exceeded our expectations and provided one of those magical moments that will linger long in our memories. As the itinerary unfolds below, you will see that you need to be in good health, rather sporty, and game to walk long distances at high altitudes and ride a horse to take advantage of this experience. However, if you enjoy the outdoors, you will be totally captivated.

Every winter millions of brilliant black-and-orange-colored Monarch butterflies brave their way through incredible hardships and flutter all the way from Canada and the northern reaches of the United States to one of about a dozen known wintering sites in the Sierra Madre mountain range in the state of Michoacán. In September when chill hits the air, swarms of butterflies start to gather (mostly in Canada) then, when they decide that the time is perfect, they take off in flocks heading south on a long flight to warmer climes. World-renowned naturalists who have studied the migration in depth generally think that their departure is based on the slant of the sun and that once they are in flight, they are then are guided by built-in magnetic compasses. They fly in daylight for six or seven hours a day at an average speed of about 12 kilometers an hour. After traveling over 4,000 kilometers, across lakes, deserts, and mountains, by November of each year, regular as clockwork, they all arrive at the same destination—an utterly remote, almost inaccessible, 3,000-meter-high mountainous area heavily forested with fir trees. The target is not large—an area of just 30 by 60 square kilometers, secreted in a cloud forest about 130 kilometers northwest of Mexico City. An estimated 100 million of these delicate creatures settle in the fir forests, accumulating in such staggering numbers that some of the sturdy tree limbs have been known to break under their weight.

This feat is even more astonishing when you realize that the butterflies that make this incredible journey have never been in Mexico before. Unlike the salmon who return to their spawning grounds, this generation taking to the air is made up of the great-great-grandchildren of ancestors who spent the previous winter in Michoacán.

For many years no one knew where the butterflies were headed. It wasn't until 1975 that the mystery was solved when a Canadian zoologist, Fred Urquhart, rediscovered the wintering grounds of the Monarchs. However, the local Indians had always known about the phenomenon and were depicting butterflies in their drawings long before the arrival of Columbus.

After the rediscovery of the wintering grounds, conservationists were extremely worried that the habitat would be destroyed as more and more forests were being cut down for

Miracle of the Monarch Butterfly

lumber but, thankfully, the Mexican government has wisely designated a large area as a Monarch butterfly sanctuary. Most of the land had been owned by *ejidos* (local communities of farmers who were granted the land after the Revolution of 1910) whose members were compensated for their loss of revenue from logging. Today most of these *ejidos* make money by acting as guides to the sanctuary.

Although extensive areas of forest in Mexico have now been set aside as safe havens for the butterflies, there is still fear that someday they might become extinct because of the threat to the milkweed plant on which they feed and lay their eggs. This flowering weed used to be ubiquitous throughout the butterflies' route, but now with subdivisions sprouting up everywhere, the milkweed is disappearing fast at the hands of the developers. The milkweed is in itself another strange story. This plant, which is the Monarch's staple diet, exudes a milky substance that is deadly to their enemies, but which is harmless to the butterflies.

Monarch butterflies begin to arrive in early November and start to leave again the end of March. The arrival coincides with one of Mexico's premier festivals, the Day of the Dead (*Día de los Muertos*) and old Indian legends say that the returning butterflies carry their ancestors' souls. Plan to make your trip sometime between late November and March. There is usually more activity in February and March as the butterflies fly about, mating in preparation for their long journey to their northern home where the females will lay up to 400 eggs, which is the survival ratio of the species. Also, the later you go in the season, the better chance there is for warm weather. Sometimes there is a frost in January so that the butterflies stay clustered in the branches of the trees and don't fly about. However, there can be a cold spell at any time, so we recommend staying several days so you can pick your day to visit the forest. When scheduling your itinerary, try to avoid visiting the butterflies on a weekend since the sanctuaries are very crowded then.

The sanctuaries are in the forests of Michoacán, located between Mexico City and Morelia. There are organized one-day bus tours during the butterfly season leaving from Mexico City, Morelia, and Pátzcuaro—all places that are wonderful destinations in their own right and described in depth elsewhere in our guide. Any of the hotels we recommend in our book should be able to steer you to a company that offers these bus tours, which leave very early in the morning and return in the evening—usually about a 12-hour trip. If you are traveling with friends and have your own small group, we recommend that you hire a guide with a car instead of taking a bus tour. If you have several people in your party, the cost isn't much greater (maybe even less) and it is a far more personal way to make the trip, as you can plan your own schedule. Again, your hotel can put you in touch with a reputable guide. If you are on a really tight budget and yet want to splurge on a butterfly spree, this too can be done. There are first-class buses from Mexico City to Zitácuaro and from there a local bus can take you to Angangueo, which is about an hour's ride beyond. Once your bus arrives in Angangueo, you can overnight at one of the simple hotels in town (the Don Bruno and the Posada Monarca are two of the betters ones) and arrange a trip to see the butterflies from there. Guides are readily available.

For a more leisurely way to see the quite remarkable Monarch butterfly migration, we offer the following suggestions:

RECOMMENDED PACING: Instead of just one day, we highly recommend spending at least three nights in the area so as to have a choice of two days (for better weather) to visit the butterflies and also a chance to see other places of interest in this beautiful and interesting niche of Mexico, so frequently missed on the normal tourist route.

ZITÁCUARO

The closest town to the butterfly sanctuaries is Angangueo, a tiny town squeezed in a narrow mountain valley where silver was mined from 1792 to 1992. The village has just one cobbled road cutting through the middle and leading up to the 3,000-meter mountaintop. Although Angangueo is the nearest town, we recommend you stay instead in Zitácuaro, which is about a 45-minute drive away. The reason we suggest staying here is twofold. Not only does it have an extremely appealing place to stay, the Rancho San Cayetano, but also you are central for other sightseeing. The Rancho San Cayetano, in a parklike setting just out of town, has much to recommend it: the lovely Lisette Span, who is French by birth, is a fabulous cook and oversees excellent meals, while her husband, Pablo, is exceptionally knowledgeable about what to see and do in the area and will be glad to help you plan your day.

From Morelia, the fastest way to reach Zitácuaro is to take the toll road 15 marked toward Mexico City. Exit at Maravatío and follow the signs toward Ciudad Hidalgo and Zitácuaro. It is about a two-hour drive from Morelia to Zitácuaro. A good detailed map is necessary since once you leave the highway, the roads are not well marked. From Mexico City take the toll road 15 west to Toluca and continue north for another 100 km. on road No. 15 (which after Toluca is no longer a four-lane highway) to Zitácuaro. It is about a two-hour drive from Mexico City to Zitácuaro.

Zitácuaro, Rancho San Cayetano

The Rancho San Cayetano is about 3 kilometers south of town on the 51 to Huetamo. When making reservations, ask for detailed driving instructions.

The first day you arrive, after settling into the inn, we would suggest a walk that takes about 15 minutes up a cobbled narrow street to visit the precious little San Pancho Church, facing a postage-stamp-sized square in the tiny hamlet of the same name. The church has a rustic interior, stone walls and a simple yet beautiful altar, and if the priest is there, he can enrich your experience by telling you about this 16th-century church's history.

CHINCUA BUTTERFLY SANCTUARY

After a leisurely breakfast, head off from Rancho San Cayetano for your butterfly adventure. There is no need to rush because midday, when the temperature is highest, is the best time to view the butterflies, which cluster in huge masses on the limbs of the trees to keep warm. They don't begin to fly about until the sun warms the air, so arriving early in the morning is of no advantage.

Most of the literature about Monarchs says that the best place to see them is the Rosario Butterfly Sanctuary. This is the best-known sanctuary since it was the original site, but it is *not* the place to go. The Rosario Sanctuary involves a 45-minute ride in an open truck over hopelessly bumpy roads, after which it is a long walk to the site. In addition, the Rosario Sanctuary is far more congested and more commercial than the one we suggest, the Chincua Butterfly Sanctuary (open in season from 9 am until 6 pm).

To reach your destination, follow your map from Zitácuaro through Ocampo and on to the tiny town of Angangueo. You might want to stop briefly to see its churches, the main plaza and visit the Casa Parker Museum covering the mining history of the town. Just up the block from the central church is an historic mural that covers both sides of the walls of a narrow, block-long alleyway.

Go through Angangueo and continue for about 8 kilometers as the road climbs up ever higher into the mountains. You will see guides along the way trying to catch your attention and entice you to let them take you to see the butterflies. Don't stop, just keeping going. Soon, on the right you will see a sign with a picture of a large Monarch butterfly and here you turn left off the road into the sanctuary, paying at the entrance for parking.

As you drive on, you soon come to the parking lot where you leave your car. It is a little confusing from here on since everything is delightfully laid-back and non-commercial, but just head toward the horses for hire and you will be approached by some of the guides. The price is set, so you don't need to worry about negotiating—everyone charges the same and included in the price is someone (usually a young boy) who will lead your horse. As well as a horse for each person in your party, you want to hire an extra guide to accompany you all the way to the butterflies, beyond where you leave your horse.

Once you are on your horse, the adventure begins. The path, dappled with sunlight filtering through the towering trees, winds up through a beautiful pine and fir forest. The altitude is over 3,000 meters, so although you can walk it is very strenuous—and the horses are great fun!

After about a 40-minute ride, you come to the "horse parking lot" and continue on foot for about another half hour, led by your guide. A narrow path twists downward through the fir and pine trees and occasionally gaps appear in the dense foliage through which you catch glimpses of beautiful faraway valleys. You will be glad you have a guide, for not only does the path sometimes split, but also it's tricky to know when you have arrived. Several times we came to small clearings filled with butterflies and we thought we were "there." However, you will *know* when you are at the site. A gentle hum in the air signals you are close. At first the hum is almost unnoticeable, but becomes louder as you approach and then, all of a sudden, the air is filled with butterflies. You can hardly see the sky through what looks like confetti in the air. You would think that there could be no more until you glance at the trees whose limbs are smothered with huge clumps of butterflies huddled together for warmth, looking like enormous nests. It's very much like being in a cathedral: the ambiance is almost ethereal and you cannot help being humbled by the experience. You will probably want to spend at least an hour here, soaking up the sublime display of nature. This is a photographer's dream, so bring lots of film to capture the magic of the moment. (Note that flash photography is prohibited.)

It will be difficult to leave this unforgettable scene, but you can't stay forever. When it is time to go, retrace your way back to your horse and the parking lot. In addition to paying the set fee, tip your guides well. They make very little money and now that logging (once their main source of income) has been halted, their yearly subsistence is dependent upon the short tourist season when the butterflies come to Michoacán.

On returning to Zitácuaro, ask Pablo Span if he will show you his excellent video about the butterflies. This will answer most of your questions about the migration and reinforce your experience of the day.

MORE SIGHTSEEING

There so are many places to visit in this part of Michoacán that if you have the luxury of time, we highly recommend at least an extra day or more here. Another advantage of spending at least two full days is that if the weather is unseasonably cold (at which time the butterflies stay clustered on the branches of the trees), you can reverse this itinerary and do your sightseeing on the first day then go to see the butterflies on the second day, when it might be warmer. Some of the places to see in the area are the following:

Cerro Pelon Butterfly Colony: Recently opened about 20 minutes southeast of Zitácuaro is a new area to view butterflies at Cerro Pelon Mountain, which has a large colony of butterflies. There are three access points: El Capulin, Macheros, and El Campamento. You can reach this sanctuary with a one-hour horseback ride, or by foot, traveling a gentle slope. The main advantage is that you will be the only visitors, and with a guide you may stay as long as you wish—one hour or all day. Detailed information is available at Rancho San Cayetano.

Enandio Waterfalls: This 100-meter spectacular waterfall is located south of Zitácuaro on the highway to Huetamo. At the 21-kilometer marker, turn right to reach the town of Enandio, a distance of 2 kilometers. Stop in this village to visit the church and its 17th-century Saint Isabel of Hungary statue. In front of the church, ask for a guide to show you the way to the waterfalls (there are no signs). You drive along a 3- to 4-kilometer dirt road, park the car, and take the 45-minute downhill walk on a path to a pool suitable for swimming. Be careful—the last 25 meters are steep and slippery.

Ocampo: The small town of Ocampo is located about 10 kilometers south of Angangueo. Its attractions include the Templo del Santo Niño, the Hacienda de Trojes, and items by local artisans who specialize in hand-worked wood.

San Felipe de los Alzati: 9 kilometers west of Zitácuaro, The town of San Felipe de los Alzati has a 16th-century church that is well known for its atrium and monolithic cross. If you are interested in archaeological sites, particularly those off the beaten path, Los Alzati is a treat. Here in a deserted field you find the ruins of once-mighty stone pyramids This was an Otomi ceremonial center, with a beautiful view of the valley below best seen in the afternoon before sunset. It is especially fun to visit this site since you will probably be the only person about.

There are in addition day trips to other attractions that include natural hot sulfur springs, Los Azufres, bat caves, and warm-water springs swimming pools in San José Purua. Information is available from Rancho San Cayetano.

Copper Canyon
A Train Adventure to Hidden Mexico

Mexico's well-known Copper Canyon (*Barranca del Cobre*) boasts statistics more impressive than the Grand Canyon in the United States. The Copper Canyon is deeper and, if you include the six canyons that make up the whole, covers more than four times the area. However, in our estimation, although the Copper Canyon's figures are more dramatic, the Grand Canyon still wins the prize for beauty and grandeur. Nevertheless, the Copper Canyon is well worth visiting. Not only is the canyon very pretty, but there are also other reasons to make the journey: you have the opportunity to take a train ride that is lots of fun; you have the chance to stay in a hotel with a breathtaking perch on a cliff overlooking the canyon; and you have the rare privilege of seeing the reclusive Tarahumara Indians whose way of life has changed little in over a thousand years.

You can make the trip any time of the year, but many prefer the fall when everything is very green and the waterfalls are gushing after the summer rains. Spring too is a lovely time to make the journey. If you go in winter, be sure to take warm clothing since the weather can be very cold and it can snow. In summer, if you hike down to the floor of the canyon, the weather is very hot and humid. Just remember, the canyon area is made up of two distinct climate zones, with the weather ranging from Alpine at the top of the canyon to subtropical at the floor.

The only easy access to the canyon is by train, which gives you various options of where to leave from and where to stop along the route. In the itinerary below we have outlined a way to have the ultimate experience in a short length of time.

RECOMMENDED PACING: We suggest two nights in El Fuerte (one before your train trip and one at the end of the train trip), and two nights in Barrancas at the Posada Mirador—a minimum of four nights total.

ORIGINATING TOWN   EL FUERTE

The Copper Canyon is so remote that for many years it was inaccessible to tourists. Only a few rugged individuals made their way by foot or on horseback to enjoy the spectacle of this masterpiece of nature. The situation changed dramatically in 1961 when the Chihuahua al Pacífico Railroad was completed, connecting the towns of Los Mochis (about 20 kilometers from the coast) on the west and Chihuahua on the east, a total distance of about 660 kilometers. You can take the train from either direction, but since the most beautiful part of the ride is that on the west side of the Continental Divide, we recommend making a round-trip journey from the west instead of going all the way to Chihuahua since the last part of the trip is a bit bland.

Because the train leaves early in the morning, you will need to spend the night before your departure at your originating town. Many passengers board the train at Los Mochis, where the train originates. However, we suggest spending the night instead in the small Colonial town of El Fuerte, which offers several advantages: El Fuerte, founded in 1564 along the El Fuerte River by the conquistador Don Francis de Ibarra, is much more charming than Los Mochis; you can sleep in later since the train leaves Los Mochis at 6 am whereas it leaves El Fuerte at 7:40 am; and El Fuerte offers the Posada del Hidalgo (featured in our guide), which has far more old-world ambiance than anything in Los Mochis.

View of the Copper Canyon

You can take a bus from Los Mochis to El Fuerte although it is easily accessible by car on a good road. Once you arrive in El Fuerte, follow signs to the large central square where you easily find the Posada del Hidalgo sitting just off one corner. If you get lost, ask anyone to point the way. Note: Although the official address of the hotel is Calle Hidalgo, the entrance is around the corner on Cinco de Mayo.

One enormous advantage of booking a room at the Posada del Hidalgo is that it is owned by the Balderrama family, pioneers of the Copper Canyon tourist industry. They were the first family to see the need for hotels and tours in the canyon area and now own most of the best hotels and offer most of the tours. They also sell train tickets, so with one telephone call to their central office (800-896-8196 from the U.S.), you can book not only hotels, but also train tickets and transfers to the train station (which is about 7 kilometers from town). You might be able to call your own cab and also purchase the train tickets for less money on an individual basis, but why do it? It is so satisfactory to have everything arranged and know in advance that everything is confirmed. Work out your dates for the Posada del Hidalgo, the Posada Mirador (second and third night on the itinerary), and the trains, and book it all at once. When you arrive at the Posada del Hidalgo, they will give you vouchers for the hotels, transfers, and train tickets. Also, when you make the reservations for the hotel, ask about leaving your car at the Posada del Hidalgo while you are away for the several days of your canyon trip.

After settling in at the hotel, take a stroll around the charming, small, historic town with its attractive central plaza studded with palm trees and narrow cobblestone streets ornamented by 17th-century buildings.

DESTINATION I BARRANCAS

Today your train adventure begins. The official time for the train to leave El Fuerte for the Copper Canyon is 7:40 am but the train is rarely on time. Request a wake-up call at the reception and ask what time you need to leave for the train. When you make your reservation, request the entire "package"—your hotels, train tickets, and round-trip transfers to the station.

It is about a 15-minute drive to the small train station. You will probably have to wait a while for the train to come, so bring a good book or postcards to write. The train, known as the Chihuahua al Pacífico, is amazingly nice. Not lavish, but far better than we had expected. It is air-conditioned, the seats are comfortable, everything is neat and tidy, and there is a bathroom in each rail car. In addition, there is a cute bar on one of the cars where you can enjoy a drink and a good restaurant with attentive service where you can get breakfast or lunch. The best views of the canyon are on the right side of the train but if you find that your seats are on the other side, you can often switch since the train is not usually full.

At first the train travels through the rather arid lowlands before gradually beginning the ascent into the Sierra Madre Mountains, where it loops and turns its way up. As you climb ever higher through the pine forests there are views of the canyon far below. The train bridges high ravines, traces surging rivers, climbs to 2400 meters, and tunnels through the mountains. Altogether, there are 86 tunnels, 37 bridges, and one 270-degree turn. The track runs mostly through the forests rather than hugging the rim of the canyon, but stay alert since stunning canyon views frequently pop unexpectedly into view. However, the very finest views await at the hotel where you will be spending the night.

Officially the train is scheduled to arrive at your stop, Barrancas, at 1:30 pm. It will probably be much later than this when the train slowly comes to a halt at what is no more than a tiny little station and a cluster of buildings. There will be a bus waiting to take you to your hotel, the Posada Mirador, which is only about a five-minute drive away. The Balderrama family, owners of the Posada Mirador, also have another hotel, the Posada Rancho, just a few steps from the train station. Although this hotel is pleasant, when making reservations be *sure* to specify the Posada Mirador since it is the one with the incredible setting.

If you visit the Copper Canyon, you just *must* stay at the Posada Mirador. The hotel seems as if it is pasted onto the steep canyon walls and has views more stunning than any you will see on your train ride. Not only is the location spectacular, but also the hotel itself is a real winner. The salmon-colored stucco building looks like a large, rugged, Indian adobe dwelling. As you approach, you will see Indian women, with their children playing beside them, sitting on the steps of the hotel weaving and selling their baskets.

The craftsmanship of their wares is outstanding and the price very low for the high quality of the work and the huge amount of time it takes to create each item.

Posada Mirador

Once inside, you find a charming, lodge-like ambiance. Low, beamed ceilings, a huge stone fireplace, tiled floors, enormous murals showing the canyon and the Indians, leather and wood furniture, woven rugs, brightly painted walls, and native crafts create a delightful rustic atmosphere. One wall of the lounge/dining room is a wall of glass and opens onto a huge deck suspended over the canyon. The views are breathtaking. The restaurant encompasses one part of the central lounge where long tables are set up family-style to serve the many tour groups, as well as individual travelers. Don't expect gourmet dining—instead, you have just good simple cooking appropriate for serving a lot of people quickly and efficiently. The waiters are friendly and there is plenty to eat.

Plan to stay two nights at the Posada Mirador—more if you want to do a lot of hiking. Your room at the inn has its own balcony where you could easily sit all day soaking up the panoramic view that unfolds below. However, there are all kinds of activities to enjoy from the hotel such as hikes down to the canyon floor, visits to Indian villages, horseback riding, and jeep excursions. You can ask at the reception desk for information on the possibilities of what to see and do here and the staff can help you with all arrangements.

This is the perfect spot to explore the Copper Canyon and there are several things you just must not miss. Be sure to take the trail that leads steeply down the canyon wall to visit a complex of Indians who are living as their ancestors have for countless generations. Their homes are perched on a narrow shelf of the canyon wall, half cave, half home. It is almost unbelievable that anyone is living like this in the 21st century. Longer walks take you deeper into the canyon where you find more Indian dwellings. Also, be sure to take the trail that makes a loop below the hotel—the views are lovely, so stop along the way to savor them. There are a few observation points en route, but whenever you pause and look down, the vista is beautiful.

One of the highlights of a visit to the Copper Canyon, in addition to experiencing the canyon itself, is the opportunity to learn more about the gentle Tarahumara Indians (also called the Raramuri), who share a common ancestry with the fierce Aztecs who settled farther to the south. They are really your hosts, having dwelled in this remote, almost inaccessible part of Mexico long before any tourists arrived. This is their home and you will be introduced to them from the beginning of your train trip since the women, colorfully dressed in their native costumes, are at all the train stations and hotels where they sit quietly weaving their baskets, which are always for sale. They bring their children with them—infants, warmly wrapped in blankets, sleep beside their mothers while older children romp and play nearby.

Tarahumaran Women and Children

Be sure to buy a few baskets—they are beautifully made and reasonably priced. The Tarahumara Indians are renowned as long-distance runners and if you walk the paths twisting along the canyon walls at what you think is a brisk pace, you will be amazed at how quickly you are passed by women and children whose speed will far surpass yours. It is said the men were able to chase deer tirelessly, following them for days at a time until their prey collapsed from exhaustion. The Tarahumara Indians used to occupy the entire state of Chihuahua. However, in the 17th century when the Spaniards arrived and began to enslave the Indians to work their mines, the Tarahumarans moved ever deeper into the remote, hidden valleys of the canyons. In winter when the weather can be very cold due to the high elevation, they move to the floor of the canyons where the climate is almost tropical. In summer, they move to higher elevations. They live in caves in the walls of the canyon or log huts, or a combination of both. Due to their isolation, their way of life, dress, food, and traditions have changed little. They are a shy, independent people, who seem to treasure their way of life. Although the government has tried to make their life easier, they seem to prefer living as they do protected against the influence of modern civilization.

DESTINATION II   BACK TO EL FUERTE

You can continue on the train, taking it the final destination, Chihuahua. However, the scenery gets less dramatic as the train goes east. There are a few stops en route to Chihuahua that are somewhat interesting. One of these is El Divisadero where the train stops for 15 minutes so that passengers can enjoy the view from a scenic overlook and buy souvenirs from Indians selling at small stalls (though the view can't surpass that of the Posada Mirador!). Another stop farther east is at Creel, a small, bland country town, popular as a base for those embarking on hiking trips into the canyons.

Our suggestion is to head back west, the same way you came (the seats on the left side of the train provide the best views). Although repeating your journey, the scenery always looks different approached from the opposite direction. The train is supposed to depart from the Barrancas station at 1:20 pm and arrive back at El Fuerte at 6:15 pm. However, the train rarely runs to schedule so ask at the Posada Mirador what time the train is expected and what time the bus leaves for the short trip to the train station.

When you arrive back at El Fuerte, there should be a taxi waiting to take you back to your hotel, the Posada del Hidalgo, in time for dinner in their cozy restaurant.

The next morning you can continue on your way or, if you want to extend your stay in El Fuerte, there are more things to see including nearby ancient petroglyphs, a local market, Indian villages, and a river float trip.

Cliff Dwelling of Tarahumaran Indians

OPTIONAL EXTENSIONS TO ITINERARY

The above itinerary covers the basic highlights of the Copper Canyon, giving you time to enjoy its major attractions. However, for those who would like to spend more time in the area and enjoy further adventures, we suggest you expand your stay to include one or all of the following extensions.

CREEL, SIERRA LODGE: About two hours east of Barrancas, the train stops in Creel. The town is not especially attractive, but the surrounding area is lovely. About half an hour's drive from the train station you can stay in the Sierra Lodge, a small hotel built on a rise just above the river (featured in the hotel section in the back of the book). Here you feel a part of this primitive, beautiful environment. The hotel has no electricity and no phones—at night the rooms are lit by kerosene lamps and warmed by pot-bellied stoves. Wholesome, hearty meals are included in the room rate and served family-style in a charming, rustic dining room with a large open fireplace. The building, made of logs and stucco and topped by a corrugated tin roof, looks like an old-fashioned motel—a long strip of rooms with a porch stretching across the front where rocking chairs are set for relaxing and enjoying the vista. The hotel is very primitive in many respects but you are not really roughing it at the Sierra Lodge. Although the price is unbelievably low, the simple accommodations are very pleasant, with hot water in the bathrooms, comfortable beds, plenty of warm blankets, fluffy bath towels tied with ribbons, and even bathrobes in the rooms.

CEROCAHUI, HOTEL MISIÓN: Owned by the Balderramas, who own most of the hotels and organize most of the tours in the Copper Canyon, the Hotel Misión adds a whole new dimension to your canyon experience. As with the other Balderrama properties, a stay here is very easy to set up since one phone call to the head office (800-896-8196 from the U.S.) completes all the needed arrangements including hotel, train, and transfer to the hotel. Spending the night here either before or after going to the Posada Mirador works in well with the above itinerary. About four hours after the train leaves El Fuerte, it stops in Bahuichivo. Balderrama tours arranges the transfer to the hotel, which is located about an hour from the train station along a very bumpy road to Cerocahui, a hamlet in a high, fertile river valley of orchards surrounded by the Sierra Madre mountains. The hotel, named for the old Jesuit mission, exudes charm. The guestrooms are cozy with beamed ceilings, carved wooden furniture, terra-cotta floors, and brightly colored hand-woven fabrics. You can take guided horseback rides, trek to the lovely Huicochi waterfall (five hours round trip), explore the many nearby trails, take a bus to the old mining town of Urique where there is a lookout with sweeping canyon views, and visit the Jesuit mission across from the hotel. The mission was founded in 1694 by Juan María de Salvatierra, a Jesuit priest from Italy who was the first European to reach the floor of the canyon and who later founded the first mission in Baja California in Loreto.

ALAMOS, HACIENDA DE LOS SANTOS: We cannot resist mentioning a side trip to Alamos. Although not located in the Copper Canyon, Alamos is a Colonial jewel very much like El Fuerte and shares a similar heritage. The Hacienda de los Santos, a remarkably charming, beautifully decorated hacienda abounding with antiques and exquisite gardens, is one of our favorite places to stay. The town is tucked into the hills about a three-hour drive north of El Fuerte, making it a convenient stopover for a few days either before or after your Copper Canyon adventure. If you have the time, go to Alamos and enjoy the spa, the food, the superb accommodations, the gardens, the swimming pools, and the tender personal attention.

Alamos, Hacienda de los Santos

Places to Play in the Sun
An Overview

Mexico has long beckoned tourists to its beautiful coastal resorts where one can play in the sun and enjoy excellent weather, beautiful beaches, splendid accommodations, and wonderful food. The quality of the resorts available is unsurpassed anywhere in the world. One need not go all the way to the South Pacific for sublime secluded beaches studded with palm trees, or to Penang for a gentle warm sea, or to the Seychelles for pristine white-sand beaches. These can all be found in Mexico. To make these beach resorts even more alluring, you find here some of the finest hotels in the world — not just super-expensive, lavish, world-class resorts (although there are plenty of these), but also charming little inns on secluded beaches. There are even several places to stay that have no road access but can be reached only by boat. How much more exclusive can you be?

We have divided the beach areas into three geographical parts: the Pacific Coast, Baja California Sur, and the Mexican Caribbean. Each of these areas has its own personality.

The Pacific Coast abounds with wide golden-sand beaches and wonderful swimming. Here you find a great variety of resorts including Mazatlán, Puerto Vallarta, Manzanillo, Zihuatanejo, Ixtapa, and Huatulco.

At the tip of the Baja Peninsula, the ultra-chic Los Cabos area is becoming more popular every day. With its gorgeous golf courses, superb lavish hotels, and excellent sport fishing, it offers something for everyone. Here you find the colorful towns of San José del Cabo and Cabo San Lucas, joined by a strip of some of the most expensive real estate in the world, called simply The Corridor.

The eastern coast of Mexico has just one main beach resort—but what a resort this is! The Mexican Caribbean on the east coast of the Yucatán Peninsula offers some of the most astounding white-sand beaches in the world, made all the more beautiful by the turquoise water that laps upon the shore. To add the finishing touch of perfection, this is the world of the Maya and you can combine visits to superb archaeological sites with your time lazing on the beach.

To help you decide where to go, in the following itinerary we give the special attributes of each area along with sightseeing possibilities. Once you decide where you want to go, study the hotel section to select from a wealth of fabulous places to stay.

Places to Play in the Sun
The Pacific Coast

Puerto Vallarta, Cathedral

Along the Pacific Coast, dense jungles sweep down to meet the deep-blue Pacific, providing spectacular backdrops for modern resort cities and smaller coastal villages. Pristine beaches stretch for miles and in some areas are snuggled in coves embraced by high bluffs. In other spots, the mountains drop right down to the sea where the surf pounds against the rocks. The waters of the Pacific are not as crystal-clear or as turquoise-blue as you find in the Caribbean, but the golden-sand beaches are some of the best in Mexico and usually safe for swimming. A profusion of modern hotels, easy air access, and a growing array of activities have transformed this region of Mexico into one of the country's premier resort areas. Although the landscape may be similar all the way along this western coast of Mexico, with wide sweeps of beaches dotted with palm trees and mountains rising just inland, the resorts here couldn't be more varied in personality. From high-energy seaside cities to pristine, primitive coves, this is the Mexico that first lured vacationers from around the globe.

Spanish conquistadors frequented the Pacific Coast, lured by its numerous sheltered coves and protected bays from which to set sail for the Far East. Years later, Mexico's first tourists found the same elements appealing and began to come for holidays.

The following beach resorts are listed geographically, starting with Mazatlán in the north and ending with Huatulco in the south.

MAZATLÁN

Mazatlán, "land of the deer" in the ancient Nahuatl language, offers 20 kilometers of sandy beaches. Hosting more than one million visitors each year, it is definitely geared towards tourists looking for casual, value-packed vacations. Most of the hotels here are high-rise and offer inexpensive, all-inclusive packages that include airfare, room, and meals. More than any other beach resort, it probably best represents the golden beaches, fresh seafood, and inexpensive vacation accommodations that launched Mexico's appeal to travelers. Most of the resorts are located on the Zona Dorado (Golden Zone) with its long expanse of shoreline, trendy restaurants, and endless tourist shops. There has been much development over the past few years and Mazatlán has become a favorite for college students at spring break.

The downtown area has an old, rather ramshackle Colonial section. Here you find the restored Teatro Ángela Peralta, named after a famous Mazatlán-born opera singer, and the cathedral, which has a Gothic exterior and a baroque interior. Both buildings date from the late 19th century. Several of the buildings around Plaza Machado have been restored and converted into artists' studios, galleries, and restaurants.

Mazatlán, Beach Scene

Mazatlán is famous for its carnival. With its pre-Lent festivals including parades, coronation parties, street dances, fireworks and floats, Mazatlán claims that this is the third-largest celebration in the world after Rio de Janeiro and New Orleans.

Bullfights are also a passion in Mazatlán and are usually held in the late afternoon on Saturdays from mid-December to April in the Plaza de Toros Monumental. The city is one of the best places on the west coast to watch a bullfight.

Several day trips are possible from Mazatlán. You can take a boat tour to the islands just off the coast for viewing wildlife and enjoying secluded beaches. You can also take a drive into the mountains or to the towns of Concordia or Copala, both about 65 kilometers away. Concordia is famous for its leather goods and furniture shops and Copala is an old mining village with whitewashed adobe homes draped with bright pink bougainvillea. Copala has been declared a national historic site and many United States citizens have retired here.

PUERTO VALLARTA

Puerto Vallarta has a scenic location on the sea with the Sierra Madre foothills behind it and the ornate crown of the Church of Our Lady of Guadalupe serving as a photogenic landmark. It is a quaint, picturesque town with cobblestone streets, Colonial buildings, traditional red Spanish-tile rooftops, and brilliant flowers. This is the second most-visited resort in Mexico (behind Cancún), boasting 43 kilometers of golden-sand beaches with many private coves accessible only by boat, great dining and nightlife, accommodations for every budget, entertainment, art galleries, shopping, world-class golf and tennis, activities and excursions galore, and fun: all this in the atmosphere of a traditional Mexican village.

In 1963 Ava Gardner and Richard Burton starred in *Night of the Iguana*, filmed in Puerto Vallarta. Burton and his new love, Elizabeth Taylor, had a wild romance during the filming (even though they were both married to others at the time). The international *paparazzi* arrived and this small seaside village was never the same again. Now with a population of over 250,000, Puerto Vallarta continues to grow as new hotels are constantly being built north of town. However, the old town retains its original, typical Mexican charm since there can be no further building—Puerto Vallarta town is bound by hills, leaving no room for expansion. In fact, there are just two main, one-way streets (usually very congested with traffic) leading through town, one going north and one south.

The majority of Puerto Vallarta's hotels are not in the town center, but just to the north. Here the hills are farther back from the coast and you find a long sweep of wide beach bound by a continuous strip of high-rise, modern hotels. Other hotels are located in small coves just south of town where the hills drop right into the sea, forming intimate, sheltered coves.

The newest tourist area is north of Puerto Vallarta, just across the border in the state of Nayarit in an area of spectacular beauty called Punta Mita. The stunning Four Seasons was the first hotel to be built here, but more are soon to follow. For some reason the beaches here are of superb white sand, surpassing by far those usually found along the Pacific Coast where the sand is coarser and golden yellow.

Puerto Vallarta offers all the usual beach-resort activities, but the river is also popular for kayaking. Also offered are expeditions along the jungle trails that lead into the mountains, which are popular for mountain biking and horseback riding.

There are many boat excursions available. During the season, whale and dolphin expeditions are popular, while another excursion involves a trip south in a boat that hugs the splendid coast to Yelapa (a private beach accessible only by boat). The town isn't special, but the trip down is lots of fun.

COSTA ALEGRE

Costa Alegre, considered one of Mexico's greatest undiscovered treasures, is becoming a favored hideaway both for celebrities and the wealthy seeking seclusion in a natural paradise. Alternatively referred to as Costa Alegre (Happy Coast) or Costa Careyes (Turtle Coast) after the many sea turtles that nest here annually, it encompasses a 240-kilometer stretch of coast that runs from Puerto Vallarta in the north to Manzanillo in the south. This entire coastal area is magical, with endless, untouched coves and secluded beaches tucked between folds of dense jungle stretching to the edge of the sea. Today the Costa Alegre is home to an eclectic array of the most unique, captivating, and exclusive places to stay, with a choice of activities including championship golf and polo.

The two-lane highway 200 connecting Puerto Vallarta and Manzanillo runs a bit inland, rarely giving a glimpse of the sea. The road is safe, but has no lighting and curves through mountains so it is best to make the drive during daylight hours. Along the way, you pass through a few nondescript villages, but the hotels are secreted within vast jungles and can be reached only by narrow lanes. Some of the hotels have built their own access roads, but others have as their only access the original dirt roads. It seems as if you are in the middle of nowhere but when you arrive, what a marvelous surprise awaits!

Costa Alegre

These resorts are tricky to find (and some are so isolated that the only approach is by boat) so it is vital that you have prior reservations and obtain detailed instructions to the hotel of your choice. The best maps, even though supposedly up to date, are not accurate. Also, many of the hotels do not want "drop-ins," so have few or no signs, and once you arrive at the entrance, you find a guard and a security gate. In the hotel section we describe the rich choice of accommodations we recommend. You will be amazed at the ultimate luxury available in such a totally remote area.

MANZANILLO

Manzanillo? Never heard of it? Except to the Canadians, who come in droves during their bitterly cold winter, Manzanillo is a relatively unknown destination. It's located on the west coast of Mexico, about 250 kilometers south of Puerto Vallarta. Manzanillo doesn't have the pizzazz of Puerto Vallarta's quaint cobbled streets or Acapulco's non-stop nightlife: its allure lies in its pristine beaches, near-perfect winter weather, and lack of commercialism. Here you feel you have found the *real* Mexico, not one prettied up for show. Downtown Manzanillo is a busy port for large cargo ships and has little appeal although an effort has been made to spruce up the central square and the promenade along the waterfront. The popular resort hotels are not in town, but located to the north. The three hotels we recommend (described in the hotel section) are in the exclusive Santiago Peninsula resort zone.

In the winter there is rarely rain, just day after day of sunshine. Summertime is also popular, especially with Mexican families. Frequently there are thunderstorms, but these usually occur in the afternoon or at night. If you enjoy swimming in warm water, you'll be thrilled to learn that in summer the temperature of the ocean hovers at 90 degrees. Absolute heaven!

Manzanillo is famous for its superb golf and is quickly emerging as a key golf destination: two of its courses were listed in the top ten of *Golf Digest* magazine. Another draw for sportsmen is deep-sea fishing. Designated the "Sailfish Capital of the World," Manzanillo is considered by many to have some of the best deep-sea fishing in Mexico.

If you want to combine a bit of archaeology with your beach holiday, you can drive about an hour east of Manzanillo up into the lush mountains to Colima. This is a clean, attractive working city with a pretty Colonial plaza where you find the excellent Museum of Archaeology. Originally this exhibit of magnificent pre-Columbian objects was a private collection housed in a rather rundown building. At the owner's death the collection came under the auspices of the Mexican National Institute of Archaeology and History and today a beautifully executed, small museum displays in great style this immense collection made over a lifetime by the original owner. The pieces, mostly of ceramic, came from burials throughout the state of Colima. Most were found by local farmers in the course of working the land and were brought to Colima for sale. Details of origin are lacking for most of the items, but the artistic value is obvious and the museum enables visitors to see a wide range of objects and styles of ancient indigenous craftsmen.

ZIHUATANEJO-IXTAPA

Zihuatanejo and Ixtapa are really two resorts in one. Ixtapa, 10 kilometers northwest of Zihuatanejo, is a modern resort full of luxury high-rise hotels set along 7 kilometers of curving beach, Playa Palmar. Zihuatanejo, in contrast, with low-rise buildings only, sits in a scenic sheltered bay (much visited by cruise ships and private yachts) and still has the intimate feel of a small fishing community. Both offer great fishing and some of the best scuba diving on Mexico's Pacific Coast. They are both also convenient starting points for exploring the spectacular deserted beaches along the surrounding coast. This dual destination tends to cater towards adults and couples rather than families (some places are off limits to those under age 16).

Zihuatanejo (which means "place of the woman" in the native Nahuatl tongue) has grown to 80,000 inhabitants but still retains the ambiance of a small village, with a lot of local color. Along its cobblestone streets are a number of cozy restaurants, grocery stores, rug shops, art galleries, and artisan markets, and you can find all levels of accommodations, though you won't find any high-rise mega hotels. The city has mandated a four-story limit to buildings in an effort to maintain its charm and village appeal. The downtown area, El Centro, is great for walking and browsing, as is the Paseo del Pescador, a brick-paved beachfront promenade along Playa Principal.

Zihuatanejo is famous for its great fishing, diving, and water sports. The area's three beaches invite all kinds of sports and the local waters are famed for their abundance of game fish, including sailfish, marlin, and roosterfish. Because it lies on a relatively small bay, the excellent beaches have clean water and are safe for young swimmers. For further recreation, do what the locals do—take

The Inn at Manzanillo Bay, Zihuatanejo–Troncones

a boat from the town pier and go to Los Gatos beach for a day of swimming and eating. There are no "great buys" these days but shopping can be fun. Bargain at the artisan market and you might come away with a very nice silver bracelet or a pretty hand-painted plate or vase.

Ixtapa is a modern, world-class resort that was created from the ground up beginning in 1968 by Fonatur (Mexico's National Tourism Development Fund). In contrast to Zihuatanejo, Ixtapa is a modern resort town with high-rise hotels along the beachfront, which is backed by a palm-lined promenade with restaurants, nightclubs, and shops. This is a good place for souvenir shopping (T-shirts and Mexican crafts). Ixtapa also offers 14 unspoiled beaches, golf courses, tennis courts, and a yacht marina. Launches explore the turtles, fish, and pelicans at El Morro de los Pericos and boat excursions tour Ixtapa Island, which served as the location for the film *Robinson Crusoe*. The town sits on a wide bay dotted with small rocky islands inhabited solely by sea birds and here you find excellent beaches with clean water (although the water is a little rougher than in Zihuatanejo). The beach in town, Playa del Mar, a 3.5-kilometer stretch of white sand, gave Ixtapa its Nahuatl Indian name, "the white place." A very special experience is to swim with dolphins at the new dolphinarium.

ACAPULCO

Acapulco was one of Mexico's first beach areas to become popular. It is no wonder these early tourists were captivated, since Acapulco has a stunning natural setting. Today, the aura of secluded bliss in the downtown area of Acapulco has faded behind rows of high-rise hotels (many of which have seen better days) and fast-food restaurants. Nevertheless, the views of Acapulco Bay, framed by mountains and beaches, are still breathtaking day or night. The towering Sierra Madre mountains are beautiful; they seem to reach right down to the shoreline. At night, the bay is magical and romantic, with millions of lights reflecting in the water like stars.

The more recently built hotels, many of them real beauties, are not in town, but tucked along the coast away from the hustle and bustle. Here golden-sand beaches, blue sea, and waving palm trees create an idyllic setting. Acapulco is non-stop, 24-hour-a-day energy. The perfectly sculpted bay is an adult playground full of water skiers and wave runners. Golf and tennis are popular, but the real attraction is the nightlife!

The nightlife scene begins at 1 or 2 am and doesn't stop until daylight. The beaches are generally wide and clean but the ocean is polluted, although it is cleaner than in years past. In the 1990s a program was instituted to clean up the water, and whales have recently been sighted offshore for the first time in years. If you do decide to swim in the sea, be aware of the strong undertow and riptides (at least two swimmers drown each year).

One of the largest and most decadent of Mexican resort towns, Acapulco leapt into the international spotlight when movie stars made it their playground in the late 1930s, but it has fallen out of favor with international visitors in the last decade.

Acapulco, Cliff Divers of La Quebrada

Today, the vast majority of visitors are Mexicans from Mexico City and Guadalajara, who pour into town in huge numbers to spend a vacation by the sea.

A visit to Acapulco would not be complete without seeing the famous cliff divers of La Quebrada who have been jumping from the rocks (about 35 meters up) into a small crevasse of ocean since 1934. Get there in time to see the spectacular sunsets and watch the divers as they plunge into the cliffs holding flaming torches. Visit the small shrine where the divers pray prior to their performances (Elvis said a few prayers himself there during the filming of *Fun in Acapulco*).

For those looking for a sightseeing excursion, a day trip can be made to the spectacular mountainside town of Taxco, although it is a rather long trip. However, if you are driving to Mexico City, Taxco makes a good stopover along the way. (For more information on Taxco, see our itinerary *Mexico City & Beyond.*)

HUATULCO

Commonly referred to as the Bahías de Huatulco (Bays of Hautulco), Huatulco is based around nine bays and 35 kilometers of beaches. After the tremendous success of Cancún, the Mexican government looked for an equivalent site to start a new tourist destination on the Pacific Coast and started building this resort in the 1980s. Located 130 kilometers south of Puerto Escondido, Huatulco is slowly building a name for itself as Mexico's authentic tourism haven. It has an 18-hole golf course and luxury resort hotels, and it also offers a growing array of ecotourism adventures that include bay tours, diving, jungle hiking tours, river rafting, and rappelling. Both dining and nightlife are limited here but it is a beautiful and relaxing setting and the nine bays include 36 beaches and countless inlets and coves for exploring. The clear blue water and golden beaches are enough of an attraction for many visitors. Its most important quality is the fact that it still isn't plagued by mass tourism, thus ensuring that your stay will be truly pleasant. (It is not easy to get to Huatulco—there are not many direct flights and it relies heavily on charter service from the United States and Canada.)

Places to Play in the Sun
Baja California Sur

The Rocks, Cabo San Lucas

The Baja Peninsula is a long, very narrow strip of land that juts like a finger down from California, creating the Gulf of California, which separates Baja from the mainland of Mexico. Until recently, because of a lack of roads, gasoline stations, sources for food, and accommodations, only a daring few in four-wheel-drive vehicles dared to venture into this desolate area. Although the road is still not top-notch, you can now drive down Highway 1 for 1,765 kilometers from Tijuana at the northern border all the way down to Cabo San Lucas at the southern tip of Baja. Most of the peninsula is like an untouched frontier, with few places for tourists to stop along the way. However the barren desert landscapes display a remarkable, austere beauty. In just about its mid section, the 28-degree parallel intersects the peninsula: to the north of the line is the state of Baja California and to the south is the state of Baja California Sur. This itinerary features Baja California Sur, highlighting the extremely popular resort area that has mushroomed along its southern tip. The government picked this area to develop as a tourist destination in 1976 due to its natural beauty and setting and their venture has indeed been enormously successful.

In 1535 an officer under the command of Hernán Cortés became the first European to land in Baja California. The reports he brought back, particularly in respect to the existence of pearls in the Gulf of California, were so tantalizing that a year later Cortés himself led settlers to the present site of La Paz. The poverty of the land and the fierceness of the Indians forced Cortés to abandon the area a few years later. The conquistadors became busy with other parts of Mexico, and all but forgot about Baja. It was not until 1697 that a permanent settlement was established: a Jesuit mission and a presidio at Loreto, 366 kilometers north of La Paz. Throughout the 18th century, the Indians in this barren land were ministered to by the Jesuits, who founded the first missions. When the Jesuits were banished from Mexico in the 1760s, the Franciscans and the Dominicans followed. But along with churches, the Spaniards brought disease and smallpox, which almost wiped out the population by the 19th century. Meanwhile, primitive settlements began to appear, but for many years the only means of access between them was by boat or on foot. Loreto remained the most important town and capital of Baja until 1829 when a hurricane leveled the town. The capital was then moved to La Paz.

One can reach Baja California Sur by plane, car, or ferry, the most popular means of transportation being by plane. There is an airport at La Paz, but since the boom in tourism in the past few years, the airport at San José del Cabo has expanded and has become the most popular access point, with many flights arriving daily, especially from Los Angeles. You can also take a ferry across the Gulf of California to or from La Paz, connecting to the mainland towns of Los Mochis or Mazatlán. If you plan to take a car or reserve a private cabin on the ferry, advance reservations are needed. Even the "deluxe" accommodations are pretty basic and if you want to take your car, there are long delays and mountains of paperwork to be filled out. Even so, the ferry is definitely faster than driving all the way north and driving back down the entire peninsula.

CABO SAN LUCAS, SAN JOSÉ DEL CABO & THE CORRIDOR

The southern tip of Baja has long been popular with wealthy sportsmen, such as the late Bing Crosby, who fly down in their private planes for deep-sea fishing. Happily, what used to be almost a private playground for the super-rich is now available for everyone. However, the area still caters to the more affluent traveler: the superb hotels and world-class golf courses here are not cheap.

This tip of the peninsula, commonly referred to simply as Los Cabos, basically consists of twin towns: Cabo San Lucas (to the west) and San José del Cabo (to the east). The 33-kilometer strip of land joining the two towns is called The Corridor, a once-barren area transformed into a verdant paradise with superb hotels perched on cliffs overlooking the brilliant blue sea, championship golf courses, colorful gardens, and dramatic beaches with waves crashing against the shore. A fine four-lane, divided road called the Transpeninsular Highway traces the coast, joining the two towns. The resorts that have sprung up along Los Cabos are exceptional. Each seems to vie with the other for originality and quality of design, gorgeous landscaping, and splendid amenities. There is nothing tacky about this area—it is obviously one of money and impeccable taste.

Because flights are so easy from Los Angeles, it has almost become a weekend retreat for Californians, and many of them have built homes here.

Although the two towns are often grouped together, they are really quite different. Cabo San Lucas became famous for sport fishing and, with a population of 25,000, is the bigger and faster-growing of the two cities. It is much more commercial and Americanized. Many people think the official language here is English!

San José del Cabo, with its pastel cottages and narrow streets, is more sedate, more charming, and still retains the feel of a small Mexican town. However, San José del Cabo has become famous by association with its neighbor and is now also growing rapidly.

Los Cabos offers some of Mexico's finest golf and great sport fishing, with the majority of visitors now coming for the world-famous championship golf courses. With a few exceptions, the sea here is not safe for swimming since the surf is often fierce and the undertow strong. Most people are content to use the beautiful swimming pools at the hotels and reserve the gorgeous beaches for walking. The contrast of the stark desert landscape with the dark blue of the sea is magnificent. Other big attractions here include kayaking, surfing, snorkeling, horseback

Places to Play in the Sun: Baja California Sur

riding, windsurfing, whale watching, and an active nightlife!

Los Cabos tends to be more expensive than other Mexican resorts and, unlike most of the other beach resort towns, the weather in Los Cabos does vary by season, although it is predictable. It is hot and sunny in the summer and can be fairly cool and windy in the winter; however, it is usually warm enough for water sports year-round and the average temperature throughout the year is 75° F. With 300 days of sunshine annually, there isn't much rain, and any rain usually comes during the month of September.

You should consider renting a car here because it is nice to be able to drive between the two towns and to explore The Corridor (taxis are expensive). Note that the coastal highway is not lit at night.

DAY TRIPS

LAND'S END & LOVE BEACH: Take a boat trip to the southern tip of the Baja Peninsula where the Pacific and the Sea of Cortez meet. Towering granite monoliths lie along the coast, including the most dramatic and famous, El Arco, a rock arch that has been carved by the waves over millions of years. The Arch is a marine refuge for hundreds of species of fish. One can often spot dolphins, sea lions, and whales (in the winter). Land's End is also a popular dive spot with underwater canyons believed to be as deep as the Grand Canyon and famous sand falls or cascades discovered by Jacques Cousteau. Diving is unpredictable given the weather and rough seas. Bring plenty of film. Many tours will also drop you off at Playa del Amor (Love Beach) where you can picnic and choose between swimming in the cool waters of the Pacific or the calm, clear waters of the Sea of Cortez.

LA PAZ: Located 183 kilometers north of Cabo San Lucas, La Paz, where Cortés landed in 1535, means "peace" and this port town does indeed have a peaceful feel. A rather large city with 200,000 inhabitants, La Paz is the capital of Baja California Sur, with a library, anthropology museum, and a theatre with performances by local and visiting artists. All of the action and tourist attractions run along the main street, Obregón, where you find restaurants, boutiques, and hotels. There is a relaxed, laid-back, old-fashioned demeanor to the town—a far cry from the trendy upscale ambiance of Los Cabos. Except for a few locals, no one much uses the narrow beach in town: the water does not look too appealing and the beach is not too clean. If you want to swim, on the road to the port where the ferries and freighters arrive, there are a few inviting coves wrapped by cactus-studded hills where the water is clear. However, most people come to La Paz for sport fishing, which is world-famous, or to take a ferry to the mainland.

TODOS SANTOS: If you want a side excursion, it is fun to take a trip to the quaint town of Todos Santos, an artists' colony located on the west coast about 70 kilometers north of Cabo San Lucas. This tiny town, dating back to the 1800s, exudes a Colonial ambiance with its central plaza, narrow cobbled streets, and whitewashed houses enhanced by rustic tiled roofs. Many expatriates, including many artists, have discovered the charm of this small town off the beaten path and have settled here to open appealing boutiques, excellent restaurants, art galleries, and a few hotels. The town is located a bit inland from the ocean, but nearby you find beautiful secluded beaches. However, swimming is frequently treacherous due to pounding surf and strong undertows. If you want to come for a few nights instead of making Todos Santos just a day trip, we recommend two hotels here, Todos Santos Inn in the heart of town and Posada La Poza just a few kilometers from town on a coastal nature reserve. Descriptions of both are in the hotel section.

WHALE WATCHING: Between January and March the gray and humpback whales are frequently seen along the coast of Baja. At this time, many tour operators offer excursions out to see these majestic creatures. However, if you prefer a more in-depth experience and want to see many more whales, you need to go to the calm lagoons farther north where the gray whales come each winter to have their babies. For this experience, refer to our *Whale Watching in Baja* itinerary.

Places to Play in the Sun
The Mexican Caribbean

There is nowhere in the world where you can find beaches that surpass those of the Mexican Caribbean. If you are looking for warm, crystal-clear turquoise water and endless stretches of soft white-sand beaches, this part of Mexico is paradise. This coast of rare beauty is found in the state of Quintana Roo, on the eastern shores of the Yucatán Peninsula, stretching from Cancún in the north to Chetumal in the south. What is quite extraordinary is the wide range of both hotels and styles of resorts found here. There is an intriguing selection of places to stay in every price range, from super-deluxe to very simple. You can also choose between secluded beaches, where the activity of the day is walking out to your hammock, and modern bustling resorts such as Cancún, where the activity is non-stop. And, in addition to the coastal resorts, the beautiful islands of Isla Mujeres and Cozumel lie just offshore, offering a further dimension of holiday possibilities.

Another tremendous bonus of the Mexican Caribbean is that the coast is protected by the Great Mesoamerican Reef, the largest coral reef in the western hemisphere. As one would expect, scuba diving and snorkeling are immensely popular and a dazzling array of fish can be seen. Adding icing to the cake, the area abounds with Mayan ruins, allowing you to easily combine a holiday in the sun with the delight of seeing some of the most stunning archaeological sites in the world, including the sensational Chichén Itzá, Tulum, and Cobá.

The resort area along the Mexican Caribbean is divided into two parts. The most developed and the larger of the two is called Riviera Maya, which begins in Cancún and stretches south to Tulum. Look in the hotel section to see the selection of wonderful places to stay that we recommend here. The second area of this coast, Costa Maya, runs from Tulum south to the border with Belize. The Costa Maya is just beginning to develop tourism and we hope to be able to offer some hotel selections here in our next edition.

From whichever hotel you choose as your base along the Riviera Maya, there are many places to visit and things to do. Listed below is information on places where we recommend hotels that you can use as your "hub," followed by sightseeing suggestions.

CANCÚN

For a no-hassle beach vacation where you can fly in, soak up the sun, eat at the Hard Rock Café, and never speak a word of Spanish or even have to exchange your money into pesos, Cancún is the place. If you want to experience some Mexican culture on your visit, you can visit a number of exceptional Mayan ruins (see "Sightseeing Suggestions" below). One of the top vacation destinations in the world, Cancún basks under year-round warm sun. This action-packed government-built Mexican resort offers pleasure seekers gorgeous white-sand beaches and clear turquoise water. There are water sports galore, as well as vigorous entertainment until the wee hours of the morning. Add excellent accommodations, gourmet restaurants, and outstanding shopping, and you've got the ultimate escape.

Cancún was just a deserted, sun-drenched spit of land off the northeast tip of the Yucatán Peninsula until the 1970s when the government chose the site to built a huge resort, offering visitors over 25,000 hotel rooms with all levels of accommodations. These hotels are located on a narrow strip of land that loops around a large lagoon, which is ideal for sailing and water sports. This 22-kilometer-long beach is lined with hotels, American restaurant chains, nightclubs, movie theaters, and shopping malls. The hotels here mostly cater to tour groups and package holidays with airfare, hotel, and food included. Although most of the accommodations are in huge, modern, high-rise hotels, they are usually ones that are well built and of imaginative architectural design. If you prefer a vacation with non-stop action, Cancún is an excellent choice. If you prefer to be away from the crowds, choose one of our other hotel recommendations along the Riviera Maya or on the islands of Cozumel or Isla Mujeres.

Cancún's beaches are excellent. The water is placid along the upper shore facing the Bahía de Mujeres, while beaches facing the Caribbean are subject to choppier water and crashing waves on windy days.

COZUMEL

Located just 20 kilometers off the coast from Playa del Carmen, Cozumel is Mexico's largest island (measuring 52 kilometers long and 15 kilometers wide). This still-unspoiled island remains only moderately developed; the rest is wild jungle populated by iguanas, foxes, deer, and other wildlife. However, it isn't the terrestrial scenery that draws visitors back year after year, it's the water. The turquoise water is so clear that visibility can reach up to 76 meters, with aquatic scenery that includes black coral and millions of exotic fluorescent fish. Cozumel's chains of coral reefs along its southwestern shore make it one of the world's best scuba-diving and snorkeling spots. During the 17th and 18th centuries, Cozumel became a favorite hideout for pirates, who ambushed and sunk many cargo ships off the island's shores, further enhancing the diving experience. What is especially remarkable here is that due to the clarity of the water, you do not have to be a diver to enjoy the underwater views. Simply put on a mask and snorkel and jump in—it will seem as if you've dropped into a tropical fish tank!

Until Cozumel was established as a major resort, the island's economy was based on chicle (used in making chewing gum), coconuts, and seafood. It remained more or less undiscovered until Frenchman Jacques Cousteau recognized the marvels of Cozumel's waters as a divers' haven in the 1960s, declaring it one of the most beautiful scuba-diving areas of the world. To protect the delicate balance of its fantastic coral reefs and abundant variety of tropical fish, in 1996 the National Marine Park of Cozumel Reefs was created, home to over 500 species of fish. Within the marine park is a saltwater lagoon called Chankanaab Nature Park where you can not only snorkel, but also watch trained dolphins perform at the dolphinarium. You can also pay to swim with the dolphins, if you so desire.

The people native to Cozumel are of Mayan descent. The Maya ruled the Yucatán for over 2000 years before the arrival of the Spanish explorers in the 16th century and the legacy of their culture survives in the ruins of the huge cities that they built during their reign. On Cozumel you can find one of the lesser-known, but interesting, sites, San Gervacio, which was once a sacred place where Mayan women journeyed to worship Ixchel, the goddess of fertility.

There are many direct flights to Cozumel or you can take the island-hopper plane from the Cancún airport. You can also travel by air-conditioned bus (about one hour) from Cancún to Playa del Carmen, walk from the bus station to the pier, and take the 45-minute ferry over to the Island. The ferries shuttle constantly between the mainland and the island.

ISLA MUJERES

Only 13 kilometers offshore and easily accessible by ferry from Cancún, Isla Mujeres, just 8 kilometers long and 4 kilometers wide, is a laid-back reprieve from Cancún's conspicuously commercialized action. This is an island of white-sand beaches and turquoise waters, complemented by a town filled with Caribbean-colored clapboard houses and rustic, open-air restaurants specializing in the bounty of the sea. Most tourists come just for the day, but there are wonderful places to stay on this small island, so if you favor a quieter, slow and easy-going vacation pace, we recommend you stay here rather than in Cancún. In the hotel section we describe some excellent accommodations.

Francisco Hernández de Córdoba gave the island its name, which means "island of the women," when he landed here in 1517 and found figurines of partially-clad females along the shore. These are now believed to have been offerings to the Mayan goddess of fertility, Ixchel, and the presence of these figurines indicates that Isla Mujeres was sacred to the Maya. Next to the lighthouse on the southern tip of the island are the ruins (not much more than a pile of rocks) of a small pyramid, which was an observatory built to the moon and goddess Ixchel.

While on the island, spend time at El Garrafón National Underwater Park, located at the southern tip of the island. This is an excellent spot for snorkeling. At the northern tip you find Playa Norte, the island's best public swimming beach.

You can take a take a ferry from Cancún's Embarcadero Pier at Playa Linda to Isla Mujeres. You might need to ask where the pier is located since it is hidden within a shopping arcade and therefore not easily visible. You can also take a ferry from the port of Punta Sam, just outside Puerto Juárez. This ferry is less expensive, but not nearly as convenient since the dock is north of town.

PLAYA DEL CARMEN

Playa del Carmen

Playa del Carmen is located on the Riviera Maya about an hour's drive south of Cancún. Many tourists' first introduction to the town is when they take a bus from Cancún that drops them off at the bus terminal from where they walk through town to the pier. This part of Playa del Carmen is congested and lacking in charm, giving the impression that the town does not have much to offer. However, this is misleading. The nicest part of Playa del Carmen is not near the port, but a few blocks north where the main street, Quinta Avenida, parallels the sea. This pedestrian-only area, several blocks long, between the Quinta Avenida and the beach, is the most attractive part of town. Here you find shops, restaurants, hotels, and lots of local color. The wide strip of beach here is outstanding, with beautiful white sand that seems to go forever. Facing this sensational beach is a string of hotels, most of which are nice, but usually quite simple, catering to travelers on a limited budget. As you go farther north along the beach, the hotels become more expensive.

All in all, Playa del Carmen gives the impression of being a relatively sleepy seaside town with a relaxed atmosphere. The town is small enough for you to walk anywhere. Save one day for an excursion to Cozumel.

SIGHTSEEING SUGGESTIONS

CENOTES

In addition to its beautiful beaches and ocean swimming, the Riviera Maya area is well known for its underground rivers that honeycomb the porous limestone of the Yucatán. In some places the limestone collapses, forming *cenotes*. A cenote is a spot where the underground river comes into view. Sometimes collapsed walls form a deep well, at other times the river runs through a cave. Because the water in these cenotes is usually pure and clear, many people come to swim in them and the really adventurous even don wet suits and follow the underground path of the river from one cenote to the next. There are major eco-theme parks, such as Xcaret and Xel-Ha, where you can swim in cenotes, but our favorites are the lesser-known ones that are far less commercial. Since these cenotes dot the countryside, ask the concierge at your hotel to suggest some nearby favorites.

COBÁ

The archaeological site of Cobá is located about 45 kilometers inland from the sea, on a road that turns west from the coastal highway 307 just south of Tulum. Cobá has very interesting and significant ruins built around a group of lakes in the middle of a jungle. Be prepared for some walking and climbing, especially if you want to see the staggering view from the top of the highest pyramid. Because it is a bit off the beaten path, there are fewer tourists here than at many other sites, making this a very rewarding excursion for those who make the effort to come. If you want to spend the night, we recommend the

Villas Arqueologicas Cobá, a simple but very pleasant small hotel near the lake, within walking distance of the ruins.

CHICHÉN ITZÁ

A favorite day trip from anywhere along the Riviera Maya is to the Mayan site of Chichén Itzá with its massive pyramids. This is one of the most-visited archaeological sites on the Yucatán Peninsula and a memorable experience, from the dizzy heights of the Pyramid of Kukulkán to the mysterious depths of the Sacred Cenote. Allow plenty of time here and be prepared for walking and climbing in the heat. If possible, visit early in the morning. There are good facilities, including bookshops and refreshments, available at the site. If you want to spend the night, we recommend two outstanding hotels: the Hacienda Chichén and Hotel Mayaland. Both are within easy walking distance of the park, which is especially convenient if you attend the Sound and Light show, which takes place at dusk each evening when lights play upon the ruins and stories of its rich history are narrated in Spanish.

ECO-THEME PARKS

There are a few natural aquariums formed by interlocking lagoons off the ocean that mix fresh and salt water, which is perfect for viewing wildlife and snorkeling. These "eco-theme parks," including Xcaret and Xel-Ha, are more "theme parks" than "ecological" parks—they are a bit like Disneyland and very popular, especially with families traveling with children. They also offer swimming with dolphins.

SIAN KA'AN BIOSPHERE RESERVE

Just a few kilometers south of Tulum, this 1.3-million-acre reserve was established in 1986 to preserve tropical forests, savannas, mangroves, coastal and marine habitats, and 115 kilometers of coastal reefs. Access is restricted and the best way to visit the area is on an excursion. Guided tours are available with biologists who can point out the amazing variety of birds and animals resident in the reserve, including crocodiles, pumas, flamingos, herons, and turtles. An unforgettable experience!

Tulum, Castle

TULUM

Tulum, a Mayan fortress built in the 10th century, has a stunning position high on a cliff above the sea, overlooking the clear turquoise water of the Caribbean below. The setting is incredibly romantic and pictures of the fortress are frequently depicted on travel posters and calendars. Until the arrival of the Spanish this was a Mayan seaport whose inhabitants traded with Cozumel, Isla Mujeres, Guatemala, and central Mexico.

Although immensely popular with tourists because of the spectacular setting, the ruins at Tulum are not large or particularly important archaeologically. The famous *castillo* (castle) overlooking the sea, used both as a fortress and a temple, is the most impressive building at the site. Try to imagine what it looked like in its heyday when covered with stucco and painted. If you want to stay near Tulum, we recommend the Cabañas la Conchita, a very primitive but charming hotel nestled on a small, secluded beach just a few kilometers south of the ruins.

Hotel Descriptions

San Miguel de Allende, Jardín Principal

Set on a hillside with beautiful views of the deep-blue water of Acapulco Bay, Las Brisas offers a romantic getaway. Add the fact that most guestrooms have their own plunge pool tucked on the terrace (the other guestrooms share a pool between two rooms) and you are in for a special treat. When we first stayed at Las Brisas over 30 years ago, we could not imagine that the brochure could be accurate: that our room would have its own private pool—we had to see it to believe it. Now other hotels have copied this extremely imaginative concept, but Las Brisas was the first with the idea and remains known worldwide as a honeymoon retreat. The guestrooms are in contemporary-style pink casitas terracing down the hillside on the 110-acre property, which spreads both above and below the main highway. The bedrooms and the Bella Vista Restaurant (a delightful place to dine with an outdoor terrace with an unbeatable view of the bay) are high on the hill. On the lower side of the highway Las Brisas has its own Beach Club with an informal restaurant called La Concha and a stunning swimming pool nestled on a terrace above the sea. The property is so spread out that it's a long way from the guestrooms to the waterfront but should you decide to leave the privacy of your own terrace, just call and one of the hotel's jaunty little jeeps will whisk you down to the Beach Club. *Directions:* Located on the main road into town, about 15 minutes from the airport.

❄ ⚏ ☕ ✂ 💳 ☎ 🍴 🚶 🐎 🍷 P 🍴 ≈ 🎿 🏌 ⛳ ♿ 🍇

LAS BRISAS
Manager: Carlos Arellano
Carretera Escenica 5255
Acapulco, Guerrero 39868, Mexico
Tel: (744) 469-6900, (888) 559-4329 USA
Fax: (744) 446-5332
*263 rooms, Double: $330–$680**
**Service: $20/day, Tax: 17%*
Open: all year, Credit cards: all major
Region: Beach–Pacific Coast
www.karenbrown.com/mex/lasbrisas.html

We cannot say enough good things about the relatively new hotel affiliation in Mexico called Quinta Real. All of their properties that we have visited are of top-quality construction, are decorated with exceptional taste, and reflect an ambiance of excellence in every detail. The Quinta Real in Acapulco is no exception. Located about a ten-minute drive from downtown Acapulco in a beautiful, exclusive area called Punta Diamante, the hotel has the benefit of being secluded, yet within easy reach of the action. However, you will probably never want to leave since here you are surrounded by everything your heart could desire: endless beach, delightful fresh-water swimming pools, tropical gardens, and wonderful restaurants. The hotel is a five-story building snuggled on a gentle hill overlooking the ocean. All of the bedrooms have a view of the sea and some suites even have their own private plunge pool. Ultimate luxury prevails with marble floors, bathrobes, and private balconies or terraces. The decor is outstanding, with creamy pastel colors blending in a quietly elegant fashion with the handsome carved furniture. Below the hotel, swimming pools face onto a lush lawn that stretches to the beach. You can lounge outside all day since food and drinks are just steps away at the palapa-style beach club. For further pampering, spa facilities are available. *Directions:* About a five-minute drive from the airport heading toward the center of Acapulco on the Carretera Escénica.

❄ ⚓ ⚔ CREDIT ☎ 🏋 Y P ⑪ ≋ 🖼 ♿

QUINTA REAL ACAPULCO
Manager: Javier Esquivel Lizarraga
Paseo de la Quinta, 6, Fracc. Real Diamante
Acapulco, Guerrero 39907, Mexico
Tel: (744) 469-1500, (800) 457-4000 USA
Fax: (744) 469-1516
*74 rooms, Double: $341–$1000**
**Tax: 17%*
Open: all year, Credit cards: all major
Region: Beach–Pacific Coast
www.karenbrown.com/mex/quintarealacapulco.html

In the '60s Acapulco was the resort of royalty and Hollywood stars and for many celebrities Villa Vera was the favorite place to stay. Elizabeth Taylor, Elvis Presley, Frank Sinatra, Lana Turner, Rita Hayworth, and Julio Iglesias all chose Villa Vera as their hideaway. It is said to have had the very first swim-up pool bar, and that makes sense—if it was to happen anywhere, Acapulco was certainly the place. Villa Vera continues to be the choice of many who are looking for a great getaway in one of Mexico's most exciting cities, especially for nightlife. Villa Vera is an oasis within the city, sitting high on a hillside overlooking the boulevard and the bay. There are both suites and individual houses available on the property, and although the hotel is not on the beach, that is not a problem as it has 17 swimming pools! The main terrace features a multi-level swimming pool with a waterfall flowing into the main pool, which overlooks Acapulco. Top-notch facilities include a racquet club and a fully equipped spa and gym, which is one of the finest in town. Throughout the resort are lush gardens with wonderful trails and walkways to enjoy at any time of day. *Directions:* In Club Deportivo residential area, five minutes from beach.

VILLA VERA HOTEL
Manager: José Eduardo Gómez
Lomas del Mar 35
Acapulco, Guerrero 39690, Mexico
Tel: (744) 484-0333, Fax: (744) 484-7479
69 rooms, Double: $165–$1200*
*Tax: 17%
Open: all year, Credit cards: all major
Region: Beach–Pacific Coast
www.karenbrown.com/mex/villavera.html

The Hacienda de los Santos is an absolute dream. If you are anywhere near the Colonial village of Alamos (a wonderful old mining town that in its heyday produced more silver than any other location in Mexico), the hotel is a must. Even if you don't have plans to be in the area, make a special trip. Not that there is much to do here: the Hacienda is a place to enjoy utter relaxation, to dine superbly, to enjoy the facilities of a lovely spa, and, best of all, to be pampered by an attentive staff. This beautiful inn is the creation of Nancy and Jim Swickard, who fell in love with Alamos, bought a 17th-century mansion there, and converted it to a jewel of a private home for themselves. It has now evolved into an outstanding inn with 25 guestrooms, splendid gardens, four swimming pools, a fabulous restaurant with four intimate dining rooms, a darling bar serving 394 kinds of tequila, an exercise room, a spa, and even a hangar for your private plane. High walls surround the entire property and guestrooms face various romantic patios. All the rooms exude the same superb taste—even the standard rooms are beautiful and have their own fireplaces. If you want to splurge, request my favorite room, Santo Domingo, which is so stunning it seems like a movie set. At the Hacienda de los Santos you enjoy the facilities of an ultra-deluxe hotel while feeling like a guest of the family—a rare combination. *Directions:* Ask for specific directions.

HACIENDA DE LOS SANTOS
Owners: Nancy & Jim Swickard
Calle Molina 8
Alamos, Sonora 85763, Mexico
Tel: (647) 428-0222, Fax: (647) 428-0367
25 rooms, Double: $165–$750*
*Tax: 15%
Open: all year, Credit cards: all major
Region: Central–Colonial town
www.karenbrown.com/mex/hacindadelossantos.html

Rancho Encantado nestles right on the edge of Laguna Bacalar, a beautiful, crystal-clear lake almost at the Belize border. This is not your standard hotel, but rather a complex of cottages tucked in amongst the trees and a large, inviting, open-air restaurant with dining tables covered with brightly colored linens, reflecting a typical Mexican motif. Breakfast and a three-course set dinner are included in the room rate. In front of the restaurant, a pier stretches out into the turquoise lake, with kayaks and canoes nearby that guests can rent. The guestrooms are in individual casitas, some in the garden and others facing the lake. In the rates shown below, we have priced only the five newer rooms facing the lake (9 through 12 and the Laguna Suite) since these are far superior to the others and well worth the relatively small difference in price. Each has a private porch in front with hammocks. Inside, you find a very spacious room, really a suite, with a separate sitting area and bedroom divided off by shelving. The décor is very pleasing, with red-tiled floor, hand-loomed bedspreads, a beautiful palapa ceiling, rattan furniture, brightly colored curtains, murals of Mayan design, and fresh flowers artfully arranged. Best of all, these lakefront units have large, louvered windows on four sides, allowing the breezes to flow through the room (there is also an overhead fan). *Directions:* On the road between Cancún and Chetumal, 2 km north of Bacalar.

RANCHO ENCANTADO
Owners: Susanna Star & Raymond Childers
Km 3, Hwy 307
Bacalar, Quintana Roo 77930, Mexico
Tel: (983) 831-0037, (505) 758-9790 USA
Fax: none
13 rooms, Double: $180–$245*
*Includes breakfast & dinner, Tax: 10%
Open: all year, Credit cards: all major
Region: Yucatán Peninsula–Laguna Bacalar
www.karenbrown.com/mex/ranchoencantado.html

Dating back to the 1960s, the Hotel Cabo San Lucas was one of the earliest resorts in the Cabo area. The hotel hasn't changed much over the years—it's a bit dated and even refreshingly old-fashioned, and makes no effort to mimic its flashy neighbor hotels along the coast, but it is much less expensive. In truth, here you will find many attributes found nowhere else: its wooded, spacious, 2,000-acre grounds can't be duplicated, the views are spectacular, and its beach is one of the safest in the area. The swimming beach is down the way a bit—you can either walk there or use the hotel shuttle. The pleasantly decorated guestrooms are located in various two-story, beige-colored buildings accented by stone pillars and red-tiled roofs. All of the guestrooms have a balcony or terrace with a view of the sea. The heart of the complex and its most outstanding feature is its dramatic restaurant, perched high on a cliff that drops sharply to the sea where mighty waves crash against huge boulders. Guests dine in the open air on a wide terrace with a 180-degree view that is nothing less than spectacular. For a romantic evening, there is no better place to dine. In chilly weather, guests eat inside in front of a roaring fire. Near the dining room there is a swimming pool on a stone terrace stretching to the edge of the cliff. *Directions:* Located at Km .5 on the San José del Cabo to Cabo San Lucas highway.

HOTEL CABO SAN LUCAS
Manager: Luis Vazquez
Km .5, Carretera Transpeninsular Hwy
Cabo San Lucas, Baja California Sur 23400, Mexico
Tel: (624) 144-0014, Fax: (624) 144-0015
67 rooms, Double: $245–$355*
*Tax: 17%
Open: all year, Credit cards: all major
Region: Beach–Baja California
www.karenbrown.com/mex/hotelcabosanlucas.html

The Casa del Mar (located in a gated community surrounded by luxurious condominiums) is one of the deluxe hotels that dot the coast between Cabo San Lucas and San José del Cabo and, although it rivals the others in beauty, the cost of the rooms is substantially less. Looking like a lovely hacienda, the pastel-ochre-colored building is accented by Moorish arched windows, wrought-iron lamps, a stone-framed doorway, and a circular fountain in front accented by colorful tile. This old-world effect is reinforced by the splendid Spanish-style interior garden courtyard, complete with a stunning stone fountain in the center, which is surrounded by an upper gallery supported by pillars. At the far end of the courtyard, a series of open arches artistically frames a gorgeous picture of tropical gardens, splendid swimming pool, swaying palms, and the deep-blue sea. The swimming pool is like a lake, dropping by a gentle waterfall from one level to the next. A path leads to a wide stretch of beach where there is a second swimming pool and beach club. The guestrooms exude great quality and are very attractively appointed with wrought-iron headboards, wicker furniture, colorful ceramic lamps, and exceptionally large bathrooms. Some of the rooms are located in two adjacent buildings, but my favorites are those in the main house, looking over the gardens to the sea. *Directions:* Located at Km 19.5. Watch the kilometer signs along the highway.

CASA DEL MAR
Manager: Mónica Díaz Serralde
Director: Claudia Vargas
Km 19.5, Carretera Transpeninsular Hwy
Cabo San Lucas, Baja California Sur 23400, Mexico
Tel: (624) 144-0030, Fax: (624) 144-0034
56 rooms, Double: $360–$410*
*Service: 10%, Tax: 12%
Open: all year, Credit cards: all major
Region: Beach–Baja California
www.karenbrown.com/mex/casadelmar.html

When Las Ventanas al Paraiso opened it doors to guests in the late 1990s, it joined the elite group of opulent hotels stretching across the tip of the Baja Peninsula. This deluxe inn is housed in a simple beige, flat-roofed building, which blends tastefully with the desert landscape, the starkness of which is relieved by majestic towering palm trees and a garden of cactus. A palapa-style thatched roof protects the lobby, which otherwise is open to the fresh sea breezes. The grounds are fabulous and highlighted by a stunning, lakelike swimming pool dropping gently from one terrace to the next in a series of waterfalls. At the bottom level there is an open-air grill by the swimming pool for casual dining. For dining in style, there is an elegant, formal dining room nearby. From the swimming pools and restaurants there is a splendid view of the deep-blue sea as the waves roll in to the creamy-sand beach. The richly appointed, lavishly decorated guestrooms, with their softly curved adobe walls, are a sensual delight. The suites overlooking the sea are spectacular, with marble bathrooms, the finest linens, sumptuous furniture, handsome fabrics, a fireplace tucked in the corner, a telescope for watching the whales go by, a little plunge pool, and a balcony that is so spacious and tastefully appointed that it seems like an outdoor living room. *Directions:* Located on the parkway between San José del Cabo and Cabo San Lucas, at Km 19.5.

LAS VENTANAS AL PARAISO
Manager: Edward Steiner
Km 19.5, Carretera Transpeninsular Hwy
Cabo San Lucas, Baja California Sur 23400, Mexico
Tel: (624) 144-0300, Fax: (624) 144-0301
*61 rooms, Double: $575–$1000**
**Service: 15%, Tax: 12%*
Open: all year, Credit cards: all major
Region: Beach–Baja California
www.karenbrown.com/mex/lasventanas.html

The deluxe Hotel Twin Dolphin is far from a traditional, old-world hotel of the kind we usually feature in our guides. Instead, it is almost like a sculpture, making a bold modern architectural statement in the barren desert landscape. However, this appealing hotel more than meets many of our criteria: it is small, intimate, and friendly, with beautiful views and lovely rooms, and, best of all, it is family-owned and family-managed. David Halliburton, grandson of Richard Halliburton, the writer who traveled to exotic faraway places, is the owner/manager. The hotel entrance, a two-story open pavilion supported by massive stone pillars, leads to a pool accented by a whimsical bronze sculpture of a pair of frolicking dolphins. Just beyond, a spacious terrace, which stretches to the edge of the cliffs, is dominated by a rectangular swimming pool with a bar at one end. In contrast to the desert ambiance, the handsome lounge with its dark tiled floors, wall of stone, heavy wooden furniture, massive fireplace, and paneled walls looks a bit like a mountain lodge. The guestrooms, located in individual clusters of buildings, are all very tastefully decorated and have large balconies or terraces looking out over a barren boulder-strewn coastline to the brilliant blue sea. There are purposely no TVs, no phones, no radios, no clocks to disturb the serenity of the peaceful natural setting. *Directions:* On the parkway between San José del Cabo and Cabo San Lucas, at Km 12.

❄ ⚓ 💳 🏋 🎣 P 🍴 🏊 🚶

HOTEL TWIN DOLPHIN
Owner: David Halliburton, Jr.
Km 12, Carretera Transpeninsular Hwy
Cabo San Lucas, Baja California Sur 23410, Mexico
Tel: (624) 145-8190, (800) 421-8925 USA
Fax: (624) 145-8196
50 rooms, Double: $350–$545*
*Service: 18%, Tax: 12%
Open: all year, Credit cards: all major
Region: Beach–Baja California
www.karenbrown.com/mex/twindolphin.html

The Hacienda Uayamón offers outstanding charm and ultimate luxury. This sumptuous hacienda has a wide, sweeping staircase leading up to a romantic veranda framed by high, open arches. Doors lead into several intimate parlors decorated with antiques, beyond which you find an enchanting dining room with large windows looking out to trees and a decorative round pond. Pathways lead from the main house through the jungle-like estate to the suites tucked about the property in brightly hued cottages. These at first appear to be basic, but looks deceive; inside, you find tasteful, appropriately simple furnishings of the finest quality. Excellent decor and quality can be found in many hotels but it is all the extra loving details that raise this hacienda to a whole new level of splendor—particularly the flowers, which decorate everything, from the bathroom toiletries, which are lavished with miniature flower designs, to the bathrobes, towels, and sheets. The bed linens appear to have delicate floral embroidery, but in fact these are fresh flowers. Other luxurious touches include an enormous, outdoor, king-sized sofa and a romantic plunge pool sprinkled with fragrant petals. There is also a gorgeous swimming pool tucked into the crumbling ruins of the old machine house. The best surprise of all comes with nightfall when all the paths are lined with what seem to be thousands of candles. Pure magic! *Directions:* Ask for detailed driving instructions.

HACIENDA UAYAMON
Innkeeper: Claudia Raymondi
Km 20, Carretera Campeche
Campeche-Uayamón, Campeche 24530, Mexico
Tel: (981) 819-0335, (888) 625-5144 USA
Fax: (999) 923-7963
12 rooms, Double: $318–$454*
*Service: 5%, Tax: 17%
Open: all year, Credit cards: all major
Region: Yucatán Peninsula–Archaeological area
www.karenbrown.com/mex/haciendauayamon.html

In Cancún, where almost all the hotels are enormous (some offering over 1000 guestrooms), the intimate, 33-room Casa Turquesa is one of the few small luxury hotels in Cancún. The white, Mediterranean-style, three-story building is decorated formally, with Mayan accents. The lobby has French-style chairs with paisley upholstery, yet the native accent is strongly evident. Colorful, large murals and stone Mayan temple carvings (reminiscent of those seen at nearby archaeological sites) enhance the walls in the sunlight-filled lounge. The bedrooms are appointed with every modern amenity and they all have a terrace or balcony with a view of the sea. All have king or queen beds, vanity mirrors, mini-bars, 90 cable-TV channels, and private, outdoor Jacuzzi tubs. The marble bathrooms are exceptionally outstanding: enormous, and beautifully outfitted. Although small, Casa Turquesa has the luxury of three restaurants: the Belle Vue offers international cuisine, El Gazebo serves breakfast overlooking the sea, and the Celebrity (temporarily closed for renovation) specializes in beef and fresh fish. The hotel's highlight is a large pool, which extends to a bluff overlooking the turquoise-blue waters of the Caribbean. Steps lead down to a beckoning, pristine white stretch of sand, one of the few semi-private beaches in Cancún. The staff of the Casa Turquesa is friendly and very professional. *Directions:* Located on Blvd. Kukulkan at 13.5 kilometer marker.

❄ ☎ ⚒ 💳 ☎ ▼ P ⍥ ≋ 👤

CASA TURQUESA
Owner: Gaston Alegre López
Manager: Ana Isabel Medina
Km 13.5, Boulevard Kukulkan
Cancún, Quintana Roo 77500, Mexico
Tel: (998) 885-2924, Fax: (998) 885-8300
33 rooms, Double: $350–$400*
*Tax: 17%
Open: all year, Credit cards: all major
Region: Beach–Caribbean Coast
www.karenbrown.com/mex/casaturquesa.html

With so many giant hotels in Cancun, it is refreshing to find this small, low-rise property. The 80 guestrooms of the Villas Tacúl are in 25 one-story, white-stucco buildings tucked in amongst the palm trees that dot the parklike, 12-acre grounds. (They don't build them like this any more—land is too expensive.) There is a somewhat dated, old-fashioned appeal to these accommodations, which seem more like a series of various-sized condominiums rather than a hotel. The choicest rooms are the few that face the waterfront where you can step out your door to the crystal-clear, turquoise sea. This is definitely a family-friendly resort: some of the units have up to five bedrooms and for those traveling with children, babysitting is available. There is also a playground for children, picnic tables, tennis courts, volleyball courts, and ping-pong tables. For water-sports enthusiasts fishing boats, Hobie cats, sailboats, kayaks, snorkeling equipment, and windsurfing boards are available for rent. One of the nicest features of the Villas Tacúl is its large, freeform swimming pool, which looks like a lake accented by miniature islands where palm trees wave gently in the breezes. Best of all, the hotel has its own small beach. Although at first appearance the Villas Tacúl seem rather laid-back and informal, the rooms have satellite TVs, direct-dial phones, and air conditioning. *Directions:* Located on Blvd. Kukulkan at 5.5 kilometer marker.

VILLAS TACÚL
Manager: Marissa Setien
Km 5.5, Boulevard Kukulkan
Cancún, Quintana Roo 77500, Mexico
Tel: (998) 883-0000, (800) 842-0193 USA
Fax: (998) 883-0349
80 rooms, Double: $220–$375*
*Tax: 17%
Open: all year, Credit cards: all major
Region: Beach–Caribbean Coast
www.karenbrown.com/mex/villastacul.html

If you really want to discover a hideaway far off the beaten path and surrounded by remarkable natural beauty, then the Eco Paraiso Xixim makes an outstanding choice. The Eco Paraiso Xixim began as a dream to preserve a long stretch of unspoiled coastline and, to make this project financially feasible, an intimate, small hotel was built along 5 kilometers of virgin beach, with 15 rooms in thatched-roof cottages tucked in amongst the sand dunes overlooking the sea. Each cottage mimics the simple style of homes built by the Mayans for over 1,000 years, but inside the similarity ends. All the delightfully spacious bedrooms are nicely decorated and extremely comfortable with two queen-sized beds, a sofa, and a desk, and in front there is a large covered porch. All the cottages have the same configuration and décor and all face the sea, but by far the best views are in 2, 4, 6, or 8. Breakfast and dinner are included in the room rate and served in an attractive dining room with a terrace overlooking the water. Activities here include excursions to visit the spectacular flocks of brilliant pink flamingos who come to feed in the nearby lagoon, kayaking, hiking, observing the sea turtles in season, fishing, and swimming in the ocean or the hotel's pool. *Directions:* When you arrive in Celestún, continue straight and one block beyond the square turn right at the last street before the sea. Continue for 10 km, following signs to the hotel (beware—this gravel road is like a washboard!).

♨ ☕ ⚒ 🏧 🏨 🏃 P ⅋ ≈ ⚡ ⚓

HOTEL ECO PARAISO XIXIM
Manager: Max Voggensperger
Km 10 de la Antigua Carretera a Sisal
Celestún, Yucatán 97000, Mexico
Tel: (988) 916-2100, Fax: (988) 916-2111
15 cottages, Double: $192*
*Includes breakfast & dinner
Open: all year, Credit cards: all major
Region: Yucatán Peninsula–Eco resort
www.karenbrown.com/mex/paraisoxixim.html

The ruins at Chichén Itzá are spectacular-absolutely not to be missed if you are the least bit tantalized by the mysteries of the Mayan world. However, during the tourist season, some of the magic is lost if you are viewing these ruins along with hordes of other tourists, so an excellent plan is to stay at either the Hotel Mayaland or the Hacienda Chichén, both right on the grounds of the site, so that you can stroll through the jungle in the early morning to savor the romantic beauty of the remains of this ancient Mayan city in relative solitude. The Hacienda Chichén is an excellent choice for accommodations, especially if you want to feel part of the history of the exploration of these ruins, because it was in this very hacienda that the archaeologists stayed when doing their original research. This nostalgic, very authentic, old hacienda and the charming gardens remain much as they must have been in their prime. You can sip a gin and tonic or have a cup of tea on the veranda after a day of exploration and just feel the excitement the explorers must have felt so long ago. The guestrooms, tucked about the property in houses built of concrete blocks, are really nice-not fancy at all, just very comfortable and tastefully decorated. My favorite was the cottage named for Dr Thomason, who was in charge of the original dig. *Directions:* Located within walking distance of the ruins. Follow signs from main road.

HACIENDA CHICHEN
Owner: Doña Carmen Barbachano
Km 120, Carretera Merida Puerto Juárez
Chichén Itzá, Yucatán 97000, Mexico
Tel: (999) 924-2150, (800) 624-8451 USA
Fax: (999) 924-5011
28 rooms, Double: $100–$120*
*Breakfast not included, Tax: 17%
Open: all year, Credit cards: MC, VS
Region: Yucatán Peninsula–Archaeological area
www.karenbrown.com/mex/haciendachichen.html

The Hotel Mayaland, with over 100 acres of parklike grounds, has an unsurpassable setting, right on the grounds of Chichén Itzá, one of Mexico's premier archaeological sites. The ruins are so close that some of the ancient temples can be seen rising above the jungle. The Mayaland is a large hotel and, because of its strategic location, attracts many sightseeing buses that bring hundreds of guests for lunch. However, it is amazing that this activity really doesn't distract from the aura of the hotel. Excellent management efficiently handles the day visitors while protecting the privacy of overnight guests. You will really feel pampered and away from the crowds if you splurge and request a room in one of the clusters of bungalows (named after famous archaeologists) that nestle in the lovely gardens. Once you are in your room, the Mayaland has the intimate feeling of a much smaller hotel. The guestrooms are very attractively decorated and there are various swimming pools on the grounds, conveniently located so that you don't have far to walk to enjoy a refreshing dip. The joy of staying at the Mayaland is that you can stroll over to the ruins before the hordes of tourists arrive in the morning, and again in the evening to watch the Sound and Light show. Many dignitaries and heads of state have stayed at the Hotel Mayaland, including Pavarotti, for whom one of the cottages is named. *Directions:* Located short walk from entrance to ruins.

❄ ☎ 🖃 ☎ 🐎 ￥ P ¶ ≋ 🖼 🔔

HOTEL MAYALAND
Manager: Fernando Barbachano Losa
Chichén Itzá, Yucatán 97000, Mexico
Tel: (998) 887-2450, (800) 235-4079 USA
Fax: (998) 884-4510
103 rooms, Double: $138–$194*
*Tax: 17%
Open: all year, Credit cards: all major
Region: Yucatán Peninsula–Archaeological area
www.karenbrown.com/mex/hotelmayaland.html

Club Med has a group of small hotels ("Villas Arqueologicas"), located close to most of the major archaeological sites in Mexico, that cater to the more adventurous travelers who want to explore Mexico's archaeological riches. Many of these sites had no hotel within the immediate vicinity, so Club Med was asked to cooperate with the Mexican government in providing good, convenient accommodations. Villas Arqueologicas are always well priced and offer clean, simple, nice guestrooms, but the one within walking distance of the rich Mayan site of Cobá stands out as a very appealing place to stay in its own right. This one-story, bright-yellow, stucco hotel with white trim is as pretty as can be. You enter into an interior courtyard, around which are shops, a library, office, and reception. Beyond is a second courtyard, enhanced by a tropical garden and swimming pool, with an open-air restaurant on one side of the quadrangle and guestrooms on the other three. The bedrooms are quite small, but tidy and nicely decorated. There are plenty of public areas in which to relax, so the size of the bedrooms should not be a problem except for long stays. A sign in front of the hotel says "no swimming" in the lake, and a sign in the village saying "beware of crocodiles" explains why swimming is discouraged! *Directions:* From Mérida, take the toll road to Cancún. Leave the highway near Valladid and continue on to Cobá.

VILLAS ARQUEOLOGICAS COBA
Manager: Jerome Lemmier
Cobá, Quintana Roo 97780, Mexico
Tel: (55) 254-7077, Fax: (55) 255-3164
42 rooms, Double: $68*
*Tax: 17%
Open: all year, Credit cards: all major
Region: Yucatán Peninsula–Archaeological area
www.karenbrown.com/mex/villascoba.html

For those who relish discovering super-deluxe hideaways far off the beaten path, the Mahakua-Hacienda de San Antonio is the perfect choice. This splendid property, originally a tobacco plantation, is really isolated, nestled beneath the shadow of a majestic volcano about a 20-minute drive into the hills from Colima. Guestrooms open off a garden courtyard, the first floor being surrounded by a colonnaded walkway and an upper gallery repeating the arched colonnades. You really don't need to choose a suite to achieve luxury, since all the antique-filled rooms are spacious and decorated with great taste. The decor has a richly masculine feel, with strong colors, tapestries, hand-woven carpets, and hand-loomed draperies. All the suites have fireplaces, terraces or patios, and beautiful bathrooms. The public rooms are vast and as you pass from room to room it seems as though you are stepping back in time and are a guest in a private home. You walk through a terraced, formal garden with reflecting pools and fountains to a gorgeous, incredibly large swimming pool. The Mahakua-Hacienda makes a wonderful retreat if you want to be alone and away from the world for a while but if you want activity, horseback riding, bird watching, nature walks, and bicycling on the 4,000-hectare property are all options. *Directions:* The room rate includes a transfer from the Manzanillo or Colima airports. If driving, ask for directions.

❄ ☎ ☕ 💳 ☎ 🐎 P ¶ ≈ 🏃

MAHAKUA-HACIENDA DE SAN ANTONIO
Manager: Angelica Paredez
Municipio de Comala
Colima–San Antonio, Colima 28450, Mexico
Tel: (312)) 313-4411, (888) 802-9127 USA
Fax: (312) 314-3727
26 suites, Double: $900–$1600*
*Includes all meals, Service: 10%, Tax: 17%
Closed: Jan, Credit cards: all major
Region: Inland–Pacific Coast
www.karenbrown.com/mex/haciendasanantonio.html

Don't take the Copper Canyon train without including a night at the Hotel Mirador. To capture the stunning canyon in all its glory, there is no place that can compare for views with the Hotel Mirador. The hotel is built into the walls of the canyon and seems to be glued against the rocks, which drop straight to the canyon floor. The tangerine-colored, adobe-plastered building blends the feel of an old Spanish mission and an Indian lodge. A stone staircase leads up to the entry and in a niche in the stepped-up roof hangs an old mission bell. Inside, the décor exudes a rustic, lodge-like ambiance with terra-cotta floors accented by Indian rugs, rough-hewn beams, richly painted thick stucco walls, large paintings of Indians, giant stone fireplaces, chairs accented by bright cushions, Indian pottery, and handmade baskets. However, the artful décor can't compete with the view from the windows, which provide an incredible panorama of the canyon from the dining room, lounge, and cozy bar. A deck extends out over the edge of the canyon, again with stunning views. All the guestrooms are attractively decorated, again reflecting the same Indian influence, and, best of all, they have balconies capturing the same breathtaking view. Walk out on your balcony at night—the stars look so close that it seems you can reach right up and pull one down. *Directions:* You will be picked up at the train station by the hotel bus.

POSADA MIRADOR
Owners: Vilma & Roberto Balderrama
Barrancas
Copper Canyon–Barrancas, Chihauhua 81200, Mexico
Tel: (668) 818-7046, (800) 896-8196 USA
Fax: (668) 812-0046
51 rooms, Double: $247*
*Includes all meals, Tax: 17%
Open: all year, Credit cards: all major
Region: Copper Canyon
www.karenbrown.com/mex/hotelmirador.html

Hotel Misión adds a whole new dimension to your stay in the Copper Canyon. From the train station at Bahuichivo, about four hours west of El Fuerte, you take a bumpy 14-kilometer ride down into the canyon to the small village of Cerocahui, nestled in a fertile valley. The hotel, set against a backdrop of the Sierra Madre mountains, is surrounded by apple orchards, gardens, and even a vineyard, which produces table wines for the restaurant. The gracious Balderrama family, who were the first to see the potential for tourism in the Copper Canyon, owns the hotel and they can arrange train tickets and bus trips for you, making everything very easy. Across the street from the hotel (and giving it its name) is a beautiful Jesuit mission, founded in 1694 by Salvatierra (the first white man to reach the floor of the canyon). This is not a luxurious hotel, nor was it ever meant to be; it exudes a cozy, rustic, inviting, lodge-like ambiance, appropriate for its setting. The guestrooms are cozy with beamed ceilings, carved wood furniture, terra-cotta floors, large chandeliers, and brightly colored hand-woven fabrics. While you stay here you can take guided horseback rides, trek to the lovely Huicochi waterfall (five hours round trip), explore the many nearby trails, or take a tour to the old mining town of Urique where there is a lookout with sweeping canyon views. *Directions:* Hotel transfer from Bahuichivo, a train stop along the Copper Canyon.

HOTEL MISIÓN
Owners: Vilma & Roberto Balderrama
Copper Canyon–Cerocahui, Chihuahua 81200, Mexico
Tel: (668) 818-7046, (800) 896-8196 USA
Fax: (668) 812-0046
42 rooms, Double: $248*
*Includes all meals, Tax: 17%
Open: all year, Credit cards: all major
Region: Copper Canyon
www.karenbrown.com/mex/hotelmision.html

The Sierra Lodge, nestled against the side of a small pine-scented valley in the Copper Canyon, is about as far off the beaten path as you can get. Here you'll find no electricity, no telephones, no TVs, no radios. The closest town is Creel, 20 minutes' drive away. The Lodge is built like a long, low, old-fashioned log cabin with a corrugated tin roof. All of the guestrooms open onto a long tiled front porch, with rustic wooden chairs outside each door so guests can sit and look out at the Cusarare River, which twists and winds its way through the valley below. Although rustic in nature, the spacious guestrooms are all surprisingly attractive with rich-red-tiled floors, white walls, Indian carpets, attractive homespun cotton bedspreads and matching drapes, beamed ceilings, Indian prints on the walls, nice bathrooms with hot water, and even bathrobes! The gentle glow of the gas lamps lends romance. Each room has a wood-burning stove to keep you warm. All meals are included in the incredibly low price and the simple, hearty food is perfect after a day of hiking. Guests dine together in a large but delightfully cozy room with a giant stone fireplace, a wonderful Indian mural, antique prints on the walls, and varnished tables. *Directions:* Take the Copper Canyon train to Creel and then a taxi to the hotel (about $25 each way).

☕ 👫 P 🍴

COPPER CANYON SIERRA LODGE
Owner: Hoteles Sierra Madre
Manager: José Luis Hernández Vega
Copper Canyon–Creel, Chihuahua 31000, Mexico
Tel: (800) 776-3942 USA, Fax: (635) 456-0036
18 rooms, Double: $100*
*Includes all meals
Open: all year
Region: Copper Canyon
www.karenbrown.com/mex/sierralodge.html

If you want to take the train going east to visit the Copper Canyon, you can board at either Los Mochis or El Fuerte. Our preference is to begin the journey in El Fuerte since you don't have to get up as early to board the train and, more importantly, it is a much quainter town in which to spend the night. One of the best choices for accommodation is the Posada del Hidalgo. This isn't a super-deluxe hotel or one that is decorator-perfect, but certainly does offer old-world quality. Built in the Colonial style, it has inner courtyards, fountains, wrought-iron gates, beamed ceilings, tropical gardens, tiled floors, shuttered windows, and some antique furnishings. There is even a small swimming pool on one of the upper terraces. My favorite feature is the quaint restaurant, which is as cute as can be with colorfully painted wood chairs, dark walls, a huge antique mirror, and a cascade of brilliantly hued paper flowers and piñatas hanging from the beamed ceiling. The guestrooms are built around various courtyards. If you make your reservations in advance, the room cost is a bit more than if you just pop in, but it is really comforting to have your accommodations secured, especially since the train leaves early in the morning. *Directions:* Located on the northeast corner of the square. The address says Calle Hidalgo but the entrance is around the corner on 5 de Mayo.

POSADA DEL HIDALGO
Owners: Vilma & Roberto Balderrama
Hidalgo 101
Copper Canyon–El Fuerte, Sinaloa 81820, Mexico
Tel: (668) 818-7046, (800) 896-8196 USA
Fax: (668) 812-0046
52 rooms, Double: $120*
*Tax: 17%
Open: all year, Credit cards: all major
Region: Copper Canyon
www.karenbrown.com/mex/posadahidalgo.html

Located a few hours south of Puerto Vallarta on the Bay of Careyes, The Careyes is one of the newest additions to the Starwood Luxury Collection in Mexico. This is one of the most beautiful bays along the Mexican Pacific coastline and is home to just two hotels with their own private beaches and spectacular hillside villas. The Careyes' guestrooms are situated around an incredible meandering pool which snakes its way through lush tropical gardens. Beyond is the bay, fantastic for swimming, sailing, kayaking, diving, or fishing. Although all the rooms have bay views, they vary in size, location, and price. Some have a private pool or Jacuzzi, others are located right in front of the beach, but all are decorated and detailed to perfection, with all the accessories you'd expect from a quality boutique hotel. For land-based fun you'll find tennis, a gymnasium and full spa, plus walking and horseback trails. However, my favorite activity was lounging and reading on the huge cushions that are placed right between the beach and the bar; my every need was met! The beachfront restaurant is the only option for dining, except for a restaurant the next beach over at Playa Rosa, but you won't be disappointed—there is a wide variety of choices and the cuisine is excellent. *Directions:* Take the coast highway south from Puerto Vallarta for about 2½ hours. You'll come to clearly marked signs and the entrance will be on your right-hand side.

THE CAREYES
Manager: Rui Reis
Km 53.5, Carretera Barra de Navidad-Puerto Vallarta
Costa Alegre–Careyes, Jalisco 48970, Mexico
Tel: (315) 351-0000, (888) 625-5144 USA
Fax: (315) 351-0100
51 rooms, Double: $296–$720*
*Breakfast not included, Service: 5%, Tax: 17%
Open: all year, Credit cards: all major
Region: Beach–Pacific Coast
www.karenbrown.com/mex/thecareyes.html

From the moment I saw it from afar, I immediately fell in love with the Casitas de las Flores. This cluster of adorable, brightly painted casitas tucked on a wooded hillside overlooking a beautiful small bay doesn't look like a hotel at all, but more like a charming, tiny, picturesque village. There are from one- to three-bedroom units available, the larger ones all having their own small plunge pool on the terrace. Although this is technically not a hotel, you enjoy all the services that you would find at a fine boutique hotel. A steep path from this "village" leads down to a sublimely beautiful, palm-tree-studded beach. In addition to the ten colorful cottages there are also seven sumptuous villas (some with as many as eight bedrooms). Each of these stupendous homes has its own swimming pool, along with many other amenities, as well as chefs and servants to make your stay extraordinary. Villa guests have access to the facilities of The Careyes Hotel, which include a full spa, gymnasium, tennis courts, and restaurant. There's also a wonderful restaurant on Playa Rosa, the villas' gathering place and private beach. Polo is played during certain times of the year, with teams from around the world taking part. Other activities include fishing, diving, and kayaking in the bay. Casitas de las Flores provides a vacation that you will not soon forget! *Directions:* The entrance is off the coastal highway at Km 53.5.

CASITAS DE FLORES
Manager: Andres Yanomé
Km 53.5, Carretera Barra de Navidad-Puerto Vallarta
Costa Alegre–Careyes, Jalisco 48989, Mexico
Tel: (315) 351-0240, Fax: (315) 351-0246
35 rooms, Double: $180–$4500*
*Service: 5%, Tax: 17%
Open: all year, Credit cards: all major
Region: Beach–Puerto Vallarta
www.karenbrown.com/mex/casitasdeflores.html

Do you dream of a romantic, secluded hideaway with crystal-clear water and a sun-drenched beach fringed by palm trees? A romantic paradise where you might well be the only person on the beach, soothed by the gentle lapping of the surf, the song of birds, and the rustle of the breeze through palm fronds? Dream no more—The Tamarindo, just such a tropical paradise, awaits! This is a secret place, which relishes its exclusivity, a hideaway of understated luxury catering to a clientele of travelers for whom discretion is imperative. From the main highway an 11-kilometer, narrow, cobbled lane meanders through dense jungle through which you catch glimpses of a brilliant-green, 18-hole golf course. The road ends at the house where you check in. The guestrooms (which are within easy walking distance of the dining room and beach) are in individual bungalows scattered amongst the jungle, their wooden exteriors and thatched roofs blending in perfectly with their setting. However, this rustic appearance is only skin-deep: inside, each of the cottages provides the ultimate in luxury and is beautifully decorated in a casually elegant style. To top it off, each has its own tiny pool plus a lazy hammock for dreaming. It seems unbelievable that such a luxurious resort with 10 kilometers of private coast could be tucked in the middle of a remote tropical jungle. *Directions:* About 45 minutes north of Manzanillo airport on the coast highway at Km 7.5 marker.

❄ ⌁ 💳 🔒 🕴 Ⓨ P ⊪ ≋

THE TAMARINDO
Manager: Rui Reis
Km 7.5 Carretera Melaque-Puerto Vallarta
Costa Alegre–Cihuatlán, Jalisco 48970, Mexico
Tel: (315) 351-5032, (888) 625-5144 USA
Fax: (315) 351-5070
29 bungalows, $373–$654*
*Service: 10%, Tax: 17%
Open: all year, Credit cards: all major
Region: Beach–Pacific Coast
www.karenbrown.com/mex/thetamarindo.html

Meson Doña Paz, a very special hideaway, was the residence of the developer of the community of Isla Navidad, which features the beautiful Grand Bay Hotel. In this gated, deluxe complex is a superb 27-hole golf course, a marina, a number of homes, and condominiums. Meson Doña Paz is secreted down a small road that passes by the Grand Bay Hotel and continues on to its own secluded cove, complete with its own beach, swimming pool, and dock. The structure is so impressive that it is hard to believe this was once a private home. You enter into a spectacular three-story house with reception area, lounge, meeting rooms, and restaurant, all fabulously decorated. This is flanked by two adjoining buildings with seven suites in each. The gracious staff strives to make you feel at home, except here you have your own chef and waiters to take care of you. Although there is a menu, the chef is happy to cook whatever you desire and usually the daily menu consists of his suggestions or perhaps suggestions you made the day before. You also have your choice of locations for dining, be it on the beach, on the jetty, near the pool, or on the terrace. Tennis courts are on site with golf, fishing, and boating available nearby. You have all the benefits of a large property, but the charm and service of an intimnate small hotel. *Directions:* From the airport turn left onto the highway. Go north to the 53.5 kilometer marker and follow signs the Grand Bay Hotel.

MESON DOÑA PAZ
Manager: Jorge Garibay
Rinconada del Capitan s/n
Costa Alegre–Isla Navidad, Colima 28830, Mexico
Tel & fax: (315) 355-6441
14 rooms, Double: $170–$500*
*Tax: 17%
Open: all year, Credit cards: all major
Region: Beach–Pacific Coast
www.karenbrown.com/mex/mesondonapaz.html

One might expect that a laid-back hotel in the middle of nowhere with tricky access, no electricity, no phones, no mini-bars, no hairdryers, no TVs, simple bathrooms, and a fickle water supply would be very reasonably priced. Not so with the Hotelito Desconocido: its rates rival those of deluxe hotels. However, for those looking for a natural paradise, this unusual hotel, elegant in its simplicity, lures guests back year after year for utter relaxation and pampering by the gentle, caring staff. This unique hotel is the dream of Marcello Murzill, a well-known Italian fashion designer, who fell in love with this remote bit of coast and bought 100 acres bordering a nature preserve with miles of remote beach. The complex mimics a simple fishing village of rustic thatched cottages. Delicious meals are served in a thatched, Tahitian-looking, open-air restaurant perched over the water. At night, when the restaurant is illuminated by candlelight, the ambiance is sheer magic. The nicely decorated guestrooms tucked around the property have colorful furnishings and fine linens. Boats are available for guests who want to row across the small estuary to the beach, which is great for walking, turtle viewing, and bird watching, but not recommended for swimming. The hotel is open all year, but our choice would be to avoid the hot, rainy summer season. *Directions:* About 100 km south of Puerto Vallarta. Four wheel-drive is needed. An airport transfer is recommended.

HOTELITO DESCONOCIDO
Owner: Marcello Murzillo
Tomatlán
Costa Alegre–La Cruz de Loreto, Jalisco 48360, Mexico
Tel: (322) 222-2526, (800) 851-1143 USA
Fax: (322) 223-0293
29 rooms, Double: $430–$690*
*Includes meals & activities, Service: 15%, Tax: 17%
Open: all year, Credit cards: all major
Region: Beach–Pacific Coast
www.karenbrown.com/mex/hotelitodesconocido.html

Las Hadas hotel in Manzanillo, the dream of billionaire tycoon Antenor Patiño, is known throughout the world, but only a lucky few know that Patiño's granddaughter, Isabel Goldsmith, created her own jewel, Las Alamandas, just up the coast. Her hotel offers the ultimate in accommodations, yet exudes a natural, understated elegance. There are no signs along the road to identify Las Alamandas: absolutely no hints that a paradise exists at the end of the narrow road through the jungle. This is not an oversight. Guests who arrive (many by private plane onto the hotel's own landing strip) cherish their privacy and Las Alamandas has become a favorite hideaway for many celebrities seeking seclusion. A beautiful beach, bound by a lush lawn studded with coconut palms, stretches in front of the hotel. There are only fourteen suites within six villas. No matter whether you have the Presidential Suite or one of the Garden View rooms, you will be pampered by the staff who seem to take great pleasure in catering to your every need. Nothing you want seems to be too much trouble, whether it be a romantic lunch served on a secluded beach or a special request for dinner. The resort is surrounded by 1,500 acres of ecological reserve with pristine beaches, exotic trees, hidden lagoons, and a myriad collection of birds. *Directions:* Located off Hwy 200, midway between Manzanillo and Puerto Vallarta. Ask for detailed instructions since there are no signs.

※ ⚓ ⚒ 🆑 ☎ 🏋 👫 🏇 ▼ P 🍴 ≈ 🏃 🖼 🛁 🐾

LAS ALAMANDAS
Manager: Domingo Castro
Hwy 200, between Puerto Vallarta & Manzanillo
Costa Alegre–Quémaro, Jalisco 48980, Mexico
Tel: (322) 285-5500, Fax: (322) 285-5027
14 rooms, Double: $430–$1320*
*Service: 15%, Tax: 17%
Minimum nights required: 2
Open: all year, Credit cards: all major
Region: Beach–Pacific Coast
www.karenbrown.com/mex/lasalamandas.html

The Playa Azul, right on one of Cozumel's best stretches of beach, is a small, moderately priced, family-run, beautifully managed hotel offering excellent value. At first glance it seems similar to many hotels built in the '50s and '60s, with a swimming pool dominating a courtyard surrounded on three sides by a four-story, pink-stucco complex, forming a U that opens to the ocean. The bedrooms look towards the turquoise-colored sea and all have at least a partial ocean view. However, once you enter your bedroom, the caring touches that make the Playa Azul so very special and distinguish it from others in its class quickly become evident. You cannot help smiling when you find the beds adorned with white towels whimsically shaped into swans and hibiscus blossoms everywhere, creating fanciful designs. The theme of fresh flowers extends into the bathroom and vanity areas, again with towels shaped in artistic designs. All of the guestrooms are air-conditioned, although frequently it is cool enough to just open the sliding glass doors and sleep to the melody of the waves with the soft fresh air flowing into the room. All of the rooms have a spacious balcony or terrace with either a direct or partial view of the sea. The beach beckons with lounge chairs shaded by thatched palapas and you can enjoy drinks in an open-air bar that extends back into the restaurant. *Directions:* Located on the beach, about 3 km north of town.

PLAYA AZUL
Owners: Martha Nieto & Fernando Beristain
Km 4, Carretera San Juan
Cozumel, Quintana Roo 77600, Mexico
Tel: (987) 872-0199, Fax: (987) 872-0110
50 rooms, Double: $175–$200*
*Tax: 12%
Open: all year, Credit cards: all major
Region: Beach–Caribbean Coast
www.karenbrown.com/mex/playaazul.html

If you are looking for deluxe accommodations on the charming island of Cozumel, we suggest the Presidente Inter-Continental. Although not small like most of the other properties we recommend, it stands out from the other large hotels that line the beach, most of which cater to groups looking for all-inclusive holiday packages. A sweeping drive leads up to the main part of the hotel, which opens to gardens and the sea. The reception area and lounges have a modern decor enhanced by many flowers and greenery. Some of the guestrooms are in this five-story section but I prefer the rooms in two wings stretching along a kilometer of beach. Ask for a room on ground level with its own private terrace leading onto the beach for the pleasure of opening your doors and stepping straight outside for a swim. Rocky escarpments divide the beach into smaller, gentle swimming areas of soft white sand, giving a secluded feel. Small piers also stretch out from the rocks for swimming access. The heart of the hotel is its enchanting, open-air, palapa-style, thatched-roof restaurant, which stretches to the edge of the water—an idyllic place to dine. Most guests seem to gravitate to the crystal turquoise sea to swim but for others there is a giant pool tucked next to the beach. Sports enthusiasts enjoy world-class snorkeling, tennis courts, and a nearby Nicklaus-designed 18-hole golf course. *Directions:* Located on the beach, about 5 km south of town.

PRESIDENTE INTER-CONTINENTAL
Manager: Guadallupe Anguiano
Km 6.5, Carretera a. Chankanaab
Cozumel, Quintana Roo 77600, Mexico
Tel: (987) 872-9500, Fax: (987) 872 9501
253 rooms, Double: $355–$455*
*Tax: 17%
Open: all year, Credit cards: all major
Region: Beach–Caribbean Coast
www.karenbrown.com/mex/presidentecozumel.html

For location, the Casa Colonial just can't be surpassed. The pink-stucco building faces onto a small street that is right in between Cuernavaca's prime sites: the Cortes Palace and zócalo are just a few minutes' walk in one direction, while the cathedral is almost next door. Another favorite, the Robert Brady Museum, is practically across the street. Netzahualcoyotl, the street that the hotel is on, is very quiet and also much more attractive than most. The hotel was at one time a private mansion and still reflects the personality and ambiance of a home. You enter through the foyer into a small reception area where you register at an antique desk. Open arched doorways lead into a garden highlighted by a large swimming pool. Beyond is a luxuriant garden with a sweeping expanse of lawn enhanced by mature shade trees and bordered by lush beds of flowers and shrubs. Artistically placed stone sculptures add further to the appeal. The entire mood is one of outdoor living, for which Cuernavaca (nicknamed "The City of Eternal Spring") is famous since its weather is so mild. The garden is definitely the heart of the hotel and all of the rooms open onto it. The living room and cozy breakfast area are both windowless, with just stone columns supporting an overhanging red tile roof. There are seventeen guestrooms: no two are alike but all are tastefully decorated with rustic antiques complemented by Mexican-style fabrics.

☎ 🍽 💳 P ≈

CASA COLONIAL
Manager: Angela Alvarez
Netzahualcoyotl, 37
Cuernavaca, Morelos 62000, Mexico
Tel: (777) 312-7033, Fax: (777) 310-0395
17 rooms, Double: $102–$230
Open: all year, Credit cards: MC, VS
Region: Central–Colonial town
www.karenbrown.com/mex/casacolonial.html

Las Manañitas fills a very special niche in my heart. My mother and father spent many happy winters in this bit of paradise, ensconced in one of the inn's loveliest suites, and I was fortunate to visit them on many occasions. Nothing much has really changed in the nearly 30 years since I first stayed there—it remains one of Mexico's most exquisite hideaways. Not only is this a superb, intimate hotel, but it is also renowned as one of Mexico's finest restaurants; people line up daily at lunchtime to dine. The entrance is most unassuming. The magic doesn't begin until you walk out into the courtyard where you are greeted by an exquisite garden with lush foliage and expansive lawns decorated with sculptures, a lily pond with a water fountain, and peacocks wandering freely throughout the property. On one side the restaurant offers both terrace and inside dining and overlooks the gardens. To the left is a very comfortable lounge and bar (primarily for hotel guests), which comes to life in the evenings. The guestrooms are very spacious, especially the garden suites, and come completely outfitted with all amenities. The corridors leading to the rooms are adorned with fine art of well-known Mexican artists and large bouquets of fresh flowers. The hotel is located just outside the historic central area, close enough to walk there, but far enough away from the hustle and bustle of the street noises. *Directions:* Five blocks from center of town.

LAS MAÑANITAS
Owner: Margo Krause
Manager: Victor Sanchez
Ricardo Linares 107
Cuernavaca, Morelos 62000, Mexico
Tel: (777) 314-1466, Fax: (777) 318-3672
*22 rooms, Double: $120–$348**
**Service: 5%, Tax: 17.5%*
Open: all year, Credit cards: all major
Region: Central–Colonial town
www.karenbrown.com/mex/lasmananitas.html

This magnificent hacienda, constructed in 1529 at the order of Hernán Cortés, was the headquarters of Emiliano Zapata during the Mexican Revolution. Today it's a spectacular hotel located about 30 minutes' drive from Cuernavaca. Surrounding the entire property are tall, thick concrete walls, through which you pass via a gated entrance opening to a cobblestone promenade flanked by giant palms and expansive lawns. The hacienda itself with its wrought-iron balconies is made even more attractive by its dense covering of vines. The main hall is full of antiques worthy of a museum and each guestroom is uniquely designed and decorated, primarily with Mexican antiques. Ruins from an old mill are still on the property, overgrown by the jungle, which creates a wonderful parklike setting. The restaurant, nestled under tall trees next to the swimming pool, serves cuisine that presents the rich flavors of the region. There is plenty to see close by, making the hotel perfect as a refuge after a day of exploring pyramids, haciendas, and Colonial towns. The wonderful grounds will also keep you busy, taking you back to the days when this was one of the largest working estates in the region. A marvelous combination of history and beauty combine to make a delightful vacation stay. *Directions:* The hotel can arrange to pick you up at the Mexico City airport or will send a map which will enable you to drive from the airport to the Hacienda.

HACIENDA SAN GABRIEL DE LAS PALMAS
Owner: Lourdes Espinosa
Km 41.8 Carreterra Cuernvaca-Chilpancingo
Cuernavaca–Amacuzac, Morelos 62642, Mexico
Tel: (751) 348-0636, Fax: (751) 348-0113
15 rooms, Double: $100–$190*
*Tax: 17%
Open: all year, Credit cards: all major
Region: Central–Colonial town
www.karenbrown.com/mex/haciendasangabriel.html

Guadalajara is a huge, bustling metropolis, but secreted within a few blocks of its heart is a section with a rich Colonial heritage. This Centro Histórico is the highlight of Guadalajara, and if you want to be within steps of its architectural wonders, there is no better choice than the Hotel de Mendoza. With a prime location next to the beautiful 16th-century Santa María de Gracia Church, the Mendoza attracts tourists from around the globe. This is a simple hotel that offers a genuinely warm welcome and pleasant facilities. From the canopied entrance, you enter an old-fashioned lobby accented by a bronze, multi-tiered chandelier and large oil paintings. To the left is a raised area with tables and chairs in a parlor-like setting. A hallway to the right leads to La Forja restaurant. The hotel is built around an inner courtyard, with an inviting swimming pool the center of attention. Some of the guestrooms overlook this courtyard, but my favorite is number 308, a smaller bedroom than many of the others, but with a romantic view overlooking the Santa María de Gracia Church. All of the bedrooms are simply furnished and have a traditional hotel look with built-in headboards. They all have good lighting, air conditioning, color cable television, and marble bathrooms. *Directions:* Follow signs to the Centro Histórico. Once there, you need a detailed city map to find the small side street where the hotel is located.

HOTEL DE MENDOZA
Manager: Raul de la Brena
Calle Venustiano Carranza #16, Centro Histórico
Guadalajara, Jalisco 44100, Mexico
Tel & fax: (333) 613-7310
87 rooms, 17 suites, Double: $86–$104*
*Tax: 17%
Open: all year, Credit cards: all major
Region: Central–Colonial city
www.karenbrown.com/mex/hotelmendoza.html

For many years we searched throughout Guadaljara for the perfect hotel, but sadly never found it. Happily, all that has changed, and dramatically so. With the opening of the Quinta Real, Guadalajara now has a hotel that is an absolute jewel: one that instantly captured our hearts. Conveniently located about a 15-minute taxi ride from the city's historic center, in the upscale hotel zone, the hotel is appealing at first glance. From the street you pass under the canopied entry into an elegant atrium highlighted by a 250-year-old elephant tree and galleried walkways above adorned with greenery. Off to the right is an indoor-outdoor garden restaurant, a real beauty, which is a favorite spot for local families to bring their children for Sunday brunch. The heart of the hotel is its inner courtyard where fountains, trees, sculptures, and immaculately groomed gardens create a magical scene. The owner of the hotel is especially fond of angels, and if you look carefully you will see tiny angel statues and ornaments tucked into the lush garden greenery. Also in the garden is a splendid swimming pool. As you'd expect, the guestrooms are elegantly appointed and top-notch in every respect. Although the Quinta Real has fabulous amenities, its crowning glory is its superb, well-trained staff who strive to make every guest's stay a happy one. *Directions:* Two blocks from the Minerva Fountain at Avenida Lopez Mateos and Avenida Mexico.

❄ 💳 ☎ ￥ P ¶ ≈ 👤

QUINTA REAL GUADALAJARA
Manager: Alfredo Aguilar
Ave. Mexico 2727
Guadalajara, Jalisco 44680, Mexico
Tel: (333) 630-1797, (800) 457-4000 USA
Fax: (333) 615-0000
78 rooms, Double: $260–$335*
*Tax: 17%
Open: all year, Credit cards: all major
Region: Central–Colonial city
www.karenbrown.com/mex/quintarealguadalajara.html

Villa Ganz is situated close to the city market and historic central area of the city. Many of the homes here are Colonial mansions that have been wonderfully restored as shops and upscale office space, or in this case, as a boutique hotel. Villa Ganz opened its doors in 2000 after undergoing a complete renovation. The result is a charming hotel that makes you feel right at home from the minute you walk through the front door. The rooms and suites are spacious and detailed, each uniquely designed and decorated. The garden at the rear of the property is a welcome escape from the busy boulevard out front, with a lounging area that's complete with a fireplace. In the mornings this is where a buffet breakfast, made up mostly of fruits, cereals and yogurts, is served. Villa Ganz does not serve lunch or dinner, however there are many restaurants nearby and copies of their menus are available at the reception. The central salon is full of books in multiple languages and there's always hot coffee in the morning or chilled Chardonnay in the afternoon. Villa Ganz delivers comfort and character with style, and is a welcome starting point for exploring Guadalajara or one of the many neighboring towns. *Directions:* In the heart of the city's commercial and financial center. One street over from main Vallarta Avenue, near the intersection with Chapultepec, near downtown and historic center.

VILLA GANZ
Owner: Klix Kaltenmark
Lopez Citilla 1739, Colonia La Fayette
Guadalajara, Jalisco 44140, Mexico
Tel & fax: (333) 120-1416
10 rooms, Double: $180–$200*
*Tax: 17%
Open: all year, Credit cards: all major
Region: Central–Colonial city
www.karenbrown.com/mex/villaganz.html

When visiting Guadalajara, if you are an inveterate shopper, you must not miss Tlaquepaque, an artisans' village on the outskirts of the city, famous for its handicrafts and colorful pottery. Though urban sprawl has grown up around it, Tlaquepaque keeps its small-town identity with a central market square enclosed by an arcaded promenade. If you choose to stay overnight, your best choice for accommodations is the Casa de las Flores, a simple bed and breakfast four blocks from Tlaquepaque's center. Located in a simple neighborhood, the lovely house stands out from all the others. Inside, you enter the private home of your extremely gracious, capable hosts, Stan Singleton and José Gutiérrez. Their home forms one wall of the most outstanding feature of the property—an enclosed inner courtyard with an impeccably manicured, flower-filled garden, lovingly tended by José (a native of Guadalajara) who spends several hours every day keeping the gardens perfect. Stan, who relocated from northern California, is both an accomplished chef and an artist whose culinary ability is evident in the breakfast served and the tasteful decor of the guestrooms. These are not luxurious, but appealingly fresh and pretty, exuding artistic good taste with hand-painted tiles, handmade brick and marble floors, and furnishings by local artisans. *Directions:* Located just on the edge of the pedestrian zone. The one-way streets make driving tricky, so ask Stan for directions.

CASA DE LAS FLORES
Innkeepers: Stan Singleton & José Gutiérrez
Santos Degollado No 175
Guadalajara–Tlaquepaque, Jalisco 45500, Mexico
Tel & fax: (333) 659-3186
7 rooms, Double: $65–$85*
*Tax: 17%
Open: all year, Credit cards: MC, VS
Region: Central–Colonial city
www.karenbrown.com/mex/casadelasflores.html

Dating back to 1862, the Hotel Posada Santa Fé is one of Guanajuato's most historic hotels. (The city's name was originally Santa Fé, hence the name of the hotel.) It faces onto the Jardín Unión, by far the prettiest plaza in the city—in our estimation, by far the choicest place to be. Just in front of the hotel is a park with a bandstand, fountains, a pedestrian-only walkway of colorful tiles, and marvelous trees that are trimmed to form a dense canopy to screen the sun. Reminiscent of a Paris scene, a line of cafés with jaunty umbrellas stretches along the street, one of these being the Posada Santa Fé's restaurant-bar, La Terraza, a prime place to sit and "people watch." The lobby lounge has a rather dark, old-fashioned, faded elegance that reflects an era of days long past. The hotel is almost like a museum, with walls enhanced by colorful murals reflecting the legends and traditions of Guanajuato. An intricate wrought-iron staircase with a delightful skylight of stained glass leads up to the guestrooms. Request one of the best rooms (such as 2,5, 7, 8, or 9). These rooms have small balconies overlooking the plaza and are far superior to the standard rooms, which are smaller and darker. However, be aware that there is much festivity in the cafés below your window, with music lasting until the wee hours of the morning. *Directions:* Guanajuato, with its underground maze of streets, is almost impossible to navigate—ask the hotel for directions. The hotel has free valet parking.

☕ CREDIT ☎ P ⑪ 👤

HOTEL POSADA SANTA FÉ
Manager: Gerardo Herrera Garcia
Plaza Principal, Jardín Unión 12
Guanujuato 36000, Mexico
Tel: (473) 732-0084, Fax: (473) 732-4653
50 rooms, Double: $107–$140
Open: all year, Credit cards: MC, VS
Region: Central–Colonial town
www.karenbrown.com/mex/hotelposadasantafe.html

Guanajuato is a national treasure, offering numerous examples of the rich Colonial lifestyle at the time when the city was one of Mexico's leading producers of silver. Its winding, narrow streets, some actually under the city itself, using the abandoned mine tunnels, and the well-preserved buildings make the city wonderful for exploring Mexico's past. A good choice for a place to stay here is Quinta Las Acacias, a family-managed small hotel located just above the downtown area, next to a dam that was once the water source for the city. It is possible to walk down into town, but since the road is steep, a taxi is best for your return. This small inn is one of the many mansions in this neighborhood that have been renovated and is a quaint and comfortable place to rest and relax after enjoying Guanajuato. The entrance/reception area, decorated with antiques and family mementoes, is very inviting. There is a small dining room on the main floor where breakfast is served and on the second floor you find a library and sitting area for guests. The guestrooms in the main house exude a Victorian formality but my favorites are those in an annex behind the hotel where there are pretty terraced gardens and a pool. These accommodations not only offer plenty of privacy, but also have a charming Mexican décor. *Directions:* Very tricky to find—ask for detailed directions.

QUINTA LAS ACACIAS
Manager: Ana Pérez Ordaz
Paseo de la Presca 168
Guanajuato 36000, Mexico
Tel: (473) 731-1517, Fax: (473) 731-1862
9 rooms, Double: $210–$310*
*Tax: 17%
Open: all year, Credit cards: all major
Region: Central–Colonial town
www.karenbrown.com/mex/quintalascacias.html

Soon after entering the town of Guerrero Negro you can't miss the Malarrimo complex where you find the headquarters of Malarrimo Eco Tours as well as the Hotel Malarrimo, gift shop, and restaurant. Guestrooms are found in separate buildings, painted deep red with white trim. The theme of whales is dominant in the décor, with headboards and chests in some of the rooms carved as whales. The guestroom are very simple in décor and appointments, but clean and comfortable. Our first choice would be one of the three guestrooms in the newest wing (numbers 16, 17, and 18), which are a bit more spacious and have more modern bathrooms. There are four rooms that are a little larger than the others and offer a sleeping loft, which would be handy if you're traveling with children. The restaurant boasts some of the best seafood in the area and we enjoyed abalone, lobster, and scallops—all reasonably priced and delicious. Although the Hotel Malarrimo is a very basic hotel, reminiscent of old-fashioned motels that used to dot the highways in the USA, it offers the best accommodations in town and we really liked it a lot. The staff is very accommodating and it is also very convenient to stay right at the point of departure for your whale-watching tour. We enjoyed a leisurely breakfast knowing we were just minutes from the bus and only had to be summoned by the courtyard bell. *Directions:* You will see the hotel to the right, just as you enter town.

HOTEL MALARRIMO
Owner: Enrique Achoy
Boulevard Zapata
Guerrero Negro, Baja California Sur 23940, Mexico
Tel & fax: (615) 157-0100
16 rooms, Double: $35–$45
Open: all year
Region: Whale watching–Baja California
www.karenbrown.com/mex/hotelmalarrimo.html

The Agua Azul La Villa bed and breakfast provides a tranquil retreat on the lovely Oaxaca coast just one bay (five minutes by car) away from the bustling Tangolunda Bay "strip" of Huatulco. Snuggled into the hillside above Conejos Bay—one of nine that the area is known for—this small B&B offers six air-conditioned bedrooms, each overlooking the bay below and the ocean beyond from shaded, private, hammock-bedecked terraces. The Canadian owners designed the Pacific Coast-style villa, combining stucco, palm thatch (the ubiquitous palapa), wood, and water, successfully achieving an intimate, original inn tucked away in a parklike setting. The main salon is attractive and welcoming, and hosts an ample Continental breakfast each morning. Each of the smallish bedrooms is simply decorated with built-in tile headboards and side tables and terra-cotta floors. Tasteful use of blue-and-white tile, punctuated with floral designs, livens up the bathrooms, and wood wall units with cubbies and hangers serve as closets. With the exception of Orca, which has two beds, each guestroom has one queen bed draped with a richly-hued Guatemalan spread. The charming, two-tiered pool in the back garden is ringed by flowering foliage and features a waterfall and wonderful view. A small, sandy, semi-private beach on the inlet below is just a three-minute walk away. *Directions:* When you make reservations, Rick will send specific driving instructions.

❄ ⌃ ☕ CREDIT ⫟ 🚶 🐎 P 🚭 ≋

AGUA AZUL LA VILLA
Owners: Brooke & Rick Gazer
Bahias de Huatulco
Huatulco, Oaxaca 70989, Mexico
Tel: (958) 581-0265, Fax: none
6 rooms, Double: $79–$99*
*Tax: 17%
Minimum nights required: 3
Open: all year, Credit cards: MC, VS
Region: Beach–Pacific Coast
www.karenbrown.com/mex/aguaazul.html

Spread throughout 27 verdant acres, 19 buildings and 3 levels overlooking Tangolunda Bay, the traditional white-stucco Camino Real Zaashila is an excellent choice for a family getaway to Mexico's Pacific Riviera. The property boasts a quarter-mile of exclusive, wide golden beach and what must be the largest (450 feet) and loveliest sculpted pool in Huatulco's nine-bay area (request poolside accommodation if you want to minimize stairs). Fully a third of the rooms feature a 196-square-foot private pool, and every room has a small, furnished balcony with a view of the bay and the blue expanse of the Pacific beyond. The rustic, off-white stucco bedrooms have green-painted ceilings and Italian-marble floors, and are large enough to accommodate a reading chair and small writing/eating table. Verdigris wrought-iron and Mexican-style pale-mahogany and rattan furniture are tastefully combined to create a light and airy ambiance. The bathrooms and closets are surprisingly spacious—a blessing at a beach resort where an extended stay is likely. Once you've undergone the bustle of check-in at the bottom of the hill, and oriented yourself and your room amidst the gardens and walkways, you'll be able to relax utterly and savor totally the natural beauty of the landscape, a myriad of water sports, tennis, nearby golf, and all the benefits of a full-service resort hotel. *Directions:* Located overlooking Tangolunda Bay.

CAMINO REAL ZAASHILA
Boulevard Benita Juárez #5
Huatulco, Oaxaca 70989, Mexico
Tel: (958) 581-0460, (800) 722-6466
Fax: (958) 581-0461
145 rooms, Double: $200–$250*
*Tax: 17%
Open: all year, Credit cards: all major
Region: Beach–Pacific Coast
www.karenbrown.com/mex/caminorealzaashila.html

Truly a grand-class resort on an intimate scale, the Quinta Real is the jewel in the tiara of hotels that crowns Oaxaca's riviera. If you're seeking an experience wherein every desire is anticipated by a staff that outnumbers the guests two to one, and every detail of your accommodation fantasy is realized, this should be your destination. From the welcoming fountain in the open-air lobby to the gorgeous tiered pool and tempting strip of private beach far below (shuttle service provided for those wishing to avoid stairs), the place caters without pretension to guests accustomed to excellence and elegance. The oversized rooms seem suffused with golden light during the day and each includes a roomy sitting area and covered terrace with lounging couch, hammock, table, and sea views. Arabian royalty would feel at home amidst the stone pillars and tables, creamy domed ceilings, niched walls, and white cement floors polished to a soft sheen and inset with dark, smooth pebbles. The decor features pale, sun-colored textiles, armoires from Michoacán hand-painted in a tropical motif, and framed original art and weavings. Spacious bathrooms contain family-size Jacuzzi tub, shower and WC in separate curtained alcoves, and every amenity you could have possibly forgotten. And, finally, the superb restaurant is justifiably proud of its creative regional and international cuisine, beautifully served inside or out. *Directions:* Located overlooking Tangolunda Bay.

❄ ⛱ 💳 ☎ ▽ ⑪ ≋ 🖼 🏄

QUINTA REAL HUATULCO
Owner: Federico Roth
Boulevard Benito Juárez Lote 2, Bahias de Huatulco
Huatulco, Oaxaca 70989, Mexico
Tel: (958) 581-0429, (800) 457-4000 USA
Fax: (958) 581-0428
*28 rooms, Double: $265–$377**
**Tax: 17%*
Open: all year, Credit cards: all major
Region: Beach–Pacific Coast
www.karenbrown.com/mex/quintarealhuatulco.html

From the moment you ring the bell and your exceptionally charming French-Canadian hostess, Danielle Michon, opens the door and welcomes you into her home, you know you are in for a special treat. You pass into a romantic enclosed courtyard, enhanced by lush tropical plants and a reflecting pool with splashing fountain. A few steps more and you are in a dramatic foyer, an open-air room with sunken sitting area. Only columns divide the room from the stunning vista beyond of a swimming pool perched on the terrace with a rimless edge that gives the illusion that its water blends seamlessly with the turquoise sea below. From the terrace, steps lead down to the water's edge where there is a pier for guests who prefer to swim in the sea. Strong architectural details and bold Mayan hues of pinks, corals, blues, greens, and purples create an artistic masterpiece everywhere you look. The individually decorated guestrooms exude a quiet, tasteful, casual charm and each has a private balcony or terrace with a view to the sea. In the morning coffee and rolls are discreetly delivered to the rooms, but the "real" breakfast, a bountiful affair, is served downstairs when guests are ready to enjoy the day. There is no restaurant but when Ms. Michon's brother, François (a talented chef), is in residence, dinner is available four nights a week (there is also a restaurant next door). *Directions:* Take a taxi from the ferry pier to the hotel.

❄ ☎ ⚓ ☕ 💳 P 🚭 ≈ 🖼 ⛵

LA CASA DE LOS SUEÑOS
Owner: Danielle Michon
Carretera El Garrafon
Isla Mujeres, Quintana Roo 77400, Mexico
Tel: (998) 877-0651, Fax: (998) 877-0708
8 rooms, Double: $250–$375*
*Service: 8%, Tax: 12%, Dinner sometimes available
Open: all year, Credit cards: MC, VS
Region: Beach–Caribbean Coast
www.karenbrown.com/mex/casadelossuenos.html

The magic of the Villa Rolandi begins when you are met in Cancún and whisked across the turquoise-blue water in the hotel's private catamaran to Isla Mujeres. The magic continues when you enter the hotel's impressive lobby richly embellished with dramatic marble columns, domed ceiling, and fresh flowers, with its distinctly Italian ambiance spiced with a tantalizing Mexican Caribbean flavor—not surprising, as the owners hail from southern Switzerland, just at the Italian border. The Villa Rolandi has a fabulous, romantic restaurant with a deck extending right over the water and steps down to a pier where in season private yachts dock, bringing the rich and famous to dine. The suites are all similar in a modern style, with leather headboards, excellent reading lights, a separate sitting area, and private terrace or balcony sporting a Jacuzzi tub. The marble bathrooms are especially outstanding, with state-of-the-art amenities like double marble showers with dual showerheads, Jacuzzi-style sprays, and a steam-bath option. Guestrooms all look out to the hotel's private beach with its soft, pure-white sand extending to the turquoise sea. For those who prefer a pool, there is an exquisite large swimming pool with a waterfall dropping down to a pond below. The wonderful staff here seems to take joy in pampering all of the guests. *Directions:* No need to worry about finding the hotel—you are picked up in Cancún and taken right to the door.

VILLA ROLANDI
Owner: Sandro Muller
Manager: Giancarlo Frigerio
Carretera Sac-Bajo
Isla Mujeres, Quintana Roo 77400, Mexico
Tel: (998) 877-0700, Fax: (998) 877-0100
20 rooms, Double: $250–$350*
*Tax: 12%
Open: all year, Credit cards: all major
Region: Beach–Caribbean Coast
www.karenbrown.com/mex/villarolandi.html

Isla Mujeres is a small island just offshore from Cancún yet here you feel far removed from the bustling commercialism of its famous neighbor. An excellent choice for accommodations on the island is the Villa Vera Puerto Isla Mujeres, which caters to yachtsmen whose sumptuous boats glide into the hotel's private marina. The hotel attracts not only wealthy sportsmen who come for a month at a time and use the resort as a hub for fishing, but also guests from around the world who come to relax and enjoy the fine accommodations. The spaciousness of the beautifully kept property sets a mood of quiet seclusion. A stunning circular swimming pool is the centerpiece around which the guestrooms are clustered in cream-colored, two-story buildings with Spanish-style red-tiled roofs. All of the rooms are suites with separate sitting areas and individual terraces. In addition to the suites, there are villas available with private plunge pools and kitchenettes. These make ideal accommodations if you are traveling with children (who stay free under the age of 12). A Continental breakfast is delivered discreetly to a little cubbyhole in the wall hidden by a cute painting. Canals wrap around the property and, any time you want, a speedboat will whisk you in five minutes to the hotel's splendid white-sand beach with its own swimming pool and palapa-style restaurant. *Directions:* Complimentary boat transfers from Cancún.

❄ 🏨 ⚓ 🛏 🚤 CREDIT 📷 🕴 🍷 P 🍴 🏊 🖼 🤿 🐾 ♿

VILLA VERA PUERTO ISLA MUJERES
Owner: Fernando Garcia Etchegaray
Manager: Javier Silva
Puerto de Abrigo, Laguna Macax
Isla Mujeres, Quintana Roo 77400, Mexico
Tel: (998) 877-0413, Fax: (998) 877-0093
24 rooms, Double: $290–$350*
*Tax: 12%
Open: all year, Credit cards: all major
Region: Beach–Caribbean Coast
www.karenbrown.com/mex/puertoislamjueres.html

If you yearn for unspoiled nature and fascinating archaeological sites, yet don't want to sacrifice creature comforts, look no further than The Explorean, where sensual delights combine with superb, understated, casual elegance. That such superb luxury can be found so far off the beaten path is quite miraculous. The complex is designed in the style of a traditional Mayan village, but there the similarity ends. The reception area, bar, and restaurant, all open to the air under a high, thatched roof, look out to a stunning terrace—an architectural masterpiece. A long, fairly narrow swimming pool and a Jacuzzi hot tub stretch across the terrace, lined by white lounge chairs and umbrellas. What makes this extraordinary is that you look out over a green expanse of lush jungle—the only structure you can see, if you look very closely, is the top of one of the pyramids of Kohunlich peeking out of the sea of green. Paths meander through the rich foliage, leading to the guestrooms, which are in thatched cottages tucked about the property. These are exceptionally spacious and beautifully furnished in elegant simplicity and all have a private terrace with sofa and hammock. As you might expect, such luxury isn't cheap, but you do get value since the rate includes all meals, taxes, tips, drinks, cocktails, and even sightseeing excursions. *Directions:* From 186, between Escárcega and Chetumal, turn at the sign for Kohunlich. The hotel is on your left after about 6 km.

❄ ☎ ⚓ ☕ 💳 ☎ 👭 P ⑪ ≈

THE EXPLOREAN
Owner: Antonio Arroyo
Zona Arqueologica de Kohunlich
Kohunlich, Quintana Roo 77981, Mexico
Tel: (555) 201-8333, (877) 397-5672 USA
40 rooms, Double: $260–$325*
*Includes all meals
Open: all year, Credit cards: all major
Region: Yucatán Peninsula–Archaeological area
www.karenbrown.com/mex/explorean.html

La Paz is a paradise for avid fishermen who come in search of the marlin and sailfish, which ply these deep-blue waters from May to November. Although the largest city in southern Baja, La Paz still has a sleepy, small-town ambiance, especially along the waterfront. Facing the sea wall is where you find most of the restaurants, shops, and hotels, including our favorite, Posada Santa Fé, a small hotel whose architecture reflects the town's early Spanish heritage (Cortés landed here in 1596). The rosy-pink, stuccoed hacienda-style building faces onto the street and it is not until you go through the wrought-iron gate that the charm of the inn is revealed. You come into an inner courtyard with a tiny, pretty, turquoise-colored swimming pool tucked into the corner, complete with tiled fountain against the far wall. Clusters of tall palm trees and potted plants enhance the scene. Steps lead up to a higher terrace where you find a guest lounge and an outdoor patio where breakfast is served overlooking the water. There are ten guestrooms, some on the lower level facing the swimming pool and others on the top floor with balconies looking out to the ocean. All are attractive and tastefully decorated, with tiled floors, colorful bedspreads, Mexican paintings, and hand-carved wooden furniture. This intimate inn is not only very well priced, but offers quality and charm. *Directions:* On Paseo Alvaro Obergón, at the corner of Via Guerrero.

POSADA SANTA FE
Owner: Edward Rose Masocco
Paseo Alvaro Obergón 440
La Paz, Baja California Sur 23000, Mexico
Tel & fax: (612) 125-5871
10 rooms, Double: $85–$125*
*Tax: 12%
Open: all year
Region: Beach–Baja California
www.karenbrown.com/mex/posadasantafe.html

The Camino Real, located in a somewhat abandoned tourist development just south of Loreto, nestles between the beach and a golf course. Designed to resemble a mission, architecturally the complex is simple, with high stucco walls on three sides embracing a large open central courtyard, pool, and terrace bar-restaurant, leaving the fourth open to the gray-sand beach. Only the bell tower pierces the horizontal lines of the complex. The reception is on the right as you enter the complex, with a boutique and restaurant opposite, and a flight of stairs leading up to the bell tower and an open terrace bar. Guestrooms are found in two wings stretching from the reception and out to the beach. The rooms' décor is similar throughout, with warm earth tones selected for the paints and tiles. Standard rooms are comfortable but the suites are a bargain for the difference in luxury provided. Junior suites have a single outdoor terrace off the bedroom while master suites enjoy a two-tiered terrace and outdoor spa tub. The Camino Real is a large hotel and seems a bit functional in design but we recommend it as an alternative to the charming Posada de las Flores in the heart of Loreto, which might often be full, and as a good location if you are traveling with children. The grounds are expansive, with an excellent large swimming pool, private beach, and two restaurants. *Directions:* Located 7 km south of Loreto on the beach.

❄ ⚒ 💳 ☎ 🏋 P ¶ ≈ 🏠

CAMINO REAL
Manager: Peter Maxwell
Paseo de la Misión S/N, Fraccionamiento Napoló
Loreto, Baja California Sur 23880, Mexico
Tel: (613) 133-0010, (800) 722-6466 USA
Fax: (613) 133-0011
156 rooms, Double: $140–$200*
*Tax: 12%
Open: all year, Credit cards: all major
Region: Beach–Baja California
www.karenbrown.com/mex/loretocaminoreal.html

On a cobbled street in the heart of Loreto, Baja California's oldest town, the charming Posada de las Flores has a prime position just a block from the mission, facing the Plaza Salvatierra. This handsome, two-story, Spanish Colonial-style building has a rich sienna-red exterior enhanced by arched windows framed by stone. Wrought-iron lamps and a multitude of potted plants in front add to the appeal. A massive door affords a glimpse into the inviting interior garden courtyard. Dramatically set under a high, two-story ceiling whose beams support the glass bottom of the upper terrace pool, the inner courtyard features a stone fountain, many potted palms, colorful Talavera ceramic pots, and groupings of overstuffed chairs. >From the courtyard a wrought-iron spiral staircase winds up to the guestrooms, each named for a flower, and higher still to the rooftop terrace where you find the restaurant and pool. Guestrooms, five of which are junior suites with sitting areas and balconies, enjoy a separate dressing area with washbasin and a closed-off shower and toilet. Although not well soundproofed, the bathrooms with their colorful hand-painted Mexican tiles are attractive and well equipped. There is a very attractive Italian restaurant on the entry level (the owners are Italian), and a second restaurant on the roof terrace, looking out across rooftops to the distant blue water. *Directions:* Facing the square in the historic center of town.

❄ ⚓ ☕ 💳 ☎ 🚶 🍷 🍴 🚭 🏊 🖼 🚤 🐾

POSADA DE LAS FLORES
Owner: Giuseppe Marcelletti
1 Madero / Salvatierra
Loreto, Baja California Sur 23880, Mexico
Tel: (613) 135-1162, (877) 245-2860 USA
Fax: (613) 135-1099
15 rooms, Double: $140–$199*
*Tax: 12%
Closed: Sep 9 to Oct 10, Credit cards: MC, VS
Region: Beach–Baja California
www.karenbrown.com/mex/posadalasflores.html

Dolphin Cove Inn is a gem. A real discovery if you are looking for a well-priced, charmingly decorated place to stay with breathtaking views that can't be surpassed anywhere in Mexico, not at any price. Enhanced by impeccably groomed gardens and brilliant displays of bougainvillea, the bedrooms are nestled in clusters of white bungalows hugging a steep hillside next to the world-class Las Hadas Resort. Dolphin Cove Inn is a select group of 24 suites (from studios to three bedrooms), which are run like an intimate hotel within a larger complex called Paraiso Las Hadas. Every room has either a balcony or terrace capturing a romantic panorama of the deep-blue bay backdropped by green volcanic hills. Every suite has a well-equipped kitchenette, a bathroom decorated with hand-painted Talavera tiles, colorful hand-loomed fabrics, and enchanting headboards carved by the Tarascan Indians. If you are economizing, the studios are fabulous, but the one-bedroom suites with huge terraces are exceptionally appealing and offer outstanding value. A maze of staircases laces the property, leading to the swimming pool and, just below, a beach. The main attraction at Dolphin Cove is just relaxing: reading a novel, sleeping late, taking a swim, a quiet stroll on the beach. However, golf and tennis are readily available. Note: Dolphin Cove's many steps make it unsuitable for those with a walking problem. *Directions:* Adjacent to Las Hadas hotel.

❋ ⚓ ⚒ 💳 🧍 🍷 🍴 ≈ 🎿 🔔

DOLPHIN COVE INN AT PARAISO
Manager: Florentino Cardenas
Ave. Vista Hermosa s/n
Manzanillo, Colima 28860, Mexico
Tel: (314) 334-1692, (888) 497-4138 USA
Fax: (314) 334-1689
24 rooms, Double: $94–$137*
*Tax: 17%
Open: all year, Credit cards: MC, VS
Region: Beach–Pacific Coast
www.karenbrown.com/mex/dolphincove.html

When we first visited and fell in love with Las Hadas many years ago, it was a small hotel, comprised of just a cluster of low cottages snuggled around a pristine, palm-ringed beach. Over the years the hotel has grown and can no longer be classified as the small, intimate type of property we normally feature. Nevertheless, it holds a secure niche in our hearts, and still has the same romantic features that captivated us so long ago. The architecture is pure fantasy, with whitewashed walls, whimsical turrets, jaunty spires, and ornate domes, reflecting the romantic concept of a Moorish village. Cobblestone pathways shaded by palm trees meander through the property where fountains, statues, fragrant flowers, and walls draped with bougainvilleas make every stroll a delight to the senses. The accommodations reflect a subdued elegance with shades of white predominating, punctuated by accents of color. The enormous, free-form swimming pool with its swinging bridge set new standards of opulence when the hotel first opened. The hotel has a marina, ten tennis courts, and an 18-hole, Pete Dye championship golf course. But, in our appraisal, one of the most outstanding features of Las Hadas is its beach—one of the finest, gentlest beaches I have ever seen for children—which fringes a private cove where the swimming is sublime. *Directions:* Coming south from Manzanillo airport, turn right at the Peninsula de Santiago and follow signs to the hotel.

❄ ⚓ 🛵 💳 ☎ 🏌 🍷 🍴 🏊 🚶 🖼 🏄

LAS HADAS
Manager: Francisco Rangel Samayoa
Ave. Los Ricos s/n
Manzanillo, Colima 28200, Mexico
Tel: (314) 334-0000, Fax: (314) 334-1950
233 rooms, Double: $215–$1015*
*Tax: 17%
Open: all year, Credit cards: all major
Region: Beach–Pacific Coast
www.karenbrown.com/mex/lashadas.html

Pepe's Paradise is a secret hideaway with a cluster of six brightly painted, thatched cottages nestled in a tropical garden of towering cacti, brilliant bougainvilleas, banana trees, and coconut palms. The lush, jungle-like property slopes down the hillside to a tiny, gorgeous, private cove enclosed with splendid rock formations. Located in an exceptionally exclusive, private, gated community next to the world-class resort Las Hadas, these cottages provide a very special spot for those who want a romantic interlude or just a secluded getaway from the cares of the world. There is a wonderful, laid-back ambiance to your stay here—a somewhat Bohemian, whimsical blend of the South Seas and Robinson Crusoe. Each of the cottages, tucked on the hillside amongst the palms, has a king-sized bed and is simply but stylishly decorated with colorful Mexican accents. All are special, but my favorites, 2, 3, and 4, are perched almost over the water where the crashing surf lulls you to sleep at night. Paths wind down to the small cove, but for ocean swimming, there is a superb beach nearby at a private beach club. A full breakfast and early supper are included in the room rate, along with cold drinks and a constant supply of margaritas. *Directions:* For those arriving by plane, Pepe will arrange an airport transfer. If driving, ask for directions, which include the delightful instruction, "Turn left into the property at the monkey cage"!

⚓ ☕ 🏌 🍷 P 🍴 ≈ 🚶 🔔

PEPE'S PARADISE
Owner: Pepe Telaraña
67 La Punta-Las Hadas
Manzanillo, Colima 28861, Mexico
Tel: (314) 333-0616, Fax: (314) 334-1690
6 rooms, Double: $250*
*Breakfast & early supper included, Service: 10%
Open: all year
Region: Beach–Pacific Coast
www.karenbrown.com/mex/pepes.html

The Balboa Club used to be a private club, an exclusive place that the wealthy called home when they flew into Mazatlán on their private planes to fish or hunt or relax by the beach. Not that it was ever opulent. Quite the contrary: it always had a laid-back, casual air—just a simple, two-story brick lodge built around an inner garden courtyard with a swimming pool. The dining room and lounge looked out to the sea, along with a few of the guestrooms. Nothing much has changed over the years—the Balboa Club looks much the same as it did when we first saw it over 30 years ago. The staff is still friendly, the food is good, and the air-conditioned guestrooms are comfortable with exposed, white-painted-brick walls, tiled floors, large bathrooms, and balconies or terraces. There is a sort of faded, dated, nostalgic charm to the property and, if you like small, low-rise hotels, this one is a winner. It also boasts a prime location facing one of Mazatlán's loveliest stretches of beach where the gentle surf is usually safe for swimming. With beachfront property so precious and high-rise hotels in every direction, it is quite amazing that the Balboa Club still exists. Plans are underway to turn the property into a timeshare and some of the maintenance has been delayed, but, at the moment, we recommend it for those looking for an intimate, small hotel with good prices. *Directions:* Located in Zona Dorada, about mid-way on Las Gaviotas Beach.

BALBOA CLUB
Owner: Fernando Madero
Avenida Camaron Sabalo, s/n Zona Dorado
Mazatlán, Sinaloa 82110, Mexico
Tel: (669) 913-5211, Fax: (669) 914-4389
40 rooms, Double: $215–$245*
*Includes all meals, Tax: 17%
Open: all year, Credit cards: all major
Region: Beach–Pacific Coast
www.karenbrown.com/mex/balboaclub.html

There is no shortage of large hotels in Mazatlán. However, there are very few small properties left since most of them have been replaced with high-rises. Looking for a hotel to recommend, we explored the best stretch of beach in town, popping in and out of every place that looked promising; the one that stood out was the Motel Los Arcos. If you are looking for luxurious accommodations with all the bells and whistles, book one of the larger hotels, but for a simple, pleasant, reasonablely-priced place to stay with a super location, you will be pleased with Los Arcos. Its architecture reflects the character of motels built in the mid-1960s, but over the years it has been very well kept up. There are various buildings on the property, including three two-story buildings facing right onto the ocean painted white, with a different color trim on each (bright purple, strong yellow, and brilliant orange). Ask for accommodations in one of these, each of which has four compact, one-bedroom apartments complete with kitchenette. The units on the top floor have private balconies, while those on the ground floor share a terrace stretching to the edge of the beach. The décor in all the guestrooms is similar, with red-tiled floors, a round dining table, a sitting area, a small bedroom with colorful bedspreads, and a tiled bathroom. Nothing fancy, but very nice—and you sleep to the sound of the waves just below your window. *Directions:* Located at the south end of Las Gaviotas Beach.

⬆️ 💳 Y P 🏄

MOTEL LOS ARCOS
Manager: Antonio Ley
Avenida Rodolfo T. Loaiza 214, Zona Dorado
Mazatlán, Sinaloa 82110, Mexico
Tel & fax: (669) 913-5066
21 rooms, Double: $80–$95*
*Tax: 17%
Open: all year, Credit cards: MC, VS
Region: Beach–Pacific Coast
www.karenbrown.com/mex/losarcos.html

When Pueblo Bonito Emerald Bay opened in 2001, it had just 78 guestrooms but will expand to 258 by about 2004. The property is a timeshare, which we don't usually feature in our guides, however it is also professionally managed as a hotel, with the guestrooms rented out in the owners' absence. When we spent the night there, we discovered that it is in fact a stunning, deluxe hotel of the highest quality with a beautifully trained, welcoming staff. The attractively decorated guestrooms are spread out on 20 acres of land in a stand of 150-year-old mangrove trees. All the rooms have a balcony or terrace, usually with a view of the ocean, which stretches in front of the hotel. The architecture of the pretty, soft-yellow buildings seems to be a quite modern interpretation of an old Mexican hacienda, a style enhanced by tall pillars and wicker furniture set on wide verandas. The foyer is built as a rotunda with light streaming through a skylight to illuminate a large fountain. From the lobby, the property steps gently down to the sea with waterfalls, ponds, manicured gardens, and a large swimming pool beautifying the landscape. The dining room is exceptionally lovely, with tall windows opening to the terrace and walls and furniture in soft shades of white, accented by potted plants. *Directions:* Go north from Mazatlán on the coast road—you see a sign to the hotel about five minutes after the road loops around the yacht harbor.

PUEBLO BONITO-EMERALD BAY
Manager: Roberto Tussi
Av. Ernesto Coppel Campana 201, Zona Cerritos
Mazatlán, Sinaloa 82110, Mexico
Tel: (669) 989-0525, (800) 990-8250 USA
Fax: (669) 988-0718
102 rooms, Double: $135–$250*
*Tax: 17%
Open: all year, Credit cards: all major
Region: Beach–Pacific Coast
www.karenbrown.com/mex/emeraldbay.html

Only 20 minutes away from Mazatlán the charming Rancho Las Moras is tucked into the foothills of the Sierra Madre mountains on an immense, 2,500-acre ranch. Michael Ruiz bought the abandoned property and restored everything with taste, preserving all the architectural heritage of the original home. The main hacienda has a wide veranda stretching across the front and a cozy, rustic ambiance inside, with a low, beamed ceiling, thick stuccoed walls, terra-cotta floors, accents of antique furnishings, beautiful old mirrors, sofas and chairs with colorful handwoven fabrics, and oil paintings adorning the walls. On a terrace behind the hacienda is a large, beautiful swimming pool with lounge chairs strategically set to capture unobstructed views of the rolling hills. The charming open-air restaurant stretches along the end of the pool. All of the 11 spacious guestrooms (60 more rooms are being planned) are exceptionally appealing and feature the finest of Mexican artisanship, with hand-crafted wood furniture, beautiful loomed fabrics, rich terra-cotta floors, and large bathrooms with Talavera tiles. Tennis courts and bikes are available and if you want to explore the countryside, the ranch has a stable of horses. Rates include all meals and activities. *Directions:* From Mazatlán, take Hwy 15 libre toward Culicán. After 9 km, turn right toward La Noira. Go about 9 km and turn left at the sign to the hacienda.

※ ⚓ 🍺 🛒 ☕ CREDIT 🏋 🚶 👫 🏇 Ⓨ P 🍴 🏊 🎣 ⛷ 🏄 ♿

RANCHO LAS MORAS
Owner: Michael Ruiz
Cocoteros no. 1, Rincon de las Palmas
Mazatlán, Sinaloa 82110, Mexico
Tel & fax: (669) 914-1346
11 rooms, Double: $280*
*Includes all meals, Service: 15%, Tax: 17%
Open: all year, Credit cards: all major
Region: Beach–Pacific Coast
www.karenbrown.com/mex/rancholasmoras.html

Located just a couple of blocks off the main square, the Casa del Balam offers a nostalgic charm. This small hotel is so closely interwoven with the beginning of tourism in the Yucatán that it could not help winning a place in our hearts. Casa del Balam was built in the early 1900s as the private home of the Barbarchano family, pioneers of tourism. It all began when Señor Barbarchano, as a young man, picked up a number of guests from a ship and took them to see some Mayan ruins, originating the idea of sharing the Yucatán's wonders with non-archaeologists. Now, three generations later, the Barbarchano family operates many of the region's buses and tour companies and owns the majority of the hotels in prime locations, including this one in the heart of Mérida. There is nothing fancy or flashy about the Casa del Balam—this is just a good, old-fashioned hotel that has excellent management and exudes the faded glamour of bygone days. The best feature is the interior courtyard, highlighted by a stone fountain and surrounded by greenery and tables and chairs. Although there is a restaurant, you can be served in the courtyard, which is more romantic. All of the rooms are comfortable so there's no need to splurge on a suite. I particularly liked 203 and 204, large rooms with wrought-iron headboards. *Directions:* Just two blocks off the main square. The streets are all numbered—odd-numbered streets in one direction, even-numbered in the other.

HOTEL CASA DEL BALAM
Owner: Doña Carmen Barbachano
Calle 60 # 488 (corner of Calle 60 & Calle 57)
Mérida, Yucatán 97000, Mexico
Tel: (999) 924-2150, (800) 624-8451 USA
Fax: (999) 924-5011
*52 rooms, Double: $85–$110**
**Tax: 17%*
Open: all year, Credit cards: all major
Region: Yucatán Peninsula–Archaeological area
www.karenbrown.com/mex/casadelbalam.html

For visitors to the rich archaeological sites of the Yucatán, the trip frequently begins in Mérida, a major airline hub. From its outskirts Mérida first appears to be a rather scruffy, sprawling, unappealing city, but don't let this put you off. At its core Mérida's Colonial heritage shines through. Like most of the cities founded by the Spaniards, there is a very grand cathedral in the center facing a lovely, tree-shaded park (zócalo) surrounded by handsome 17th-century buildings. Two blocks from the park sits the Hotel Mision de Fray Diego, an intimate, appealingly appointed, charming inn that we just love, and although its street isn't one of the prettiest in Mérida, just a few minutes' walk takes you to the center of all the activity. You enter into the hotel's delightful courtyard, which is as pretty as can be with a fountain in the middle, an exuberant display of flowers and greenery, and a statue of Fray Diego, the Catholic brother for whom the hotel is named. The reception area and restaurant face this patio. A few more steps bring you to a second patio, this one highlighted by a lovely swimming pool surrounded by a garden. The guestrooms wrap around this courtyard in a three-storied, colonnaded wing enhanced by a wrought-iron balcony. All of the fresh-looking, uncluttered guestrooms are equally pleasing and provide modern amenities. *Directions:* Two blocks from the zócalo on Calle 61, between Calle 64 and Calle 66.

❄ ☎ 💳 ☎ ⅄ P ⅋ ≈ 🖼

HOTEL MISION DE FRAY DIEGO
Owner: Jorge Torre
Calle 61, 524
Mérida, Yucatán 97300, Mexico
Tel: (999) 924-1111, Fax: (999) 923-7397
27 rooms, Double: $83–$138*
*Tax: 17%
Open: all year, Credit cards: all major
Region: Yucatán Peninsula–Archaeological area
www.karenbrown.com/mex/misionfraydiego.html

When Monica and Hernandez Gonzalez purchased the 17th-century Hacienda Katanchel in the 1990s it had been abandoned for many years. Years of labor and love have brought it back to its original grandeur and today you find a deluxe hotel snuggled behind high walls in a vast 740-acre estate. A doorway through a deep Mayan-red wall opens onto a garden and a building that houses the reception. However, the heart of the property is a second, far grander hacienda located quite a way from the entrance. Here you find an elegant dining room and grand salon with ornate furnishings, brilliantly colored walls, arched doorways, and soaring ceilings. The guestrooms are scattered throughout the tropical, jungle-like property in romantic, colorfully painted, private cottages that used to house the plantation workers. All are imaginatively furnished in a minimalist style and exude a modern, uncluttered appeal, with the main focus being a four-poster white-iron bed. No need to worry about the cottages being too far-flung—there are tracks meandering throughout the property that were once used to transport the sisal to the plantation factory and today, just as in the past, donkeys still pull little trams along them, but instead of hauling sisal, they bring guests to dinner. *Directions:* Located 26 km east of Mérida, on the road toward Cancun.

HACIENDA KATANCHEL
Owners: Monica & Anibal González
Km, 26, Mérida-Cancun Hwy
Mérida–Katanchel, Yucatán 97470, Mexico
Tel: (999) 923-4020, (888) 882-9470 USA
Fax: (999) 923-4000
52 rooms, Double: $250–$400, Service: 10%, Tax: 17%
Minimum nights required: 2
Open: all year, Credit cards: all major
Region: Yucatán Peninsula–Archaeological area
www.karenbrown.com/mex/haciendakatanchel.html

Of all the alluring haciendas in the Yucatán, the Hacienda Santa Rosa is perhaps the prettiest—an appealing, 17th-century building delightfully decorated in blues, reds, and ochres. The first thing you see as you drive up is the owner's mansion, enhanced at the front by a long row of arches, which form a romantic veranda. On arrival, you are cordially welcomed with a glass of fresh juice and a refreshing cold towel. As you step inside, years seem to slip away—the antique furnishings re-create to perfection the ambiance of a wealthy plantation owner's home. The luxurious guestrooms, in various buildings around the property, live up to all expectations: each has its own personality, but all have tremendous charm. The suites have individual plunge pools adorned with floating flower petals. The most unusual accommodation is a Mayan-style, thatched-roof cottage where the king-sized bed is suspended from the ceiling like a hammock. The lovely young girls in native costume who care for the rooms create incredible designs with the flowers that adorn the robes, the towels, the bed linens, the baskets of shampoos and lotions, the bathmats, the dishes—everything is magic. The food is delicious and dining a special treat in an open-air porch with the jungle almost at your fingertips. *Directions:* 70 km from Mérida airport. Because maps are inaccurate we suggest you arrange a transfer from the airport. Otherwise, ask for detailed driving instructions.

❄ ☎ 💳 ☎ 🏇 ▼ P ¶ ≋ ▣

HACIENDA SANTA ROSA
Manager: Karsten Lemke
Mérida–Santa Rosa, Yucatán 97800, Mexico
Tel: (999) 950-1262, (888) 625-5144 USA
Fax: (999) 923-7963
11 rooms, Double: $299–$419*
*Service: 5%, Tax: 17%
Open: all year, Credit cards: all major
Region: Yucatán Peninsula–Archaeological area
www.karenbrown.com/mex/haciendasantarosa.html

The 17th-century Hacienda Temozón is a superb hotel with the warmth and charm of a private home, which is exactly what it once was. Not only is it convenient to the Mérida airport (about a 45-minute drive), but it also makes an excellent hub for exploring some of the Yucatán's most popular archaeological sites. Using the Hacienda Temozón as your home base, you can visit off-the-beaten-path Mayan ruins, convents, stunning old haciendas, and breathtaking cathedrals—the possibilities are endless. The hacienda has been renovated with meticulous care and love, maintaining its marvelous features such as soaring ceilings, wood beams, thick walls, sweeping verandahs, lovely tiles, and arched windows. However, all creature comforts have been added: air conditioning, direct-dial phones, mini-bars, the finest linens, excellent mattresses, beautiful decor, and wonderful bathrooms. Many of the guestrooms have an individual plunge pool and the Presidential Suite even has a private swimming pool. In addition, there is a huge, 48-meter pool with a swim-up bar. A floodlit tennis court is tucked into the estate's old stockyard and, for joggers, a path leads through the hacienda's 37-hectare garden. The Hacienda Temozón has more guestrooms than its "sister" hacienda-hotels, but it maintains the same intimacy, charm, and incredible service. *Directions:* 35 km south of Mérida. Ask for directions when making reservations.

❄ ☎ 💳 ☎ 🏋 🍸 P 🍽 ≈ 🏃 🖼

HACIENDA TEMOZON
Manager: Herman Reeling Brouwer
Km 182, Carretera , Mérida-Uxmal, Temozón Sur
Mérida–Temozón, Yucatán 97825, Mexico
Tel: (999) 923-8089, (888) 625-5144 USA
Fax: (999) 923-7963
28 rooms, Double: $299–$605*
*Service: 5%, Tax: 17%
Open: all year, Credit cards: all major
Region: Yucatán Peninsula–Archaeological area
www.karenbrown.com/mex/haciendatemozon.html

The intimate Hacienda San José exudes charm and offers incredible service. What a surprise to find luxurious accommodations so far off the beaten path. Although as you drive to the hotel it seems very remote (near Tixkokob, the hammock capital of the Yucatán), this is actually a great location for visiting the Colonial city of Mérida and taking trips to see the many rich archaeological sites nearby. However, you might not want to stray from this alluring, utterly romantic property. The rooms all exude a quiet elegance and are appropriately decorated with simple furnishings of the very highest quality. Many of the bedrooms have a private plunge pool, but in addition there is a dramatic, large swimming pool with a very special bottom coating that makes the water shimmer like the sea. When restoration began on this abandoned sisal property, the hacienda was no more than a shell but lots of money and, more importantly, impeccable taste have transformed it into a dream of a small hotel, while avoiding over-renovation. Although offering the ultimate in luxury, the colorful old hacienda and its surrounding buildings still ring true to their romantic origins. As you dine exquisitely on the terrace with large arches opening to the gardens, you feel as pampered as the owners of this wealthy sisal plantation must have felt so long ago. *Directions:* About 45 minutes east of Mérida. Ask the hotel for detailed instructions.

❄ ☎ ▣ ⚒ CREDIT ☎ 🏇 �托 P ⊪ ≋

HACIENDA SAN JOSE
Manager: Veronique Timsonet
Mérida–Tixkokob, Yucatán 97470, Mexico
Tel: (999) 950-1272, (888) 625-5144 USA
Fax: (999) 923-7963
15 rooms, Double: $299–$507*
*Service: 5%, Tax: 17%
Open: all year, Credit cards: all major
Region: Yucatán Peninsula–Archaeological area
www.karenbrown.com/mex/haciendasanjose.html

One of the pleasures of traveling on the Yucatán Peninsula is the opportunity to stay in one of the beautifully restored haciendas dotted throughout the area. A gem in this collection is the superbly restored Hacienda Xcanatún. Built in the mid-18th century, the hacienda was once owned by a wealthy local family and used to produce sisal ("green gold"). When the sisal market collapsed, the property fell into ruins and was abandoned for many years until the present owners purchased it and began an arduous five-year restoration project. The result is much like a work of art as the owners used only the best master craftsmen and materials in the region. The spacious guestrooms are richly decorated, many with antiques, and have simply incredible bathrooms featuring Jacuzzi bathtubs complete with a waterfall. Each room is unique: some are hacienda-style with wide, covered terraces outside, while others enjoy romantic private gardens with outdoor Jacuzzis. The grounds include lush tropical gardens, a large fishpond, and two swimming pools. The hotel's very popular restaurant, the Casa de Piedra, offers gourmet cuisine that fuses European techniques with regional cooking styles. This is a wonderful oasis for pure relaxation and also a great starting point for exploring the incredible Mayan sites and other haciendas in the area. *Directions:* Located about 12 km north of the center of Mérida on the highway to Puerto Progreso.

※ ☎ 📧 ☎ ♿ 🏋 🚶 🐎 Ⴤ P ⑪ ≈ 🚶

HACIENDA XCANATUN
Owners: Jorge Ruz Buenfil & Cristina Baker
Km. 12, Carretera Mérida-Progreso
Mérida–Xcanatún, Yucatán 97300, Mexico
Tel: (999) 941-0213, Fax: (999) 941-0273
18 rooms, Double: $195–$240*
*Service: 5%, Tax: 17%
Open: all year, Credit cards: all major
Region: Yucatán Peninsula–Archaeological area
www.karenbrown.com/mex/haciendaxcantun.html

Casa Vieja is perfectly situated on a quiet side street in the popular district of Polanco, within walking distance to many sites of interest. Avenida Masyrik (often known as the Rodeo Drive of Mexico) is just a block away, plus Chapultepec Park and Avenida Reforma, both well worth visiting, are within walking distance, while the historical central part of the city is an easy taxi ride away. Casa Vieja, an ochre-colored, two-story mansion, draped with ivy and enhanced by blue trim, oozes Mexican charm. It doesn't look like a hotel at all, but rather like a very old, enchanting private hacienda. Inside, brilliantly-colored stucco walls, cheerful bouquets of flowers, beautiful ceramic vases, tinkling fountains, masterful craftsmanship, original Mexican paintings, sculptures, Mexican folk craft, beamed ceilings and hand-crafted quarrystone floors harmonize to create a magical old-world mood. Each sumptuously decorated, luxurious suite is unique and complete with every amenity imaginable, including a kitchenette. Rooms are very spacious, especially the two-bedroom Lolita Suite, named after the famous owner of the hotel. The top floor overlooks the street and features an open terrace restaurant/bar with excellent cuisine, as well as a meeting/entertainment room off to one side. *Directions:* Centrally located a block from Ave. Masyrik in Polanco. Turn on Eugenio Sur and the hotel is less than one block before the Chapultepec Park.

CASA VIEJA
Manager: Luis Fernando Sosa
Eugenio Sue 45, Colonia Polanco
Mexico City, D.F. 29230, Mexico
Tel: (55) 282-0067, Fax: (55) 281-3780
10 rooms, Double: $350–$850*
*Tax: 17%
Open: all year, Credit cards: all major
Region: Central–Colonial city
www.karenbrown.com/mex/casavieja.html

La Casona is a treasure—a charming, beautifully managed small hotel nestled in a lovely residential area. Staying here, you would never believe you were in the world's second-largest city: instead, you feel as snug as can be, pampered with such loving attention that you feel like a guest in a private home. Indeed, facing a quiet street with a tree-lined parkway in the middle, the pretty, two-story, pink hotel looks like a charming private residence. Inside, the ambiance continues, with an intimate lounge with lovely slip-covered sofas and chairs, a grand piano in the corner, soft lighting, bouquets of fresh flowers, and nicely framed paintings decorating the walls. The bedrooms too look like those in a private home. Each is individually decorated, but all exude the understated elegance reminiscent of a bedroom in an English country estate. Rooms are not large but adequate in size and have all the most modern conveniences. La Casona has a musical theme throughout and the bedrooms each display a musical instrument. The hotel has a cute restaurant with checked tablecloths, humorous paintings of dogs in fancy dress, and an exterior courtyard with fountain for outdoor dining in balmy weather. La Casona is not in the center of town, but taxis quickly whisk you to wherever you want to go, then after all your sightseeing you have the pleasure of returning to your oasis of comfort. *Directions:* Four blocks south of the Reforma, one of Mexico City's main boulevards.

LA CASONA
Manager: Ines Macedo
Durango No. 280 at Cozumel, Colonia Roma
Mexico City, D.F. 06700, Mexico
Tel: (55) 286-3001, Fax: (55) 211-0871
29 rooms, Double: $125*
*Tax: 17%
Open: all year, Credit cards: all major
Region: Central–Colonial city
www.karenbrown.com/mex/lacasona.html

If you want to sample of bit of Mexico's rich historic past, the Hotel de Cortés is your best bet. In fact, it is the only choice for accommodations in a building that dates back to the 17th century. Well located just across from the Alameda Park and only steps from the Palace of Fine Arts, the hotel is a richly adorned, baroque stone building constructed in the early part of the 17th century as a hospice for the Order of the Agustinians. From the beginning, the monastery welcomed weary friars who used this as a resting place on their journeys. Over the handsome stone entry is a charming carving of Santo Tomás de Villanueva, patron of the needy, shown bestowing his gentle blessing on all who enter. Inside, the most inviting feature of the Hotel de Cortés becomes immediately evident: the building is constructed around an exceptionally cheerful interior courtyard adorned by a central fountain, flowers, trees, and potted plants. There is an indoor restaurant but on sunny days the sheltered patio is the heart of the hotel where guests dine at colorfully set tables. Most of the bedrooms overlook the courtyard and are appropriately simple in their decor. This is not a deluxe hotel: the guestrooms are plain but very pleasant and the bathrooms are a bit dated but spotlessly clean. *Directions:* Located on the corner of Hidalgo Avenue and Reforma Boulevard, in front of Alameda Park.

HOTEL DE CORTES
Manager: Sebastian Rincon Gallardo
Av. Hidalgo 85, Colonia Guerrero
Mexico City, D.F. 06300, Mexico
Tel: (55) 518-2184, Fax: (55) 512-1863
29 rooms, Double: $120*
*Tax: 17%
Open: all year, Credit cards: all major
Region: Central–Colonial city
www.karenbrown.com/mex/decortez.html

We normally feature small hotels, especially those secreted off the beaten path. The Hilton Aeropuerto hotel, with 129 rooms and smack in the middle of Mexico City's airport, certainly doesn't fit our usual criteria. However, by any standards this hotel is a real winner, especially if you are overnighting in Mexico City and have an early-morning flight. Few cities can boast of a hotel truly inside an airport, which is exactly where you find this Hilton. When the elevator doors open, you enter into a grand lobby, charming in its simplicity. No clutter here—just a large open room with green-marble floor, a sitting area accented by modern sofas and chairs, a bar tucked into one corner, and, along one side, a restaurant, discreetly cordoned off by potted palms. The most special feature of the decor is a wall of glass overlooking the airport runways. This foyer has an air of tasteful simplicity, with one dramatic accent of a huge bouquet of colorful fresh flowers on a table in the center of the room. Wide hallways carpeted in a deep-green color, which complements the green marble in the foyer, lead to the beautifully equipped guestrooms. Be sure to request one overlooking the runways for the fun of watching the endless parade of planes taking off and landing just below your window. *Directions:* Go to the "F" sign in the airport lobby and take the escalator up one floor, then the elevator marked to the hotel.

HILTON AEROPUERTO
Manager: Omar Santillanes
Benito Juárez International Airport
Mexico City, D.F. 39306, Mexico
Tel: (55) 133-0505, Fax: (55) 133-0500
129 rooms, Double: $160*
*Tax: 17%
Open: all year, Credit cards: all major
Region: Central–Colonial city
www.karenbrown.com/mex/hiltonaeropuerto.html

For location, the Hotel Majestic just can't be beat—not at any price. It overlooks Mexico City's colorful zócolo(main square), national palace, and spectacular cathedral. However, it is not just location that makes the Majestic such a winner: it brims with character. From the moment you walk into the lobby, which glows with soft light, you are transported back to another era. Here you find a handsome red-tile floor, a beamed ceiling, arched coves, intimate sitting niches, elaborate bouquets of fresh flowers, potted palms, a stone fountain, and richly-hued mosaics—predominantly blue and white with a touch of yellow. These beautiful mosaic tiles are the hallmark of the Hotel Majestic and richly enhance the staircases, hallways, and public rooms. You reach the guestrooms, which are simple, with a 1930s-style decor, by an old-fashioned elevator or up a winding staircase. Don't expect luxury, but the rooms are very comfortable and have air conditioning, security boxes, mini bars, cable TVs, and telephones. Be sure to ask for a room overlooking the zócolo. The Majestic's renowned restaurant, the Terraza, located on the seventh floor, has a stunning balcony around two sides, which affords a prime view of the cathedral. A bountiful buffet breakfast (included in the rate) is served here each morning. Although not super-deluxe, the Majestic offers incredible value and is one of our personal favorites. *Directions:* On a corner overlooking the main square.

HOTEL MAJESTIC
Manager: Miguel Salgado
Madero 73, Centro
Mexico City, D.F. 06000, Mexico
Tel: (55) 21-8600, Fax: (55) 512-6262
85 rooms, Double: $85–$273*
*Breakfast not included, Tax: 17%
Open: all year, Credit cards: all major
Region: Central–Colonial city
www.karenbrown.com/mex/majestic.html

The popular Polanco district is the perfect place to situate yourself for enjoying Mexico City. It is close to many of the city's landmarks, offers great shopping opportunities, and has many wonderful restaurants nearby. Residencia Polanco is a small boutique hotel offering casual but comfortable accommodations and its location on a quiet side street ensures that the noises of one of the world's largest cities will not be a bother during your stay. There are 23 spacious one-bedroom suites decorated with Mexican handicrafts and furnished with rustic Colonial-style furniture, each providing a separate sitting/living area and a small kitchenette. The size of the rooms and the amenities that are included make this hotel perfect for longer stays to really get to know this amazing city. The upper floor of the hotel features a large terrace for sunbathing and enjoying the open-air Jacuzzi, and the restaurant Los Gernios, open for breakfast, lunch, and dinner. Next to the restaurant is a pleasant bar and lounge, a wonderful gathering place before or after dinner. Each floor is accessed by an elevator as well as a wide staircase that winds its way up the front of the building. On the main floor, next to the reception, is a small deli selling pastries, fresh coffee, and sandwiches. *Directions:* Situated in the exclusive Polanco area, ask for specific directions if driving.

RESIDENCIA POLANCO
Manager: Oskar Palavicini
Calle Newton 272, Colonia Chapultepec Morales
Mexico City, D.F. 11570, Mexico
Tel: (52) 5250-8018, Fax: (52) 5203-8145
23 rooms, Double: $155–$735
Open: all year, Credit cards: all major
Region: Central–Colonial city
www.karenbrown.com/mex/residenciapolanco.html

Hotel Los Juaninos's central location, right across from the plaza and the cathedral, is perfect for exploring the streets of Morelia. This small boutique hotel with 33 rooms, once the Episcopal palace and then the Royal Hospital of San Juan de Dios, opened its doors in 1986, with major renovations taking place in the late 1990s. The lobby is enhanced by stained-glass windows, beamed ceiling, stone arches, numerous religious icons, floral bouquets, Victorian-style furniture, and a huge basket of colorful glass balls. A steel, freestanding elevator dominates the end of the entrance hall, but there is also a handsome curved stairway whose stone steps are well worn from centuries of use. The spacious bedrooms feature vaulted, wood-beam ceilings, wood floors, and lace curtains. One of our favorites, 214, is a junior suite with a view of the cathedral. Each floor looks out over a central courtyard, hacienda style, with wide passageways lined with finely carved doors and doorways framed in stone. On the rooftop, La Azotea, a renowned gourmet restaurant and bar with excellent regional cuisine, offers live music on weekends and lovely views of the plaza and church. Adjacent to the restaurant is an appealing small lounge, solely for the enjoyment of hotel guests. Morelia has many museums and fine examples of Colonial architecture to discover, as well as markets where local handicrafts are sold. *Directions:* Overlooing the cathedral.

LOS JUANINOS
Owner: Lorena Morales
Morelos Sur 39
Morelia, Michoacán 58000, Mexico
Tel: (443) 312-0036, Fax: (443) 313-4256
33 rooms, Double: $120–$260*
*Tax: 15%
Open: all year, Credit cards: all major
Region: Central–Colonial town
www.karenbrown.com/mex/losjuaninos.html

Snuggled on a hillside overlooking Morelia lies one of our favorite inns, the charming Villa Montaña. For many years it has been known as one of the finest small hotels in all of Mexico. The entrance sets the mood of refinement and good taste with an enormous stone fireplace, massive oil paintings, exuberant bouquets of fresh flowers, an antique reception desk, and a huge wrought-iron chandelier. The magic continues in the parklike grounds, which are stunning: everywhere you look there are treasures—from whimsical fountains to romantic statuary—all lovingly chosen by the artistic owner whose passion for handicrafts and antiques is obvious in every tiny detail. Brick pathways lace the property, leading to the 35 suites, each different in layout and distinct in design with wood furniture, handcrafted accessories, and fine European antiques. The ceilings are vaulted with thick wood beams and supported by carved columns. Fireplaces make the rooms cozy at night in winter, while sunny afternoons can be enjoyed poolside with a beautiful panoramic view of the city of Morelia below. The restaurant is gourmet, featuring both international and local dishes, with a wonderful ambiance and fine cuisine. On balmy evenings dinner is served outside on a terrace with an incomparable panorama. Other amenities include a tennis court, tours to nearby Colonial towns, and a golf course nearby. *Directions:* In the hills above the city. Ask for directions.

VILLA MONTAÑA
Manager: Margarita Murillo
Patzimba 201, Colonia Vista Bella
Morelia, Michoacán 58090, Mexico
Tel: (443) 314-0231, Fax: (443) 315-1423
35 rooms, Double: $207–$518*
*Service: 7.5%, Tax: 15%
Open: all year, Credit cards: all major
Region: Central–Colonial town
www.karenbrown.com/mex/villamontana.html

If when visiting Morelia you would prefer a country setting rather than being in the center of town, the Villa San José makes a good option. Perched on a hill in parklike grounds of over an acre, the Villa San José has lovely views of Morelia, which nestles in the valley below. The hotel shares the hillside with its neighbor, the Villa Montaña, but the Villa San José with its conference rooms and business center has more of a commercial feel and would probably be the better choice if you are traveling with children (there is even babysitting service available). The guestrooms are not in one building, but grouped in various casitas connected by paths that weave throughout the property. The construction is contemporary (the hotel was built in the 1950s) but the architecture reflects the Mexican rustic style with brick walls accented by red-tiled roofs. All of the guestrooms are delightfully decorated with Mexican artifacts and whimsical paintings on the walls and, best of all, each has its own fireplace to warm you on chilly evenings. One of our favorite rooms, number 29, is a junior suite with an elevated terrace that captures a view out over the rooftops to the spires of Morelia's beautiful cathedral. The hotel has a swimming pool, tennis courts, and access to a nearby golf course. *Directions:* On a hill above Morelia. Ask for directions.

VILLA SAN JOSE
Owner: Juan Manuel Abud
Patzimba 77, Colonia Vista Bella
Morelia, Michoacán 58090, Mexico
Tel: (443) 324-4545, Fax: (443) 315-1736
43 rooms, Double: $128–$282*
*Tax: 15%
Open: all year, Credit cards: all major
Region: Central–Colonial town
www.karenbrown.com/mex/villasanjose.html

The Virrey de Mendoza, a wonderful hotel exuding old-world refinement and understated elegance, has an unparalleled location looking across the picturesque Armas Square to Morelia's exquisite cathedral. The original building was a simple stone home constructed in the 16th century but over the years it was greatly enhanced and became one of the most magnificent mansions in town. The hotel is built around an attractive three-story arcaded courtyard crowned by a beautiful large stained-glass skylight. The lobby has an air of stately grandeur, with a handsome Oriental carpet accenting a gorgeous parquet floor, a huge bouquet of flowers, fine oil paintings, potted palms, soft lighting, a grand piano, and intimate groupings of leather sofas and chairs. There is a romantic, formal dining room with rich paneling halfway up the walls, a beamed ceiling, and antique-style chandeliers. The rather compact standard bedrooms are all pleasantly decorated with traditional-style furniture and tasteful artwork. The suites are more spacious and many are decorated with lovely antiques. The quietest bedrooms overlook the interior courtyard, but those facing the street, although noisier, have more sunlight. For a splurge, request one of the five suites that face the cathedral—these have incredible views of the cathedral and at night, when it is gently illuminated, these suites are truly magical. *Directions:* Facing the cathedral, across Armas Square.

HOTEL VIRREY DE MENDOZA
Owner: Ramon Toca Narro
Manager: Margarita Murillo Hurtado
Av. Madero Pte. 310
Morelia, Michoacán 58000, Mexico
Tel: (443) 312-0633, Fax: (443) 312-6719
55 rooms, Double: $102–$268*
*Tax: 17%
Open: all year, Credit cards: all major
Region: Central–Colonial town
www.karenbrown.com/mex/vireydemendoza.html

If you are looking for luxurious accommodations without sacrificing one iota of charm, the Camino Real is an incomparable choice. Not only is this spectacular hotel a real beauty, but it also boasts the finest location in town-between two of Oaxaca's prime targets: the zócalo (main square) with its gorgeous cathedral and the lovely Santo Domingo. This former convent of Santa Catalina dates back to the 16th century, when it was constructed for the order of the Dominican nuns. Happily, nothing has been over-renovated: the building has been tenderly restored, preserving its stunning architectural features and authentic grace while subtly adding deluxe amenities. Time slips by as you step into the first superbly romantic garden courtyard, bound by massive arched colonnades. Quiet tiled corridors enhanced by faded original frescoes lead to two additional sun-drenched courtyards: one features a pretty stone fountain where the nuns used to do their washing, while the other has a lovely swimming pool. The guestrooms vary in style and size due to the age of the building, but all are most appealing and decorated with great taste using native weavings, hand-loomed fabrics, and colorful Mexican tiles in the bathrooms. As would be expected in a luxury hotel, all rooms are air-conditioned and offer all modern amenities. *Directions:* On Calle 5 de Mayo, one block south of Santo Domingo.

❋ ☎ 🛋 🃏 ☎ 🏌 🏃 🐎 ▼ P ¶ ⇌ 🖼 🐾 ♿

CAMINO REAL OAXACA
Manager: Alexandre de Brouwer
Calle Cinco de Mayo No. 300
Oaxaca 68000, Mexico
Tel: (951) 516-0611, (800) 457-4000 USA
Fax: (951) 516-0732
91 rooms, Double: $205–$305*
*Tax: 17%
Open: all year, Credit cards: all major
Region: Central–Colonial town
www.karenbrown.com/mex/caminorealoaxaca.html

The Casa Cid de León is a mirror of the vibrant personality of owner/operator Lety de Cid de León and indeed, each of the four guestrooms follows a theme taken from some aspect of, or time in, Lety's life. The decoration and design are at once eclectic but delicate, and sophisticated. Lety cares profoundly about her small bed and breakfast and takes great care in selecting only the finest linens and top-quality furnishings, and ensuring that fresh flowers abound in all the rooms. You could literally spend days in your room and still be discovering something new. If you are traveling with family, Lety can certainly accommodate you, as a couple of the rooms offer additional space or a connection with other rooms. The hotel has three floors, with the third being a rooftop terrace that serves as the dining room, lounge and bar. Although there is no restaurant on the premises, Lety has made arrangements with a couple of restaurants close by that deliver anything on their menus. Casa Cid de León is located right in the heart of downtown Oaxaca, making it perfect for exploring this truly wonderful city. There are so many markets and shops in Oaxaca and nearby, that staying somewhere right in the middle is extremely convenient. *Directions:* The hotel is easy to find as it is on one of the major streets (Morelos) in downtown Oaxaca. Two blocks from the square.

CASA CID DE LEON
Owner: Leticia de Cid de León
Avenida Morelos 602
Oaxaca 68000, Mexico
Tel: (951) 514-1893, Fax: (951) 514-7013
4 rooms, Double: $220*
*Tax: 17%
Open: all year, Credit cards: all major
Region: Central–Colonial town
www.karenbrown.com/mex/casaciddeleon.html

The Casa Conzatti, a mustard-colored Colonial-style building, is a moderate-sized hotel on the edge of the historic section of Oaxaca. The hotel was the home of Cassiano Conzatti, a renowned Italian botanist who lived in Oaxaca at the end of the 19th century. Grateful for his remarkable work, the city named the garden where he did his research Jardín Conzatti. The Casa Conzatti faces the park and has a roof garden overlooking it. Like so many of the properties in Oaxaca, it reflects its early heritage with massive wooden beams, arched passageways leading to the guestrooms, and thick 200-year-old wooden double doors giving onto a central courtyard. To the right as you enter is a popular restaurant with tables and chairs overflowing into the patio, a very popular place to eat with the locals. Rustic wooden furniture and rich-colored fabrics decorate the bedrooms, all of which offer many amenities such as hairdryers, room safes, cable TV, air conditioning, and telephones with modem ports. The master suites have the added bonus of Jacuzzi tubs. Care has been taken to preserve all the architectural details of the Colonial era to maintain the historic flavor of Oaxaca while offering a high level of comfort. The Casa Conzatti's sophisticated ambiance and similarly decorated rooms lend it more of a commercial air than some of the other hotels we feature in Oaxaca. *Directions:* Three blocks from Santo Domingo Church, facing Conzatti Park.

CASA CONZATTI
Manager: Marco Díaz Hermández
Gómez Farias, 218
Oaxaca 68000, Mexico
Tel: (951) 515-8500, Fax: (951) 513-0777
45 rooms, Double: $100–$213*
*Tax: 17%
Open: all year, Credit cards: all major
Region: Central–Colonial town
www.karenbrown.com/mex/casaconzatti.html

La Casa de Mis Recuerdos is a simple, but delightful, well-located bed and breakfast. You enter into a blissful courtyard whose walls are laced with a brilliant display of bougainvilleas. Cheerful canaries add their song to the idyllic scene. For two generations Casa de Mis Recuerdos has been the family home of Concepción Arroyo de Valencia who welcomes her guests like friends. You cannot help falling in love with Concepción whose gentle kindness and exceptional warmth make a stay here very special. She speaks no English (though her daughter and son-in-law do) but her hospitality has no language barriers. Some of the guestrooms are in an annex facing a courtyard in the back of the inn, but my favorites are the four at the front. Some of these are quite small, but all are sweetly decorated and furnished with great care and good taste. Fabrics are handmade and little touches such as embroidered pillows and fresh flowers are everywhere. If you want more space, request the bedroom with two beds in the main house overlooking the garden. Concepción does her own baking for breakfast, which is served either in the garden or, on chilly days, inside in a most appealing dining room with colorful Talavera plates adorning dark-red walls. This is a simple B&B, but a marvelous choice for those looking for a charming, intimate place to stay in the heart of Oaxaca. *Directions:* Located four blocks west of Santo Domingo on Pino Suárez.

LA CASA DE MIS RECUERDOS B&B
Owner: Concepción Arroyo de Valencia
Pino Suárez, 508
Oaxaca 68000, Mexico
Tel: (951) 515-5645, Fax: (951) 515-8483
9 rooms, Double: $65–$74*
*Tax: 17%
Open: all year
Region: Central–Colonial town
www.karenbrown.com/mex/misrecuerdos.html

Superbly located in the heart of town, the Casa Oaxaca offers an old-fashioned style of personal service and a sophisticated, gentle refinement—far beyond what you would expect in such a tiny hotel. This simple, unadorned, bright-blue, stuccoed house is typical of the buildings found throughout Oaxaca. The heart of the hotel is its open garden courtyard, which is surrounded by a white-columned arcade. Whereas most of Oaxaca's courtyards exude a cheerful, colorful, busy ambiance with many potted plants and fountains, Casa Oaxaca's is much less cluttered and, with its dazzling white walls, carefully placed accent trees, and rattan tables and chairs, has an almost Oriental look. In fact, throughout the hotel there is a most refreshing, minimalist, modern simplicity. The guestrooms have modern furnishings and white walls accented by well-framed photographs of Indian villages. Most of the guestrooms have doors opening onto the courtyard, but the suite faces a second patio with swimming pool. The hotel has an excellent, intimate restaurant where the talented chef, Alejandro Ruiz Olmedo, upon sufficient prior notice, will prepare a menu of your choice. Like the décor in the rest of the hotel, the small restaurant has a delightfully fresh look, with white walls and modern furnishings. A Continental breakfast including homemade breads is served each morning in the tranquility of the courtyard. *Directions:* Four blocks from the square.

CASA OAXACA
Manager: Peter Kaiser
Calle Garcia Vigil 407
Oaxaca 68000, Mexico
Tel: (951) 516-4412, Fax: (951) 514-4173
7 rooms, Double: $175–$265*
*Service: 12%, Tax: 17%
Open: all year, Credit cards: all major
Region: Central–Colonial town
www.karenbrown.com/mex/casaoaxaca.html

Just before Christmas in 2000, your gracious young host, Ernesto Suárez, opened the doors of Casa San Felipe, a new hotel in Oaxaca. "New" isn't exactly the proper word since the hotel is within a centuries-old, Spanish-style home built around a central courtyard. This small hotel with a brick-red stucco façade with doors and windows framed in white stone faces a busy, one-way street, about five blocks from the zócalo (main square). Double wooden doors lead into a small, simple courtyard with walls painted a cheerful butter yellow and with green plastic chairs surrounding small tables. Potted palms and red geraniums add color. The guestrooms open off the courtyard, some on the ground level and others off an upper gallery with a wrought-iron railing. The junior suites are extremely spacious, but even the standard rooms are pleasant. Windows are insulated by double glass but for the greatest quiet, request accommodations upstairs away from the street. All of the bedrooms are nicely decorated in a tasteful, uncluttered, attractive style. They have fresh white walls, wrought-iron-and-wood headboards, good lighting, hand-loomed fabrics, and original paintings by local artists. This is a simple hotel, but provides great value for the amenities offered such as Internet connections in all the rooms, excellent bathrooms, and air conditioning. *Directions:* From the main square, go four blocks on Av. Hidalgo and turn right on Xicotencatl.

CASA SAN FELIPE
Owner: Ernesto Suárez
Xicotencatl No. 212, Col. Centro
Oaxaca 68000, Mexico
Tel & fax: (951) 514-8800
8 rooms, Double: $92–$156
Open: all year, Credit cards: MC, VS
Region: Central–Colonial town
www.karenbrown.com/mex/casasanfelipe.html

The Hostal de la Noria has a prime location just two blocks from the zócalo (main square). From first glance, you see that this handsome, deep-pink-colored 17th-century mansion with white trim and wrought-iron balconies oozes authentic, old-world charm. You walk through the front door into a charming courtyard framed by white marble columns supporting a series of arches. Here you find a flower-bedecked fountain in the center surrounded by many potted plants and attractive wrought-iron tables shaded by white awnings with pretty lacy trim. Guests can dine in the courtyard but there is also a cozy inside dining room with a ceramic tiled floor, beamed ceilings, hanging chandeliers, and attractive French-style chairs. The food is delicious and not expensive. The guestrooms, off the courtyard, have no air conditioning and the decor is a bit dated but all of them are spotlessly clean and comfortable, with many amenities such as marble bathrooms, hairdryers, cable TV, and direct-dial phones. My favorite, 206, a junior suite, is an especially attractive corner room. It has very appealing wood furniture hand-carved by artisans from the state of Michoacán and is further enhanced by light streaming in from windows on two sides. If you are looking for a hotel right in the heart of town with a wonderful faded old-world charm, you'll love the Hostal de la Noria. *Directions:* From the zócalo take Av. Hidalgo for two blocks. The hotel is on a corner on the left.

HOSTAL DE LA NORIA
Manager: Manuel Franco Trueba
Av. Hildago 918
Oaxaca 68000, Mexico
Tel: (951) 516-7844, Fax: (951) 514-3992
50 rooms, Double: $143–$260
Open: all year, Credit cards: all major
Region: Central–Colonial town
www.karenbrown.com/mex/hostaldelanoria.html

The Parador del Dominico is a well-located hotel that can be depended upon for quality and service. The hotel rooms are similar in style and furnishings and although it is perhaps not quite as quaint as some of our other hotel recommendations in Oaxaca, it has the advantage that, whichever room you are in, you are assured of consistent standards. The guestrooms are furnished in a typical hotel style, with wooden headboards, writing tables, and chests of drawers. All offer air conditioning, good lighting, nice bathrooms, mini-bars, satellite TV, direct-dial phones, and room service. Facing onto one of Oaxaca's main streets, the hotel looks the same outside as so many of the town's Colonial-era buildings: an unadorned, one-story, colorful, stuccoed building with windows and doorway bound by stone and an entrance enhanced by antique wrought-iron light fixtures. Not until you step inside does the personality of the hotel appear. The enclosed interior courtyard has a pretty zigzag-patterned brick floor, an old stone well, potted plants, and even a large old shade tree. A contemporary wooden bar tucked against one wall of the courtyard provides refreshments to guests sitting at the modern glass tables and wrought-iron chairs. There is also a restaurant at the front of the hotel with bright-white walls and beams. *Directions:* From the square go east 4 blocks on Ave. Hidalgo to Pino Suárez. Turn left and go to # 410.

PARADOR DEL DOMINICO
Manager: Flor Gomez
Pino Suárez 410
Oaxaca 68000, Mexico
Tel & fax: (951) 513-1812
32 rooms, Double: $126
Open: all year, Credit cards: all major
Region: Central–Colonial town
www.karenbrown.com/mex/paradordominico.html

There seem to be two ways to explore Oaxaca: stay either downtown where you are close to everything but have to put up with the hustle and bustle of city life, or just outside the city limits, in one of the more established and quiet neighborhoods, at a recently renovated hacienda. Both work well, but Hacienda Los Laureles offers a few extras that make it worth the ride into town when you wish to explore. Well-known hotelier Peter Kaiser finally, after years of operating hotels for some of Mexico's finest hotel chains, realized his dream of having his own boutique hotel. Los Laureles is situated around a beautiful garden with majestic trees and colorful flowers. The setting is soothing and relaxing, especially when enjoyed from the hacienda's wide verandah, which leads to the spacious guestrooms. Also overlooking the garden is the restaurant patio, where you can enjoy wonderful meals for breakfast and lunch and gourmet cuisine in the evening. Los Laureles has a small gymnasium as well as a mini-spa offering on-site massage services. After a day of exploring the markets, it's a treat to return for a swim in the pool or even a temazcal cleansing. Oaxaca is wonderful and exciting, but returning to the tranquility offered at Los Laureles at the end of the day makes your visit all the more enjoyable. *Directions:* Best to ask the hotel—they will fax you detailed instructions.

❈ ☎ 🐾 ☕ 💳 ☎ 🗡 🧍 🍸 P 🍴 ≈ 🏞 ♿

HACIENDA LOS LAURELES
Owner: Peter Kaiser
Hidalgo 21
Oaxaca–San Felipe del Agua 68020, Mexico
Tel: (951) 501-5300, Fax: (951) 501-5301
25 rooms, Double: $200–$355*
*Service: 12%, Tax: 17%
Minimum nights required: 3
Open: all year, Credit cards: all major
Region: Central–Colonial town
www.karenbrown.com/mex/haciendalaureles.html

Palenque is a "must-see" site for all who are enthralled by Mayan ruins, so it is not suprising that the Chan-Kah Resort Village (the closest good place to stay near the ruins) is extremely popular—with both individual travelers and tour groups. However, although the hotel is usually bustling with activity, it exudes the personal intimacy of a family-owned hotel. When you first arrive, the Chan-Kah appears to be a normal hotel—but just wait! This is a very special property within 50 acres of ecological reserve: a lush jungle paradise with the Michol River winding through it. Best of all, the rooms are in individual cottages tucked artfully around the grounds. Except for the suites, all of the rooms are identical in configuration. The décor is simple, but the rooms themselves are really nice, with two walls of windows looking out to the dense foliage, two double beds, a stone floor, writing desk, chairs and table, a large bathroom, and a wonderful covered porch with two comfortable rocking chairs. If possible, be sure to request one of the rooms snuggled deepest in the jungle, such as 35, 36, 40–45, and 63–74. All of these are very special, but my very favorite is room 39. When you stay here you feel like Tarzan, high in a treehouse in the jungle. The hotel also has three stunning lagoon-type swimming pools. *Directions:* Follow signs for the ruins. Before you arrive, the hotel is prominently marked on the left side of the road.

❄ ☎ ▦ ☎ P ⫪ ≋

CHAN-KAH RESORT VILLAGE
Manager: Roberto Romano Huerta
Km 3, Carretera Ruinas, Zona Arqueológica
Palenque, Chiapas 29960, Mexico
Tel: (916) 345-1100, Fax: (916) 345-0820
77 rooms, Double: $99–$150
Open: all year, Credit cards: all major
Region: Southeast–Archaeological area
www.karenbrown.com/mex/chankahvillage.html

For years we looked in vain in the wonderful Colonial town of Pátzcuaro for a charming place to stay. At last, in 2001, we discovered a recently-opened gem, the enchanting Casa Brunson. This small bed and breakfast is snuggled next to the Casa de Los Once Patios (a picturesque collection of handicraft shops), just a block off the square. You will fall instantly in love with this fabulous little inn, which exudes charm, quality, and outstanding taste. From the street it looks nondescript but, like so many of the homes built in the 1800s in the classic Colonial style, its beauty is hidden behind massive wooden double doors. Across the spacious entrance is an idyllic patio, highlighted by a stone fountain and an immaculately groomed formal garden, with two guestrooms facing onto it. Each is appealingly decorated with beautiful furniture and the floors, combining both mosaic and tiles, are especially handsome. These two bedrooms are both quite wonderful but unless you are on a tight budget, we highly recommend requesting the suite, which is stunning and worth the splurge. It has a pretty sitting room plus a separate bedroom opening onto its own secluded, romantic garden with ivy-draped walls and a pretty fountain guarded by a stone angel. *Directions:* One block from Don Vasco de Quiroga square. Ask directions for Los Once Patios (Casa Brunson is just beyond the steps that lead to Los Once Patios).

☎ ☕ P 🚭

CASA BRUNSON
Owner: Phyllis Skaglund
Doctor Coss, 13
Pátzcuaro, Michoacán 61600, Mexico
Tel: (434) 342-3903, Fax: none
3 rooms, Double: $100–$135*
*Service: 10%
Minimum nights required: 3
Open: all year
Region: Central–Colonial town
www.karenbrown.com/mex/casabrunson.html

Just a short drive from the picturesque village of Patzcuaro, the Hacienda Mariposas is an intimate, exceptionally appealing small inn, secreted in a serene, 25-acre woodland. What an unexpected pleasure to discover such a rustically deluxe, expertly run inn offering outstanding amenities so far off the beaten path! The main house, with its thick-tile roof, wraparound veranda, ceramic pots of cheerful red geraniums, and aged wood columns, resembles a wonderful old Spanish hacienda. Some of the guestrooms are in this building, while others are in a row of cottages tucked under the towering pines. Whatever room you choose, the accommodations are not only comfortable, but display excellent taste. The décor exudes a rustic elegance with corner fireplaces, beamed ceilings, loomed fabrics, colorful ceramic lamps, wrought-iron beds, fine linens, hand-carved tables, and lovely Talavera-tiled bathrooms. On top of this, the friendly staff (dressed in traditional costumes) pamper guests like royalty and the food is fantastic and beautifully prepared. There is not much structured activity at Hacienda Mariposas, but long walks in the forest, horseback riding, forays into Patzcuaro, and trips to nearby Indian villages and archaeological sites are readily available. Note: Smoking is strictly forbidden anywhere on the property. *Directions:* From Patzcuaro, take the road to Santa Clara de Cobre. About 3 km after the bridge, look for a sign on the left.

❄ ☎ ☕ CREDIT ⛹ 🐎 P ⍩ 🚭

HACIENDA MARIPOSAS
Owner: Rene Ocana Rivera
Km 3.5, Carretera Patzcuaro-Santa Clarea del Cobre
Pátzcuaro, Michoacán 61600, Mexico
Tel: (434) 342-4728, (800) 573-2386 USA
Fax: (707) 575-1166 USA
12 rooms, Double: $110–$222*
*Tax: 17%
Open: all year, Credit cards: all major
Region: Central–Colonial town
www.karenbrown.com/mex/haciendamariposas.html

Dating back to the 17th century, the handsome Hotel Mansión Iturbe has a rich history. In 1830 it was given as a dowry gift by Francisco de Iturbe to his daughter, Paca, when she married Francisco de Arriaga y Peralta and the home has been in the same family ever since that time. It has now been converted into a small hotel, but the interior still reflects its past grandeur. As is typical with these beautiful Colonial buildings, the house sits directly on the street with many of the rooms facing onto an interior garden courtyard with a galleried walkway on the second level. Inside, the Spanish-style décor features heavy carved furniture and walls painted in deep tones of mustard yellow and red. The hotel's most outstanding attribute is its unsurpassable location—it is absolutely center stage, overlooking Pátzcuaro's stunning Plaza Vasco de Quiroga, without a doubt one of the most beautiful squares in Mexico. Best of all, in three bedrooms facing the plaza you can open wide your French doors and step out onto a small wrought-iron balcony to savor the ever-changing scene before you. Because these rooms are less spacious than the others and have smaller bathrooms, they are not considered prime but in my mind these are without a doubt the best. Ask for 11, 12, or 14 (11 is a bit smaller, but has the same view). *Directions:* Facing Plaza Vasco de Quiroga square.

☎ ▬ 🆑 ☎ P 🍴 👤

HOTEL MANSIÓN ITURBE
Owner: Margarita Pedraza Arriaga
Porto Morelos, 59, Plaza Vasco de Quiroga
Pátzcuaro, Michoacán 61600, Mexico
Tel: (434) 342-0368, Fax: none
14 rooms, Double: $85–$110
Open: all year, Credit cards: MC, VS
Region: Central–Colonial town
www.karenbrown.com/mex/mansioniturbe.html

The Camino Real Puebla, situated in the historic center of the beautiful city of Puebla, is housed within a beautiful convent dating back to 1593. It was built by the local priest, Don Leonardo Ruiz de la Peña, to fulfill a promise he made to the Virgin for saving his life after a flood ravaged the city. The Convent of Immaculate Conception allowed into the order only girls who came from families of a pure Spanish bloodline. Their fathers had to pay to have them accepted, and this accounts for why the rooms in the hotel vary so in size—the girls from wealthy families received the largest rooms (these are now the suites), while those whose fathers were less affluent received smaller quarters (now the standard rooms). A few of the guestrooms have some of the original 16th-century frescoes and four have amateurish but quite interesting paintings on the walls that were done by soldiers who were barracked here in 1865. On the rooftop is a Jacuzzi pool and terrace with a great view of the city. My favorite guestroom, 407, is a standard room but quite special and private, with a door opening onto this terrace. The hotel is built around various interior courtyards, the main one enhanced by a large fountain in the middle and surrounded by an arcaded portico, a favorite place to dine on balmy days. There are two dining rooms plus a cozy bar. *Directions:* Just a few blocks from the cathedral, on Calle 7 Poniente, between 16 de Septiembre and Calle 3 Sur.

☎ ✗🖃☎ ᴴ ⅄ P ⅋ 🖼

CAMINO REAL PUEBLA
Manager: Miguel Mestas Torres
7 Poniente 105, Centro Histórico
Puebla 72000, Mexico
Tel: (222) 229-0909, (800) 722-6466 USA
Fax: (222) 232-9251
84 rooms, Double: $190–$243*
*Tax: 17%
Open: all year, Credit cards: all major
Region: Central–Colonial town
www.karenbrown.com/mex/caminorealpuebla.html

The Hotel Colonial, with a prime location one block from Puebla's main square, dates back to 1668 when it was built as a Jesuit monastery. Not only is the mustard-yellow building with white trim and wrought-iron balconies attractive, but it also has another great bonus: it faces onto a pretty cobblestone, pedestrian-only street adorned by a fountain and shade trees. The hotel is not deluxe or sumptuous, but it exudes a quiet air of quality. Officially designated as a three-star hotel, in our estimation the Hotel Colonial soars far above this rating. You enter into a spacious reception foyer whose vaulted ceilings, arched doorways, thick walls, and handsome stone floors attest to the building's origins. The hotel is built around a central courtyard where meals are served at tables with handsome wood-and-leather chairs. A lovely antique stone fountain accents one of the walls and the room is gently illuminated by an exceptionally pretty domed skylight, which has colorful Talavera tiles dividing the sections of glass. Talavera tile is also used on the staircase that leads up to the guestrooms, which are surprisingly spacious and pleasantly decorated in a simple way. Best of all, most of the guestrooms have a small wrought-iron balcony where you can step out and enjoy the view. If you are looking for quality and location at a reason price, you can do no better than the Hotel Colonial. *Directions:* One block south of the main square.

❄ ☎ ⚒ CREDIT ☎ ⛉ Ⴘ Y ¶ ▣

HOTEL COLONIAL
Manager: Maria Luisa Ortiz de Montellano
4 Sur 105
Puebla 72000, Mexico
Tel: (222) 246-4612, Fax: (222) 246-0818
70 rooms, Double: $55
Open: all year, Credit cards: all major
Region: Central–Colonial town
www.karenbrown.com/mex/colonialhotel.html

History whispers from the walls of this 16th-century building, the affable Espinosa family's second hotel in Puebla. Like its sister hotel, Mesón Sacristia de la Compañia, it's in Puebla's centro histórico, perfectly located for walking tours. Antique dealers for four generations, the Espinosas have applied their talent to faithfully restoring the former residence of an aristocratic family to a most extraordinary seven-room hotel. The worn edges of times past lend character to a contemporary palette of white, aquamarine, and citrine on the walls against which the display of antiques and religious artwork is dramatic. All guestrooms are spacious with different layouts and unique furnishings from the family collection. The effect is unexpectedly avant-garde while respecting the building's historic roots. In the hotel's intimate restaurant the food parallels the design—a contemporary interpretation of international classics—and is served in a serene room with a sleek, modern finish. An adjacent small bar features a broad list of specialty tequilas. The hotel also caters to business travelers with rooms equipped with writing desks and coffee makers. *Directions:* Take the Boulevard Hermanos Serdan entrance to Avenida Juárez then drive down the Paseo Bravo to 9 Oriente Street (the other name for Capuchinas).

☎ ☕ ♨ 💳 ☎ 🚶 P 🍴 🍷

MESON SACRISTIA DE CAPUCHINAS
Manager: Leobardo Espinosa
9 Oriente 16
Puebla 72000, Mexico
Tel: (222) 232-8088, Fax: (222) 246-6084
7 rooms, Double: $170–$200*
*Tax: 17%
Open: all year, Credit cards: all major
Region: Central–Colonial town
www.karenbrown.com/mex/sacristiacapuchinas.html

To stay at Mesón Sacristia de la Compañia is to experience the essence of Puebla's history and culture and the warmth of its people. This inn looks like a simple Colonial building with typical terraces and heavy wooden doors, though its deep-blue façade hints at a certain panache of design within (the 18th-century building formerly housed an antique gallery and warehouse). Your hosts will greet you in the reception room to the right, which leads to the still-existing antique gallery beyond. An atrium courtyard cocoons the restaurant, known to offer some of the city's finest Pueblan cuisine, and a small door leads to its amusingly named bar, El Confesionario. One guestroom is located on this level, with another seven suites upstairs. Eclectic and comfortable, all eight rooms differ in layout and colorful decor, with religious relics typically found in sacristies, antiques, and abundant Talavera pottery. It's important to note that live Pueblan music, featured most nights in the bar, drifts up to the rooms. Los Sapos Street is lined with handicraft and antique shops and the hotel is a short half block from the Los Sapos market and two blocks from the much larger El Parian market. *Directions:* Take the Boulevard Hermanos Serdan entrance to Avenida Juárez then drive down the Paseo Bravo to 9 Oriente Street. Take 9 Oriente to Boulevard 5 de Mayo, turn left on Avenida 3 Oriente and turn left again on the Callejon de los Sapos.

☎ ☕ ♨ CREDIT ☎ 🚶 P 🍴 🍷

MESON SACRISTIA DE LA COMPAÑIA
Manager: Leobardo Espinosa
6 Sur 304
Puebla 72000, Mexico
Tel: (222) 242-3554, Fax: (222) 232-4513
8 rooms, Double: $170–$200
Open: all year, Credit cards: all major
Region: Central–Colonial town
www.karenbrown.com/mex/sacristiacompania.html

The Casa Claudia is a fabulous find for those who want to be close to Puerto Vallarta's shopping and colorful restaurants, while being just steps from the beach. Most of Puerto Vallarta's hotels are large, nondescript properties to the north of town, definitely not within walking distance of the center. If you are looking for a super deluxe hotel, these might appeal to you, but this gem of a small, family-run hotel has it all: location, price, and charm. It sits just across from Playa Camarones and has its own laid-back, open-air beach club. The building's style reflects the mood of old Mexico with a stuccoed exterior, red-tiled roof, beamed ceilings, tall palm trees, and traditional furnishings: pretty, hand-crafted wooden furniture, bright, colorful accents, and hand-loomed fabrics. The decor is in excellent taste and the amenities far surpass what you would expect for the price. Each unit has a well-equipped kitchenette with lovely Mexican pottery. All the rooms are inviting, but our favorites are suites 8 and 10—either would make an excellent choice for a long stay in Puerto Vallarta. The three-story complex wraps around a small inner courtyard accented by a free-form swimming pool and a lush lawn studded by palm trees and brightened by colorful plants. *Directions:* From the north, go past the airport and the hotel zone and into town. Turn right at Nicaragua Street (at the Hotel Buenaventura) and go one block. Turn left on Paraguay. The hotel is on your left.

CASA CLAUDIA
Owner: Alejandro Velasco
Paraguay 1290, Col. 5 de Diciembre
Puerto Vallarta, Jalisco 48350, Mexico
Tel: (322) 222-4400, Fax: (322) 222-3630
12 rooms, Double: $100–$170*
*Tax: 17%
Open: all year, Credit cards: MC, VS
Region: Beach–Pacific Coast
www.karenbrown.com/mex/casaclaudia.html

The lavish, Moroccan-style Quinta Real Puerto Vallarta (previously named Hacienda Cora) is located within Marina Vallarta, a beautiful Marina development close to the airport. Though it primarily appeals to those looking for an escape from the hustle and bustle of the city, just minutes away are Puerto Vallarta's wonderful restaurants and nightlife. An 18-hole golf course drapes itself around the hotel, providing privacy and solitude. The hotel's enclosed lobby features tropical plants and pleasant seating arrangements, and adjoining it in the rear is a sitting area—the lobby bar, overlooking the swimming pool. The pool area is the highlight of the hotel: it is surrounded by lush gardens and tall, majestic palms and is set with very comfortable lounge chairs and white-canopied tents that offer shade from the tropical sun. Next to the pool is the gourmet restaurant El Candil, which serves wonderful blends of Mexican and international cuisine. The rooms are spacious and tastefully decorated, with separate sitting areas and in some cases terrace Jacuzzis. Amenities include a gymnasium, tennis courts, and jogging and biking trails, while the marina nearby is great for walking, admiring boats from around the world, and enjoying the shops, cafés, and restaurants. *Directions:* Located a few minutes from the airport. Follow signs south to Puerto Vallarta and take the Marina Vallarta exit. Signs will lead you to the hotel.

❄ ⛼ ▭ ☎ ☖ ⚘ ♦ ❢ ≈ ⚐ ▣ ⚓

QUINTA REAL PUERTO VALLARTA
Manager: Philip Vidal
Calle Pelicanos 311, Marina Vallarta
Puerto Vallarta, Jalisco 48354, Mexico
Tel: (322) 221-0800, (800) 457-4000 USA
Fax: (322) 221-0801
67 rooms, Double: $260–$880*
*Tax: 17%
Open: all year, Credit cards: all major
Region: Beach–Pacific Coast
www.karenbrown.com/mex/haciendacora.html

If you prefer to be on a secluded beach close to Puerto Vallarta yet far removed from its crowds, then the Casa Blanca, about a 20-minute drive north of town, might be just your cup of tea. It is an attractive, two-story white stucco building, with a superb setting right on a beautiful stretch of beach, which houses six two-bedroom, pleasantly decorated apartment-suites, each having two bathrooms, a living room, fully-equipped kitchen, eating area, large balcony, and a view out over the swimming pool in the patio and beyond to the sea. The property extends to a grassy lawn with a quiet terrace perched at the edge of the creamy-white-sand beach. As commodious as these apartments are, what really won our hearts is the honeymoon suite, a very special guestroom in its own small brick cottage topped by a thatched roof. The cottage has its own private terrace, plus its own garden that extends to the edge of the beach. The interior exudes a romantic, charming allure with tiled floors, hand-woven bedspreads, colorful pillows, Talavera lamps, a queen-sized, and Mexican handicraft accents. You also have your own fully-equipped kitchen, but for dining out, there is a wonderful restaurant just across the street from the hotel. At $120 per night, this cottage is a fabulous value. *Directions:* Drive north from Puerto Vallarta, turn left at the first stoplight after the Flamingo golf club then when the road ends, turn right. At Galeana, turn left one block to the hotel.

❄ ⏛ ⚗ 💳 🐴 🍸 ≋ 🤽

CASA BLANCA
Manager: Roberto Velasco
Galeana 12
Puerto Vallarta–Bucerias, Nayarit 63732, Mexico
Tel: (329) 298-0428, Fax: (329) 298-0285
7 suites, Double: $120–$150*
*Tax: 17%
Open: all year, Credit cards: MC, VS
Region: Beach–Pacific Coast
www.karenbrown.com/mex/casablanca.html

Part of the fun of the Majahuitas resort is just getting there! Located on the coast just south of Puerta Vallarta, the hotel is reachable only by boat. It's a beautiful cruise from Boca de Tomatlan, ending at a small cove with a pristine beach backed by jungle and the bungalows of Majahuitas. Don't expect luxury; the facilities are a bit primitive. But, if you've ever dreamed of being shipwrecked on a Robinson Crusoe-style deserted island with someone to pamper you, this is about as close as you can get. There are seven bungalows, each unique in decoration, construction, and location. Our favorite is Los Arcos, a two-bedroom unit close to the beach. Electricity is limited: candles usually are used at night and the shower is heated by coconut husks! Days are spent lazing around, reading that book you've always wanted to finish and working on your tan. When you want to go to town for shopping, the boat is ready to take you there. The food at Mahajuitas is always wonderful, but dinnertime is very special. The beach is lit up with candles and the cocktail hour gives everyone a chance to meet their neighbors and mingle before a feast of the catch of the day and later a bonfire on the beach. *Directions:* Call them first! South of Puerto Vallarta there is a small cove (50 minutes from the airport) called Boca de Tomatlan. Majahuitas staff will pick you up from here or you can take a water taxi (a 15-minute ride).

🛏 🛋 ⚓ 💳 🏋 👫 🐴 🍴 🏄 🔔

MAJAHUITAS
Manager: Livio J. Gonzalez
Playa Majahuitas
Puerto Vallarta–Majahuitas, Jalisco 48399, Mexico
Tel & fax: (322) 221-5808
7 rooms, Double: $325*
*Includes all meals, Tax not included
Open: all year, Credit cards: all major
Region: Beach–Pacific Coast
www.karenbrown.com/mex/majahuitas.html

Casa Las Brisas is truly a treasure. Tucked on a small peninsula about half an hour's drive north of Puerto Vallarta, next door to the super-deluxe Four Seasons Hotel (where golf and tennis privileges can be arranged), the intimate, tastefully decorated Casa Las Brisas offers not only a gorgeous white-sand beach and a lovely swimming pool, but also fabulous dining and genuine warmth of welcome. Best of all, the rate is extremely fair— in our estimation, one of the best values in Mexico. This delightful small inn is owned by Marc Lindskog, your charming host who fell in love with Mexico many years ago and has made it his permanent home. The hotel has just six guestrooms, each individual in size and decoration. All are oceanfront and have handcrafted furniture, patchwork quilts from Hawaii, beautiful tiled bathrooms with huge showers, and terraces overlooking the sea. The pool, positioned by the beach, is the heart of the hotel. Next to the pool is the restaurant where three wonderful meals a day (included in the room rate) are served. Several choices of entrée are available and there is even a special pastry chef. Marc wants each guest to truly feel like a friend in his home, so even drinks are included in the room rate. In addition, each guestroom has a refrigerator stocked with complimentary cold drinks. There is a minimum five-night stay, but you will quickly decide that this is too short. *Directions:* Marc will pick you up at the airport. If driving, call for directions.

CASA LAS BRISAS
Owner: Marc Lindskog
Playa Careyero
Puerto Vallarta–Punta Mita, Nayarit 48324, Mexico
Tel: (322) 306-2122 (cell), Fax: (322) 225-4364
6 rooms, Double: $315*
*All meals & drinks included, Tax: 17%
Open: all year
Region: Beach–Pacific Coast
www.karenbrown.com/mex/casalasbrisas.html

The luxurious Four Seasons is larger than hotels we normally feature, but there is no way we could possibly not share this gem with you. Although it has many guestrooms, the ambiance is one of a small, intimate, boutique hotel. We love it! Don't expect to drop by to "take a look"—security is absolute. You must have a reservation to be admitted through the front gates. This is to protect the privacy of the guests, many of whom are very high-profile. However, the joy is that, once you enter the property and drive through the spectacular manicured grounds, you receive such a warm reception that it would seem you are in a small, family-run hotel. You feel the mood of refined luxury, ultimate quality, and superb décor as soon as you enter. The reception area extends on to become a beautiful lounge with a peaked palapa-style ceiling and a color scheme of creamy beiges and whites accented by a few well-placed sculptures and splendid bouquets of fresh flowers. The guestrooms continue the same degree of quality and refinement. However, my absolute favorites are the rooms in small cottages right on a tiny, palm-studded beach with a crescent of sand just outside your door. Sports are a big deal here, with world-class golf courses, tennis, and all water sports instantly available. *Directions:* Drive north from Puerto Vallarta following signs to Punta Mita. You cannot miss the dramatic entrance to the hotel on the right-hand side of the road.

FOUR SEASONS
Manager: Ricardo Acevedo
Bahía de Banderas
Puerto Vallarta–Punta Mita, Nayarit 33734, Mexico
Tel: (322) 291-6120, (800) 332-3442
Fax: (322) 291-6121
146 rooms, Double: $590–$2750*
*Service: 15%, Tax: 17%
Open: all year, Credit cards: all major
Region: Beach–Pacific Coast
www.karenbrown.com/mex/fourseasonspuntamita.html

Verana is a truly unique resort: a secluded hotel that has an intriguing blend of primitive simplicity and subtle sophistication. A 25-minute drive south from the Puerto Vallarta Airport to the tiny fishing village of Tomatlán, a half-hour speedboat ride to Yelapa (accessible only by sea), followed by a 20-minute hike up a mountainous path through the jungle bring you to a nondescript gate with a small sign, "Verana". As you turn back and look down across the dense foliage, you get a breathtaking view of blue sea with a crescent of beach edged by the colorful village of Yelapa. The hotel has just six guestrooms, four in individual cottages and two sharing one house. Each is unique in style and eclectic in furnishings—some rooms are ultra-modern, some cozy with antique accents—but each is extremely appealing to the eye. All of the bungalows have a close-to-nature mood, but my favorite, the Palapa, is really special. It is like luxury camping, with waist-high stone walls, no windows at all, various levels of sitting and sleeping areas, a large terrace, and a shower open to the stars. Breakfast and a set-menu dinner are included in the room rate and lunch is also available. Meals are served on a terrace with a glorious view of the bay where, in season, whales can often be spotted. Guests enjoy relaxing by the stunning swimming pool, which seems to float over the jungle. *Directions:* You will be picked up by boat at Tomatlán and taken to the resort.

VERANA
Owners: Veronique & Heinz Legler
Yelapa Beach
Puerto Vallarta–Yelapa, Jalisco 48300, Mexico
(800) 677-5156 USA, Fax: none
6 rooms, Double: $320*
*Includes breakfast, dinner & taxes, Service: 10%
Minimum nights required: 5
Open: Nov to mid-July
Region: Beach–Pacific Coast
www.karenbrown.com/mex/verana.html

At the end of an 18-kilometer dirt road, hugging the length of a rocky promontory, is the gorgeous Posada de las Flores (sister hotel to the Posada de las Flores in Loreto). The setting is stunning and the hotel brilliantly designed to maximize bay and water views. Standard rooms are in a cluster of buildings overlooking an attractive rock and cactus garden, while spacious junior suites are found in a one-story building that stretches across a low bluff right at the water's edge. Each suite has a private patio and stone arches in front, which frame a marvelous view of the sea. Definitely splurge and request one of these suites; they are so special that you will be disappointed if you don't. The suites have terra-cotta tile floors, a small sunken sitting area in front of a closed-off fireplace, and large picture windows capturing a magnificent sea view. Coffee and sweet cakes are set out each morning on tables just outside each guestroom. Wrapping around the hotel, a stone terrace set with comfortable teak lounge chairs shaded by white umbrellas looks out to the turquoise-blue water of the bay. Down from the guestrooms is a charming outdoor bar and restaurant with tables set under a protective palapa. On the other side of the restaurant is a beautifully landscaped pool whose water seems almost an extension of the bay. *Directions:* On the east coast of Baja, 48 km north of Mulegé, 54 km south of Santa Rosalia.

❄ ⚓ ☕ 📷 🏋 🍷 P 🍴 🚭 ≈ 🚶 ⚓

POSADA DE LAS FLORES
Owner: Giuseppe Marcelletti
Punta Chivato, Baja Califormia Sur 23880, Mexico
Tel: (615) 153-0188, (877) 245-2860 USA
Fax: (615) 155-5600
20 rooms, Double: $160–$260*
*Includes breakfast & dinner, Tax: 12%
Closed: Sep 9 to Oct 10, Credit cards: VS
Region: Beach–Baja California
www.karenbrown.com/mex/posadapuntachivato.html

La Casa de la Marquesa, located in the heart of Querétaro, is an enchanting, 17th-century palace, richly embellished with an ornately sculpted roofline, windows framed by lavishly carved stone, a family crest above the door, and wrought-iron wall lamps. The legend goes that the original owner fell in love with a beautiful nun who asked him to build the most sumptuous home in Querétaro, La Casa de la Marquesa. You would almost think you have stepped into the palace of a Moorish prince: graceful arches, colorful tiles, wrought-iron balconies, potted plants, enormous chandeliers, giant floral bouquets, lace curtains at the windows, antique furniture, and a dramatic staircase create a mood of amazing splendor. The hotel is built within two lovely homes across the street from each other. Guestrooms are found in both, but those in the second home exude more of an antique ambiance in their furnishings. Snuggled in the courtyard of this second house there is an absolutely charming restaurant with deep-blue walls, an arched colonnade, potted plants, bright-red geraniums, wrought-iron tables, and, in the center, a romantic stone fountain adorned by a gigantic bouquet of fresh flowers. This lovely property is owned by the exceptionally charming Maria del Carmen Gonzalez Cosio de Urquiza, who runs her small inn like a fine home and overlooks no detail to assure guests' comfort. *Directions:* In the historic center. One block west of Jardín Obregon.

LA CASA DE LA MARQUESA
Manager: Juan Pablo Urquiza
Madero 41
Querétaro 76000, Mexico
Tel: (442) 212-0092, Fax: (442) 212-0098
25 suites, Double: $170–$350*
*Tax: 17.5%
Open: all year, Credit cards: all major
Region: Central–Colonial town
www.karenbrown.com/mex/casamarquesa.html

Although this is a sprawling urban area, you find at Querétaro's center a rich Colonial heritage—beautiful churches, centuries-old buildings, tree-lined streets, and pretty little squares replace the modern buildings on the outskirts of town. The Mesón de Santa Rosa, built in the 1700s for horsemen, sits in the heart of the historic center and its romantic charm is immediately apparent. As you enter the lobby there is an intimate, antique-filled parlor to your left and ahead a positively delightful courtyard surrounded by red walls laced with greenery and with a vine-covered trellis above to filter the bright sun. Enhancing the scene are potted plants, tables set with fine linens, and a lovely old stone fountain. Many Spanish-style mansions have not just one, but a series of courtyards, and such is the case with the Mesón de Santa Rosa, where you discover a delightful tile-lined swimming pool, surrounded by potted plants and accented by colorful geraniums, tucked into another courtyard. Most of the simply furnished guestrooms face onto this courtyard and are a bit dark because there is not much sunlight coming through the windows. Another wonderful feature of this small hotel is that just across the street is Independence Square, a jewel of a little park surrounded by charming, arcaded old buildings. *Directions:* In the historic center, facing Independence Square.

☎ 🛴 💳 ☎ 🕴 👭 🍸 P 🍴 ≈ 🖼 🔥 🐾 🍇

MESON DE SANTA ROSA
Owner: Pasquale Del Prete Capasso
Manager: Marco A. Del Prete T.
Pasteur Sur 17, Centro Histórico
Querétaro 76000, Mexico
Tel: (442) 224-2623, Fax: (442) 212 5522
22 rooms, Double: $120–$190*
*Tax: 17.5%
Open: all year, Credit cards: all major
Region: Central–Colonial town
www.karenbrown.com/mex/mesonsantarosa.html

If you want to be right in the middle of the action in Playa del Carmen, you can do no better than stay at El Faro. From morning until night, the beach in front of the hotel is a constant show: people walking up and down, vendors selling souvenirs, children playing, water activities, sunbathers, swimmers. You will never be bored. However, when you want more peace and quiet, you can retreat to the hotel and just observe the show from your lounge chair by the exceptionally beautiful, lagoon-like swimming pool perched above the beach. Next to the pool is a very attractive, open-air, palapa-style restaurant. There is a wide variety of rooms available. The least expensive are cabaña rooms, which are very small and somewhat dark. Unless you are desperately trying to save money, by all means opt for one of the superior rooms or above. If you want to splurge, the oceanfront rooms, right on the beach, are really lovely. The hotel's landmark is a lighthouse on the property, which makes finding the hotel very easy. It also houses a bedroom, which is quite romantic, but very small. El Faro is a lively hotel and when we visited, seemed very popular with young couples. It is definitely very appealing, particularly for those who want to be right on the beach and just a few blocks from the pedestrian-only shopping streets of busy Playa del Carmen. *Directions:* Easy to find as the streets are numbered. Located on Calle 10 Norte where it meets the ocean.

❄ ☎ ⚓ ☕ ⚙ P ⑂ ≈ ⚓

EL FARO
Manager: Bernd Dürrmeir Calle
10 Norte
Riviera Maya–Playa del Carmen
Quintana Roo 77710, Mexico
Tel: (934) 873-0973, (888) 243-7413 USA
Fax: (934) 873-0968
*28 rooms, Double: $110–$210, *Tax: 12%*
Region: Beach–Caribbean Coast
www.karenbrown.com/mex/elfaro.html

If your idea of a Caribbean paradise doesn't include high-rise hotels, when you arrive at the Cancún airport, head straight south to Playa del Carmen. The downtown part of Playa del Carmen is rather congested, but your target, Las Palapas, lies about a kilometer north of the city. There are quite a few places to stay here along a heavenly stretch of soft white-sand beach, which seems to stretch forever, but in our estimation Las Palapas is the star of them all. This isn't an intimate, boutique-style hotel, but a laid-back, moderate-sized complex of one- and two-story rustic, thatched cottages tucked in amongst the palm trees. All of the guestrooms are very pleasant in a simple, uncluttered style and have very nice tiled bathrooms. Rooms do not have TVs, phones, or air conditioning, but who wants to watch television when you can sit under a palapa on one of the most beautiful beaches in the world? And who needs air conditioning when you can open your windows to the fresh ocean breeze? There are several categories of accommodations available, but this is the time to splurge: request one of the seven ocean cottages that sit right on the beach. These don't cost a lot more and are actually a tremendous bargain when you realize you have your own idyllic, romantic cottage steps from the crystal-clear turquoise sea. *Directions:* Located on a road that parallels the sea, about 1 km north of Playa del Carmen.

LAS PALAPAS
Manager: Jacques Novel
Calle 34 North
Riviera Maya–Playa del Carmen
Quintana Roo 77710, Mexico
Tel: (984) 873-0584, Fax: (984) 873-0458
75 rooms, Double: $158–$196*
*Includes breakfast, taxes & tips
Open: all year, Credit cards: all major
Region: Beach–Caribbean Coast
www.karenbrown.com/mex/laspalapas.html

Newly opened in 2002, the Playa Xcalacoco brings new heights of luxurious, understated elegance to the Riviera Maya. There is nothing ostentatious about this beautiful small property: in fact, there is very little about the hotel that hints of any commercialism. No signs boldly point the way; only a privileged few who have secured a reservation in advance will ever find their way to this intimate hotel secreted down a gravel lane in a lush wooded park that stretches to the beach. Once you arrive you are greeted personally by either the exceptionally gracious manager, Nicolás Dominguez, or one of his able assistants. Paths meander through the property to the guestrooms, each an individual villa tucked into the rich foliage with a small private pool in front and beautiful private terrace, your own romantic hideaway. The décor of the bedrooms reflects the kind of quiet simplicity that exudes top quality and refinement. Nothing is cluttered or busy. You have just a king-sized bed with sumptuous linens, a soaring thatched ceiling, beautiful hardwood floors, a cabinet hiding televsion, stereo, and VCR, and a top-of-the-line bathroom with a second shower in the garden. Paths wind down to a splendid stretch of white-sand beach where a beautiful pool and restaurant with gourmet dining complete the scene of perfection. *Directions:* About 3 km north of Playa del Carmen.

❄ ☎ ⚓ ☕ 💳 ☎ 🐎 ⛾ P ⑂ ≈ 🖼 🏄

IKAL DEL MAR
Manager: Nicolás Dominguez
Playa Xcalacoco
Riviera Maya–Playa Xcalacoco
Quintana Roo 77710, Mexico
Tel: (984) 877-3000, (888) 230-7330 USA
Fax: (984) 877-3009
29 suites, Double: $475, Service: 10%, Tax: 12%
Open: all year, Credit cards: all major
Region: Beach–Caribbean Coast
www.karenbrown.com/mex/ikaldelmar.html

With 126 rooms, the Ceiba del Mar, which opened in December 2001, is definitely larger and more contemporary in feel than the properties that we usually include in our guide, but we think it will appeal to many of you looking for a pretty beachfront property away from the crowds. From the moment you enter into the low-rise reception area with its thatched roof and open-air reception lounge, it is obvious from the very attractive furnishings that good taste abounds. A huge, wrought-iron chandelier dominates the room, which is furnished with handsome sofas, chairs, and tables brought from Guadalajara. The guestrooms are located in eight three-story buildings that form a loop around two swimming pools. Each of the buildings is fresh and pretty, with white stucco walls, wood trim, and a thatched roof. All guestrooms are attractively decorated and offer every amenity. One of my favorites, 1832, has an especially romantic view of the turquoise sea. In addition to the swimming pools, each building has a rooftop garden with a Jacuzzi pool for guests. You also find a spa, beauty parlor, bikes for guests, an exercise room, and even a library where guests can check out books or videos for use in the VCRs in the rooms. However, during the day one certainly wouldn't want to sit inside and watch movies with that glorious white-sand beach stretching in front of the hotel! *Directions:* Just at the north end of Puerto Morelos. Well marked with signs.

❄ ☎ ⬆ ☕ CREDIT ☎ 🍴 🍸 P 🍴 🏊 🖼 ⛵ ♿

CEIBA DEL MAR
Manager: José Manuel Ugalde
Av. Niños s/n
Riviera Maya–Puerto Morelos
Quintana Roo 77580, Mexico
Tel: (998) 872-8060, (877) 545-6222
Fax: (998) 872-8061
126 rooms, Double: $285–$515, Tax: 12%
Open: all year, Credit cards: all major
Region: Beach–Caribbean Coast
www.karenbrown.com/mex/ceibadelmar.html

Less than an hour's drive south of Cancún (yet light years away in mood), the Maroma is an intimate, luxurious, beachfront hotel where the pampered guests are known and greeted by their first name. The owners consider the Maroma their home: a home with guestrooms for visiting friends, which is how the tale began. In 1980, your delightful hostess, Sally, made a brief trip from Chicago to Cancún. While there, she fell in love with the gentle beauty of the Caribbean and with José Luis Moreno, who took her to see a gorgeous property he owned with dense jungle growing to the edge of an endless stretch of stunning white-sand beach. Sally and José Luis married and their hideaway cottage grew into a permanent residence, always filled with friends. When rebuilding after a devastating hurricane in 1988, it seemed the perfect opportunity to add more bedrooms and transform Maroma into a hotel. Guestrooms are individual in decor, yet all exude a quiet, tasteful, rustic appeal, with native handicrafts used throughout. Hammocks swing lazily from the porch or balcony, enticing one to forget the cares of the world. The beach is superb and studded by small palapas, which shade comfortable lounge chairs. Nearby you find a lovely swimming pool, an open-air restaurant, and an elegant, gourmet restaurant with truly outstanding food. *Directions:* Included in the room rate is a transfer from the Mérida airport. If driving, ask for detailed instructions.

❄ ☎ ⚒ CREDIT P ⛶ ≈ ⚓

MAROMA
Owners: Sally & Jose Luis Moreno
Riviera Maya–Punta Maroma
Quintana Roo 77501, Mexico
Tel: (998) 872-8200, Fax: (998) 872-8220
36 rooms, Double: $360–$630*
* Service: 10%, Tax: 12%
Open: all year, Credit cards: all major
Region: Beach–Caribbean Coast
www.karenbrown.com/mex/maroma.html

If you yearn for a thatched hut facing an idyllic white-sand beach studded with coconut palms, the Cabañas la Conchita is your dream come true. However, this bit of paradise is not for everyone: you must be young at heart and have a bit of a bohemian spirit since the guestrooms have no phones, no air conditioning and the lights come on only briefly for a couple of hours in the late afternoon, generated from a solar panel. The flip side is that when you arrive at the Cabañas la Conchita, you leave the real world far behind and fall into a routine of pure bliss, doing nothing more than reading a good book, napping under the palapa on the beach, swimming in the crystal-clear turquoise water, and enjoying evenings by candlelight. This tiny, romantic hotel is owned by Cynthia James and Jorgé Rosales, who originally intended it to be their vacation hideaway, but people kept begging to rent space on their beach, so the idea of a proper inn just evolved. Gifted local craftsmen replaced the decrepit shacks with beautifully built, sturdy, thatched-roofed cottages. The simple guestrooms exude the perfect blend of comfort, style, and simplicity, thanks to Cynthia's artist's eye for color and fabrics. All the cottages are steps from the sea, but the prize is number 1, right on the beach. *Directions:* Just south of the Tulum archaeological site. At the junction to Cobá, turn left to the beach and at the end of the road turn right. The hotel is on the left after 1 km.

CABAÑAS LA CONCHITA
Owners: Cynthia James & Jorgé Rosales
5 Km, Carretera Tulum-Boca Paila
Riviera Maya–Tulum, Quintana Roo 77780, Mexico
Tel: none, Fax: (415) 680-2394 USA
8 rooms, Double: $85–$135*
*Includes breakfast & all taxes
Open: all year
Region: Beach–Caribbean Coast
www.karenbrown.com/mex/cabanasconchita.html

Stretched along the splendid coast between San José del Cabo and Cabo San Lucas there is a breathtaking choice of sumptuous hotels, most of which are very, very expensive. However, there is one remarkable exception: the Cabo Surf, which is not only well priced, but also has a fantastic location. This was previously a private home, which perhaps accounts for its privileged position on the bluff overlooking Acapulquito, a world-class surfing beach. The original house, an attractive white-stucco building, has a reception area, a small parlor, and a large open lounge extending out to a spacious terrace restaurant-bar partially covered with a thatched roofed. Here guests sip a cool drink or dine to the sound of the surf while enjoying an incredible view of the sea. In this main building you find two very spacious guestrooms with great balconies and lovely views. The other guestrooms are located in an adjacent, two-story wing. Those on the top floor have the choice views, my favorites being rooms 3 and 4. Tall palms dot the grounds and nestled on a terrace is an idyllic swimming pool with an infinity edge creating the illusion that the water blends into the sea. Lounge chairs dot the lawn around the pool where you can relax and watch some of the finest surfers in the world just below you. *Directions:* The hotel is signposted near km. 28 on the coastal highway between San José del Cabo and Cabo San Lucas.

CABO SURF HOTEL
Owner: Mauricio Balderrama
Carretera Transpeninsular, Km. 28, Playa Acapulquito
San José del Cabo, Baja California Sur 22676, Mexico
Tel: (624) 142-2666, Fax: (624) 142-2676
10 rooms, Double: $150–$175*
*Service: $4.00 a day, Tax: 12%
Open: all year, Credit cards: all major
Region: Beach–Baja California
www.karenbrown.com/mex/cabosurfhotel.html

For a charming, intimate hotel in the heart of San José del Cabo, you can do no better than the Casa Natalia, which boasts a restaurant so outstanding that guests from many of the super-exclusive resorts nearby come here to dine. The hotel is owned by Natalie and Loic Tenoux, from Luxembourg and France respectively, who combine the colorful ambiance of Mexico with the quiet elegance of Europe in their small inn. From the street you see a simple, squarish, beige-colored building and it is not until you step inside that the appeal of the hotel is revealed. After passing through the foyer, you come to a small sitting area to the left with white slipcovered sofas splashed with color by brightly embroided pillows and colorful ceramics set on simple wooden tables. An outdoor thatched-roofed bar extends to the dining terrace, which is studded with tall palm trees. Guestrooms are in several buildings forming one side of a walled garden, which features an especially attractive half-circle swimming pool embraced by tall, pillarlike palm trees. All of the individually-decorated bedrooms exude a charming Mexican ambiance with loomed fabrics, embroidered pillows, hand-crafted wooden furniture, hand-carved sconces or lamps, original artwork, and luxurious amenities. No detail has been overlooked to pamper the guests. All of the guestrooms have balconies and the two suites have Jacuzzi tubs. *Directions:* On main street in downtown San José del Cabo

CASA NATALIA
Owners: Nathalie & Loic Tenoux
Boulevard Mijares N.4
San José del Cabo, Baja California Sur 23400, Mexico
Tel: (624) 142-5110, (888) 277-3814 USA
Fax: (624) 142-5100
18 rooms, Double: $225–$350*
*Service: $5, Tax: 12%
Open: all year, Credit cards: all major
Region: Beach–Baja California
www.karenbrown.com/mex/casanatalia.html

When wealthy sports fishermen first discovered Cabo, the Hotel Palmilla was one of the original luxury hotels built along this fabled tip of Baja. It has aged with grace and remains the grande dame of them all, exuding a quiet, old-world elegance that the newer properties cannot match. Surrounded by manicured grounds, the low-rise building has a Spanish feel with its white façade, red-tiled roof, watchtower, arches, and dramatic stone fountain at the entrance. The hotel sits on a gentle rise overlooking the sea and has a lovely swimming pool meandering through the gardens. Guests need never move from this idyllic oasis since a bar and casual palapa-style restaurant are available, though there is also an elegant restaurant for formal dining. Comfortable lounge chairs are strategically positioned on the lush green lawn dotted by tall, swaying palms where you can relax in utter tranquility overlooking the surging sea. A path winds down to the beach, which has secluded nooks for sunbathing cleverly tucked in amongst the boulders. The luxurious guestrooms, located in nine separate buildings, are all very large and offer the ultimate in good taste plus all amenities of the best quality. The suites with large terraces overlooking the coast are especially outstanding. Golfers will enjoy the Jack Nicklaus golf course next door. *Directions:* The hotel is signposed near Km. 1 on the coastal highway between San José del Cabo and Cabo San Lucas.

HOTEL PALMILLA
Manager: Gonzalo Franyutti
Km 1, Carretera Transpeninsular
San José del Cabo, Baja California Sur 23400, Mexico
Tel: (624) 144-5000, Fax: (624) 144-5100
115 rooms, Double: $430–$1295*
*Service: 15%, Tax: 12%
Minimum nights required: 3
Open: all year, Credit cards: all major
Region: Beach–Baja California
www.karenbrown.com/mex/palmilla.html

The Antigua Villa Santa Monica is truly a treasure, a marvelous, intimate hotel exuding friendliness, refinement, charm, and excellent taste in a quiet, unostentatious manner. This enchanting 200-year-old villa, once the home of Mexico's famous opera singer, Padre José Mohica, has just 14 rooms, some around the flower-filled courtyard and others opening onto the garden near the swimming pool. All vary in size and décor, but all have a similar romantic ambiance, with wrought-iron beds, tiled floors accented by Indian rugs, beamed ceilings, richly hued walls, abundant use of colorful hand-made tiles, beautiful Talavera lamps, and handsome loomed fabrics used as bedspreads and draperies To top it all off, all rooms but one have a cozy, wood-burning fireplace. My very favorite master suite, 12, is fabulous, with a king-sized bed, huge bathroom, and private patio. If you prefer a standard room, 3 is delightful, with a queen-sized canopy bed and doors opening to a large terrace. The hotel is also famous for its restaurant where guest dine in casual elegance around a gorgeous flower-filled courtyard with the song of birds in fanciful cages serenading the guests and the gentle tinkling of a stone fountain banked by tiers of colorful potted plants. *Directions:* Opposite Benito Juárez Park near the center of town.

⊟ 💳 P ¶ ≋

ANTIGUA VILLA SANTA MONICA
Manager: Pedro Perez
Baeza 22
San Miguel de Allende 37700, Mexico
Tel: (415) 152-0247, Fax: (415) 152-0518
*14 rooms, Double: $180–$230**
**Tax: 17%*
Open: all year, Credit cards: all major
Region: Central–Colonial town
www.karenbrown.com/mex/villasantamonica.html

Because of San Miguel de Allende's strict building regulations, protecting the Colonial charm of the town, Casa de Sierra Nevada consists of six renovated mansions located close to one another near the downtown area. This only adds to the appeal of the hotel, where the reception is on one side of the street, the restaurant on the other, your room perhaps a few doors up the street, and the fully-equipped spa a few doors down! The most recently added guestrooms are slightly out of town (but within walking distance) in another superbly renovated mansion near a park. For years the hotel has been famous for its distinct décor and design, with antiques and handicrafts from around Mexico, and it is also well known for its fine cuisine: gourmet at the central restaurant and excellent Mexican dining at the park location. Breakfast is most enjoyable poolside at another small restaurant with a wonderful view of Allende's famous church steeple. The Casa de Sierra Nevada was founded many years ago by Peter Wirth (whose family owns the stunning Hassler Hotel in Rome). His idea (at the time quite unique) of an intimate, charming, antique-filled hotel snuggled within a graceful, romantic Colonial building has spread throughout Mexico. Casa de Sierra Nevada is now part of the prestigious Quinta Real affiliation. *Directions:* The hotel has two sections, one facing Benito Juárez Park, the other 3 blocks from the square.

CASA DE SIERRA NEVADA
Owners: Marta & James Sprowls
Hospicio 35
San Miguel de Allende 37700, Mexico
Tel: (415) 152-2337, 800-457-4000 USA
Fax: (415) 152-7040
37 rooms, Double: $185–$370*
*Tax: 17%
Open: all year, Credit cards: all major
Region: Central–Colonial town
www.karenbrown.com/mex/casadesierranevada.html

If you are looking for an impeccably kept bed and breakfast with romantic charm, lovely gardens, gorgeous swimming pool, unbeatable location, and warmth of welcome, you will find nowhere better than the Casa Schuck Boutique B&B. It is truly a jewel, with amazingly low rates for such quality. Like so many beautiful old Colonial homes, the exterior gives little hint of the beauty inside, but behind the thick front door you discover a charming, flower-filled garden courtyard whose lower terrace gives onto some of the guestrooms and a dining room. If you are staying for a while, I recommend requesting one of the upstairs suites, which are exceptionally spacious, some with large balconies, others a terrace, and definitely a bargain. My favorite is the suite just above the swimming pool. Speaking of swimming pools, this one is really a dream: cozily tucked into an old stone wall and bounded on one side by a carved balustrade, it is enhanced by masses of potted geraniums, has a dear statue of Mary and baby Jesus, and, to top it off, is guarded by a friendly lion sculpture. The Casa Schuck is not a hotel, so if you are looking for the amenities of a deluxe resort and decorator-perfect décor, this might not be for you, but it is a rare find for those looking for charm, quality, and location. *Directions:* Located 4 blocks southeast of El Jardín (the main plaza). There is an excellent map on their website; link through www.karenbrown.com.

CASA SCHUCK BOUTIQUE B&B
Owner: Susan Cordelli-Easter
Garita 3
San Miguel de Allende 37700, Mexico
Tel & fax: (415) 152-0657
6 rooms, Double: $115–$165*
*Tax: 2%
Open: all year
Region: Central–Colonial town
www.karenbrown.com/mex/casaschuck.html

For a a small, moderately priced hotel with a superb location, the Posada Carmina makes an excellent choice. This is not a deluxe hotel, but exudes the flavor and charm of old San Miguel de Allende. It was built in the 18th century as a private house with the same stone as that used in the nearby cathedral. The exterior is a square, mustard-colored building with tall windows crowned by carved stone and enhanced by small wrought-iron balconies. As with many Colonial-style buildings, once you step into the lush enclosed courtyard, the appealing heart of the hotel, the mansion's magic is revealed. The courtyard is highlighted by a lovely old stone fountain adorned with potted geraniums, while walls laced by colorful bougainvillea, potted orange trees, wrought-iron chairs, and round tables shaded by white umbrellas complete the romantic scene. Most guests choose to dine here but there is also an interior restaurant tucked into the former stables. The simple, old-fashioned guestrooms are located off the arcaded walkway around the courtyard. Windows in the doors opening to the patio provide the light for many of the bedrooms, but my favorites are the few rooms that face outside and have windows with an exterior view. Some of the bedrooms have a few accents of antique furnishings, but by and large the appeal of this hotel is in its wonderful location, fabulous interior courtyard, and old-world charm. *Directions:* Half a block south of the main square.

POSADA CARMINA
Manager: Rodrigo Garcia
Cuna de Allende 7
San Miguel de Allende 37700, Mexico
Tel: (415) 152-8888, Fax: (415) 152-1036
12 rooms, Double: $85–$120*
*Tax: 17%
Open: all year
Region: Central–Colonial town
www.karenbrown.com/mex/posadacarmina.html

Tucked in the hills above San Miguel de Allende, La Puertecita has an air of seclusion yet is within walking distance of town (though you might want to take a cab for your return uphill). La Puertecita is a contemporary stucco-and-stone building accented by a series of arches that form a canopy stretching over the parking area. You can see from the outside that everything is meticulously kept, but it is not until you walk down the steps into the hotel that its lush beauty is revealed. The property slopes gently down a wooded hillside, accented by terraces and lovely gardens. The especially attractive restaurant not only serves fabulous cuisine, but is perfectly positioned to take the ultimate advantage of this beautiful landscape. One of the two swimming pools is near the restaurant on a terrace surrounded by gardens. The accommodations are found in various buildings, some in condominum apartments, which offer more space, including kitchenettes. However, my favorite by far is a romantic little cottage tucked away all by itself. It looks like a fairy-tale house with its white-stuccoed façade laced with ivy and climbing roses, a red-tiled overhang above the entrance, a carved wooden door, a whimsical circular window, and even its own little birdbath. Inside, the décor is most attractive, with a terra-cotta floor, handsome carved headboard, rustic wood furniture, and hand-loomed fabrics. *Directions:* Ask for driving instructions.

LA PUERTECITA
Owner: John Kay
Manager: Donato Ortega
Santo Domingo 75
San Miguel de Allende 37740, Mexico
Tel: (415) 152-5011, Fax: (415) 152-5505
35 rooms, Double: $160–$420*
*Tax: 17%
Open: all year, Credit cards: all major
Region: Central–Colonial town
www.karenbrown.com/mex/puertecita.html

Villa Rivera, wonderfully located for exploring the streets and central plaza of San Miguel de Allende, is situated just a block from the town's famous Arcángel Church and surrounded by shops, boutiques, and great restaurants. This intimate, well-run hotel, blending contemporary elements and rustic furnishings, was previously a private residence and reflects the homey ambiance of its heritage with just 12 guestrooms. The heart of the inn is a perched garden terrace highlighted by beds of well-tended flowers, mature shade trees, and a delightful swimming pool. This terrace is snuggled into the walls that back up to the Arcángel Church and captures fabulous views of the town and church towers. Facing onto this appealing garden is a charming restaurant serving a fusion of Italian and Mexican cuisine. The guestrooms on the upper floor of the hotel give splendid views of the church and town, while the other bedrooms are well situated next to the pool and garden. Most rooms have a fireplace. The owners have lovingly decorated each room in a personal style with a liberal use of local handicrafts. San Miguel de Allende, registered as a national monument, has been superbly preserved as the thriving silver town it once was. It is one of Mexico's loveliest Colonial cities, with its old mansions and flower-filled patios making strolling along the winding cobblestone streets a delightful activity in itself. *Directions:* One block from the main square.

VILLA RIVERA
Owner: Jesús Manuel Calvo
Cuadrante 3
San Miguel de Allende 37700, Mexico
Tel & fax: (415) 152-2289, (800) 024-4789 USA
12 rooms, Double: $160–$220*
*Tax: 17%
Open: all year, Credit cards: all major
Region: Central–Colonial town
www.karenbrown.com/mex/villarivera.html

Taxco is a Colonial town clinging to a hillside with narrow cobblestoned streets twisting in a maze-like fashion up the steep incline. The fun of being here is to be right in the heart of town where you can experience what Taxco was like in all its glory in the 16th century when the Spanish achieved enormous wealth from the silver mines. The delightful Hotel Santa Prisca is perfectly located only a few minutes' walk from the cathedral, just off the Plaza de San Juan. This is not a deluxe hotel, but a simple one that is freshly painted, immaculately kept, and exudes remarkable taste and charm for its modest price. The exterior is white with black wrought-iron trim. Inside, the mood is set by a cheerful color scheme of white, blue, and bright yellow. As you enter there is a small reception area and, just beyond, a charming dining room which is as pretty as can be with large windows letting in lots of sunlight and brightly painted yellow chairs set around tables covered with fresh white cloths adorned by fresh flowers. Most of the guestrooms face onto a central garden courtyard with a fountain in the middle. The standard rooms are quite small, but if you request one of the two suites (which are a great value), you will be treated to a large room and a stunning view out over the whitewashed buildings and red-tiled roofs to the magnificent spires and dome of the cathedral. *Directions:* Two blocks from Plaza Border. Ask hotel for directions.

☎ 🍴 💳 P ¶

HOTEL SANTA PRISCA
Manager: Maria Elena Ocampo
Cena Obscuras 1, Plaza de San Juan
Taxco, Guererro 40200, Mexico
Tel: (762) 622-0080, Fax: (762) 622-2938
31 rooms, Double: $46–$65
Open: all year, Credit cards: all major
Region: Central–Colonial town
www.karenbrown.com/mex/santaprisca.html

Perhaps you have never heard of Tlaxcala—it isn't well known as a tourist destination but you should put it on your priority list of places to see. If you like Colonial towns, you will be instantly captivated: Tlaxcala is a real jewel. Happily, it also has an excellent hotel, the Posada San Francisco, which exudes great old-world ambiance and charm. Its location is perfect, facing onto the gorgeous Plaza de la Constitución, one of the most beautiful in all of Mexico, and, in keeping with the other architectural masterpieces that line the square, the oldest sections of the Posada San Francisco date back to the 16th century. It is a two-story, handsome stone building with arched windows and doorway. Whereas the exterior has a somber appeal, as soon as you enter into the large lobby, formerly an interior courtyard, the mood changes to a joyous one with bright-yellow walls, a terra-cotta floor, a fountain, bouquets of flowers, and sun streaming in through a ceiling of stained glass. An arched passage leads to an inviting restaurant with dark-green wicker tables and chairs, bright-yellow table linens, yellow walls, and a skylight for its ceiling. (Another restaurant upstairs overlooks the plaza.) As you continue on, you come to a garden courtyard and a large swimming pool, around which you find most of the guestrooms. Rooms on the first floor have French doors opening to the pool area and those on the second floor have balconies. *Directions:* Facing the main square.

☎ 🏌 ☕ 💳 🛎 🐎 🍸 P 🍴 🏊 🚶 🖼 🐾 ♿

POSADA SAN FRANCISCO
Manager: Minerva Flores Mendez
Plaza de la Constitución 17
Tlaxcala, Tlaxcala 90000, Mexico
Tel: (246) 462-6402, Fax: (246) 462-6818
68 rooms, Double: $90–$145
Open: all year, Credit cards: all major
Region: Central–Colonial town
www.karenbrown.com/mex/posadasanfrancisco.html

Libusche and Juerg Wiesendanger left successful careers in Zurich and moved to Mexico with the goal of creating a small, deluxe inn offering the fine food and accommodations, combined with personal attention and charm. They built their dream a ten-minute drive from the quaint town of Todos Santos, taking great care not to disturb the natural beauty of the pristine natural wonderland they found. The restaurant, headed by a top-notch chef, serves a creative blend of Mexican and Swiss cuisine in an attractive dining room with potted plants, a whimsically painted fireplace, windows capturing a view of the sea, and walls adorned with original paintings by Libusche, who is a very talented artist. In warm weather, most guests dine outside on a large terrace, looking out through the cactuses and palm trees to the lagoon and beyond to the sea. The seven guestrooms, located in two adjacent buildings, are all beautifully appointed and have excellent bathrooms. The décor takes advantage of the many beautiful Mexican fabrics but the fine linens and pillows were brought from Switzerland. The two master suites, each with a Jacuzzi right outside the room, are especially nice. All rooms have air conditioning, CD players, refrigerators, direct-dial phones, and even binoculars—but no TVs. Guests enjoy a magnificent large swimming pool and birdwatchers in particular delight in the estuary, which is a natural sanctuary. *Directions:* On the coast. Ask for directions.

POSADA LA POZA
Owners: Libusche & Juerg Wiesendanger
Todos Santos, Baja California Sur 23305, Mexico
Tel: (612) 145-0400, Fax: (612) 145-0453
7 rooms, Double: $140–$510*
*Tax: 12%
Open: all year, Credit cards: MC, VS
Region: Baja–Eco resort
www.karenbrown.com/mex/posadalapoza.html

When you arrive at the Todos Santos Inn, you will be warmly greeted by your gracious host, Robert Whiting. His experience working at hotels inspired him to open his own small inn, though it wasn't easy to find just the right piece of property, in just the right spot, at just the right price. An article in Travel & Leisure alerted him to the great potential of Todos Santos, a tiny, low-key village in Mexico with old-world character, lovely weather, art galleries, great restaurants, colorful boutiques, low-cost real estate, and a beach nearby, but, best of all for him, there was no good hotel. So in the mid-1990s Robert moved to Todos, bought a 19th-century hacienda in the middle of town, and went to work. All of his efforts have paid off brilliantly. The derelict but once-grand, old brick home has been transformed with great sensitivity into a charming small inn. The two standard guestrooms are in the original part of the house, while the other four are air-conditioned garden suites located in two buildings built with such skill that you would never know they were new. All of the spacious rooms exude great taste, with terra-cotta floors, beamed ceilings, hand-carved furniture, heavy French doors, Oriental rugs, antique prints on the walls, great bathrooms accented with Talavera tiles, and very comfortable beds. *Directions:* Three blocks off the main square.

TODOS SANTOS INN
Owner: Robert Whiting
Calle Legaspi #33
Todos Santos, Baja California Sur 23305, Mexico
Tel & fax: (612) 145-0040
6 rooms, Double: $95–$135*
*Tax: 12%
Closed: mid-Aug to mid-Oct
Region: Baja–Eco resort
www.karenbrown.com/mex/todossantosinn.html

Uruapan is well known as the avocado capital of the world, but the congested downtown area is not too pretty and lacks any historical ambiance. However, the pine-covered hills surrounding Uruapan are lovely and on the outskirts of town is a real prize—the 1315-acre Eduardo Ruiz Parque Nacional, a wooded natural preserve with countless sparkling clear springs that form the source of the Cupatitzio River. The Hotel Mansión has a prime setting just on the edge of the park, capturing views of it from the large windows of the charming dining room. The architecture of the mansion mimics the Colonial style and has a charming rustic appeal. Mexican handicrafts and regional artwork decorate the walls and are used throughout in the furnishings. The bedrooms are spacious, bright, and cheerful, with large windows looking out to the garden, and all have very attractive fine, dark-wood furniture hand-painted with birds and other popular native motifs. All the rooms have satellite TVs, telephones, safes, hairdryers, and radios. The hotel, which wraps around a splendid central garden highlighted by a very large swimming pool, is justifiably famous for its gardens, which are outstanding—no matter what the season, you find gorgeous beds of flowers and hanging plants everywhere. The flower theme continues throughout the hotel with fresh flowers in all the rooms. *Directions:* On the northwest edge of town, next to the Parque Nacional.

HOTEL MANSIÓN DEL CUPATITZIO
Owner: Manuel Montoy Gómez
Km 2.3, Carretera a Huetamo, Parque Nacional
Uruapan, Michoacán 60000, Mexico
Tel: (452) 523-2060, Fax: (452) 524-6772
57 rooms, Double: $98–$250*
*Tax: 17%
Open: all year, Credit cards: all major
Region: Central–Colonial town
www.karenbrown.com/mex/mansioncupatitzio.html

The Lodge at Uxmal is blessed with an unsurpassable location, just across from the archaeological site. However, location is not all this hotel has to offer; it's a real charmer in every way. Your introduction begins when the receptionist, dressed in colorful Mayan costume, welcomes you in an open-air, thatched-roof palapa. The Mayan theme continues in the cluster of five two-story, brightly colored, thatched-roof buildings that house the guestrooms. All of the accommodations are appointed with materials of the finest quality throughout. The woodwork is especially remarkable—highly polished hardwood floors, beautiful cabinetry, and handsome louvered plantation shutters. My favorite rooms are the corner units and my favorite buildings are those overlooking the lakelike swimming pool (there is a second pool located near the restaurant). Because of its strategic location so close to the ruins, the Lodge is naturally a target for busloads of tourists who come to eat lunch in its open-air restaurant. This is really no problem, since if you have a room overlooking the pool, you are ensured tranquility. In addition to being such a lovely small hotel, the Lodge has another super advantage: you can visit Uxmal first thing in the morning before the buses arrive then return to the hotel in the heat of the day to relax by the comfort of the pool. *Directions:* The inn is directly across from the entrance to the ruins.

LODGE AT UXMAL
Manager: Angel Amador Cortazar
Zona Arqueologica
Uxmal, Yucatán 97840, Mexico
Tel: (997) 976-2012, (800) 235-4079 USA
Fax: (997) 976-2011
40 rooms, Double: $160*
*Tax: 17%
Open: all year, Credit cards: all major
Region: Yucatán Peninusula–Archaeological area
www.karenbrown.com/mex/lodgeuxmal.html

For those who want to delve in depth into the rich history of the Spanish conquest of Mexico, then Veracruz, which still exhibits its Spanish heritage, is a key city to visit. It was here that Cortés landed in 1519 and, after burning his ships to discourage his soldiers from trying to return home, made his first settlement in the New World. The best place to stay in town is the Fiesta Inn, which opened in 2001, a modern, four-story hotel whose architecture conveys a vague Spanish feel with its stucco walls, red-tiled roof, and balconies. Inside, the hotel exudes a quiet, soothing, contemporary ambiance with cream-colored marble floors, indirect lighting, tasteful furnishings, and fabrics in tones of creams and rusts. You enter into a spacious lobby with a restaurant to the right offering a choice of quick buffet-style meals or à-la-carte menu selections. The hotel caters both to businessmen with its business center and conference facilities, and to families with its beautiful large swimming pool and children's playroom. Even though the Fiesta's amenities are first-rate, its finest attribute is its setting. Not only are you just steps from most of the major sights in town, but you are also right on the promenade that runs along the waterfront—a prime location that offers splendid views from many of the bedrooms (be sure to ask for a room with a balcony that looks out to the harbor, such as 426, 428, or 430). *Directions:* In the historic center, next to the bay.

❄ 🤿 💳 ☎ 🛗 🍽 P ≈ 🖼

FIESTA INN
Manager: Raul Rodriguez
General Figueroa 68, Paseo del Malecón
Veracruz 91709, Mexico
Tel: (229) 923-1500, Fax: (229) 923-1509
92 rooms, Double: $185–$250
Open: all year, Credit cards: all major
Region: Southeast–Colonial town
www.karenbrown.com/mex/fiestainn.html

Most tourists who are attracted to Villahermosa have a very special interest in archaeology since it is conveniently close to the extraordinary archaeological site of Palenque and has two excellent archaeological museums. One of these, Parque Museo de la Venta, is located within a pretty park that also has an outdoor museum displaying colossal Olmec stone carved heads. This is one of the prettiest parts of Villahermosa and, happily, the most charming hotel in town, the Hotel Cencali, is nearby. Although of contemporary construction, the hotel uses a brilliant Mayan color scheme and in the lobby huge, bold murals of Indian mythology cover the walls, surrounding an intimate sitting area. Steps lead down to a lower level where you find the dining room, La Isla, its walls of glass looking out to a particularly delightful swimming pool in a lush, jungle-like setting, with mango, cocao, and palm trees stretching to the edge of Las Ilusiones Lagoon. (This is the same lagoon that meanders through the park where you find the Olmec carved heads.) All of the attractive guestrooms are spacious and similar in décor, with built-in headboards, color-coordinating drapes and bedspreads, good lighting, and comfortable beds. By far the most attractively located bedrooms are those in the back with a balcony overlooking the lagoon (such as rooms 229, 231, 233, 235, 237)—be sure to ask for one of these. *Directions:* Facing the lagoon near Parque Museo de la Venta.

❄ ☎ ☕ 🧺 CREDIT ☎ P ⚟ ≋ 🖼

HOTEL CENCALI
Manager: Jorge Bacha Padilla
Juárez y Paseo Tabasco
Villahermosa, Tabasco 86040, Mexico
Tel: (993) 315-1999, Fax: (993) 315-6600
113 rooms, Double: $100–$112*
*Tax: 17%
Open: all year, Credit cards: all major
Region: Southeast–Archaeological area
www.karenbrown.com/mex/hotelcencali.html

Until the Chicanná Ecovillage opened in 1995, there weren't any good accommodations near the newly accessible, fascinatng archaeological treasures of Río Bec. In fact, the roads in this remote area were so bad that one had to be truly motivated to dare to make the trip. All that has changed. The roads are good and a few more hotels are coming on the scene, but none can surpass the central location of the Chicanná Ecovillage. The developers indeed displayed great foresight in putting such excellent accommodations in an area where there was no tourism and is even now almost unknown. This is not a deluxe, trendy resort; nor is it meant to be. Instead, what you find is a pleasingly casual complex of pastel-hued, thatched cottages tucked in a jungle-like setting. Some of the cottages are one-story with two guestrooms, others are two-story with four guestrooms. There is no air conditioning, just ceiling fans, and rooms on the upper level have more of a breeze. Each spacious bedroom is nicely furnished, has a very good bathroom, comfortable beds, and its own private deck or terrace. Paths meander about the property, one of them going to a small swimming pool, which has real allure for guests after a day of sightseeing. This is a casual hotel—no need to dress up for dinner in the thatched-roofed restaurant. *Directions:* On 186, between Escárcega and Chetumal, just west of Xpujil.

☎ 🛵 💳 🚶 P 🍴 🏊

CHICANNÁ ECOVILLAGE
Manager: Richardo Trueba
Km. 144, Carretera Escárcega-Chetumal
Xpujil, Campeche 24000, Mexico
Tel: (981) 816-2233, Fax: (983) 871-6075
32 rooms, Double: $115
Open: all year, Credit cards: all major
Region: Yucatán Peninsula–Eco resort
www.karenbrown.com/mex/chicannavillage.html

This wonderful hotel, located in the rather less-visited town of Zacatecas, may well be the most spectacular boutique hotel in all of Mexico. It was built within an old stone bullring just on the outskirts of the historic central area of this once-thriving mining town. Today the town is delightful, with narrow, winding streets lined with recently restored Colonial classic buildings. The small chain of Quinta Real hotels prides itself on offering very personalized service, gourmet cuisine, and fine examples of hotel design and architecture. Each property is unique, with this impressive hotel certainly being the most extraordinary of the group. The architect was a master at combining old and new: built into the surrounding walls of the bullring are the bedrooms, the lobby, and a gourmet restaurant, all situated to take in the wonderful views of this ancient structure. Even more unique is the bar, situated on the ground level looking out over the ring, which uses what were once the bullpens for small sitting areas. Dining at any Quinta Real restaurant is always a pleasure but the view, the setting, and, of course, the cuisine, make this dining experience truly wonderful, especially when the ring and its walls are lit up at night. The Quinta Real is so special that it definitely warrants a splurge when visiting Zacatecas. *Directions:* Located 8 blocks from the center of town, in the old bullring facing the aqueduct.

※ ☎ 💳 ☎ ♿ P 🍴 🖼 🐾

QUINTA REAL ZACATECAS
Manager: Carlos Rocha Franco
Ave. Rayon 434
Zacatecas, Zacatecas 98000, Mexico
Tel: (492) 922-9104, (800) 457-4000 USA
Fax: (492) 922-9105
49 rooms, Double: $197–$208*
*Tax: 17%
Open: all year, Credit cards: all major
Region: Central–Colonial town
www.karenbrown.com/mex/quintarealzacatecas.html

Casa Buenaventura, a stark-white building enhanced by colorful almandras and bougainvilleas, is a beautiful bed and breakfast. Its architecture displays an elegant combination of a Mediterranean-style structure and unique Mexican touches. There are seven bedrooms, one located on the first level, near the swimming pool and dining room. Ascending the circular staircase, you reach six more rooms, all with sitting areas, full baths, and terraces with the proverbial hanging hammocks. Single bedrooms each have a king-size pedestal bed, double rooms each have two matrimonial-size beds, and the furniture in all of them reminds you of the simplicity of old Mexican-style houses. Although the rooms have ceiling fans and no air conditioning, the bay breeze brings cool, fresh sea air. All rooms come equipped with a mini-bar filled with complimentary bottled water and soft drinks. The blue-tiled pool invites you for a refreshing dip and is also a good spot for watching the tropical sunsets. Breakfast is included and features fresh-squeezed juice, assorted tropical fruits, granola, yogurt, eggs, breakfast meats, and Mexican favorites. Worth mentioning is the spectacular view of Zihuatanejo Bay from every corner. Note: The B&B's hillside location makes it inaccessible for wheelchair-handicapped persons. *Directions:* Located above Playa La Ropa.

☎ ⏇ ◨ Ⴤ ≋

CASA BUENAVENTURA
Owner: Elia Laura Rodriquez
Carretera a Playa la Ropa
Zihuatanejo, Guerrero 40880, Mexico
Tel & fax: (755) 554-2855
7 rooms, Double: $200*
*Tax: 17%, Lunch &dinner on request
Open: all year
Region: Beach–Pacific Coast
www.karenbrown.com/mex/buenaventura.html

Like a star in the night sky, Hotel Casa Cuitlateca sits on the highest point overlooking Zihuatanejo Bay. This unique four-room boutique hotel is reached by a steep driveway and a swaying suspension bridge, but for those afraid of heights, there are steps wandering through the gardens and up to the main reception area. Two of the bedrooms are found in the main house sharing a comfortable lobby. One of these rooms is a suite with a living area, and the other one has a deck overlooking the Bay of Zihuatanejo. Both have fairly large bathrooms and double beds. The other two guestrooms are in an adjacent building, each with a king-size bed, a sitting area, and a deck with a built-in chaise and a spectacular view. There is a private terrace and a hot tub at the very top of this building. The main area is comprised of a sundeck, dining area, kitchen, bar, and a stunning infinity swimming pool made of local small river rocks and surrounded by a tropical lily pond. On one side of the pool sits a palapa-shaded gazebo where you can while away the day without being disturbed. A full breakfast is included in the room price, and lunch and dinner are provided upon request. The truly personalized service includes picking you up at the airport with a welcome refreshing drink and driving you to town or to the beach on request. *Directions:* Ask for directions when making reservations.

☎ ⊤ ☕ 💳 ≋

CASA CUITLATECA
Innkeeper: Rogelio Herrera
Calle Playa La Ropa
Zihuatanejo, Guerrero 40880, Mexico
Tel: (755) 554-2448, (877) 541-1234 USA
Fax: (755) 554-7394
4 rooms, Double: $340*
*Tax: 17%, Lunch & dinner on request
Open: all year, Credit cards: all major
Region: Beach–Pacific Coast
www.karenbrown.com/mex/casacuitlateca.html

This lovely all-suite hotel, featured in the movie When a Man Loves a Woman, is spectacularly set into a cliff above Zihuatanejo Bay. La Casa Que Canta ("the house that sings") derives its name from the sounds echoing through the open windows and down the hallways, and each of its suites is named for a Mexican song. The air-conditioned guestrooms all have unique personalities, privacy, serenity, and stunning views. All have ceiling fans, a mini bar filled with complimentary bottled water, soft drinks, and beer, and a marble bathroom with double sink and walk-in shower. Some have terraces and others private pools, and all have the proverbial hammock. The textured walls are embedded with bits of straw and are painted a wonderful terra-cotta color. Furnishings for the hotel were collected from the best artisans throughout Mexico. The palapa roof, typical of this tropical area, is outstanding by its size and shape. Meandering stairs lead from the lobby to the restaurant below, past the beautiful infinity pool, and down to a saltwater pool on the ocean level. Special features of the hotel include beautiful designs crafted from fresh flower petals and leaves that the maids create on the bedspreads and a wonderful gift shop in the lobby. Breakfast and lunch are reserved exclusively for guests, while dinner is open to all by reservation. *Directions:* On hill overlooking Playa La Ropa, 3 km from town.

LA CASA QUE CANTA
Owner: Jacques Baldassari
Carretera a Playa la Ropa
Zihuatanejo, Guerrero 40880, Mexico
Tel: (755) 555-7030, (888) 523-5050 USA
Fax: (755) 554-7900
24 suites, Double: $375–$680, Service: 10%, Tax: 17%
Minimum nights required: 7 (in high season)
Open: all year, Credit cards: all major
Region: Beach–Pacific Coast
www.karenbrown.com/mex/casaquecanta.html

According to the owner, Eva Bergtold, Hotel Catalina was the first "fancy" hotel built in Zihuatanejo, way before Zihuatanejo was "discovered"—when it was just a small fishing village and La Ropa Beach was just an empty, quiet paradise nearby. The contemporary-looking Hotel Catalina and its neighbor, the larger Hotel Sotavento, were run as one property until 2002, when they separated into individual hotels. The 40 guestrooms, decorated with simple modern furnishings, have white walls and yellow and hot-pink spreads on the double beds. Each bedroom has a sitting area and is equipped with a small refrigerator. The tiled bathrooms are small but adequate. The terraces are spacious and have hammocks and loungers for sunbathing. The outstanding feature of this hotel is its superb view of Zihuatanejo Bay and the surrounding hills. Built on a landscaped hillside with lush tropical gardens overlooking La Ropa Beach, the Catalina has many steps meandering down to the swimming pool and onto the beach far below. The sunset bar is a great favorite of locals who come to relax with a drink and enjoy the spectacular sunsets. Children and pets are welcome here. There is no air conditioning but the rooms are cooled by sea breezes and overhead fans. *Directions:* Located on the hill above Playa La Ropa.

☎ ♨ 🚼 💳 ☎ 🐕 🕴 👫 🏇 Ⴢ P 🍴 ≋ 🏄 ⛳

HOTEL CATALINA
Owner: Eva Bergtold
Carretera a Playa la Ropa
Zihuatanejo, Guerrero 40880, Mexico
Tel: (755) 554-2137, Fax: (755) 554-9327
40 rooms, Double: $55–$130*
*Service: 10%, Tax: 17%
Open: all year, Credit cards: all major
Region: Beach–Pacific Coast
www.karenbrown.com/mex/hotelcatalina.html

When one heads to the tropics for a vacation, falls in love with the sun and sea, then contacts the home office to tell them, "I'm never returning!" the Aussies say, "He's gone troppo." This is how the small hotel La Quinta Troppo acquired its name. Rene and David Ferguson started building this hotel in the mid-1990s as a vacation home. It is now their primary residence and a place where they offer guests a tranquil setting on the beautiful Mexican coast in uniquely decorated rooms filled with Mexican art and handicrafts. All the bedrooms offer something special: some have balconies; one a private garden; another a beautiful bath with two showerheads and a headboard painted by local artisans; others have a magnificent view of Zihuatanejo Bay. The beds are made with cotton sheets, which are a must in warm weather, and each guest receives a pair of terrycloth slippers to slip into after taking a shower. The lap pool with its pre-Hispanic-style fountains is located in the dining area and is a perfect place to exercise or relax after a full day on the beach. The dinner menu—for guests only—changes daily (kitchen closed Wednesdays) and a wonderful tropical Continental breakfast is included in the room rate. The hotel has no TV, but does offer guests a dedicated computer line. *Directions:* La Quinta Troppo is located on the hillside above the sea: at most a five-minute walk to La Ropa Beach.

LA QUINTA TROPPO
Owners: Rene & David Ferguson
Managers: Pablo Neri Garcia & Erica Islas Gonzalez
Camino Escenico a Playa la Ropa
Zihuatanejo, Guerrero 40880, Mexico
Tel: (755) 554-3423, Fax: (755) 554-7340
8 rooms, Double: $140–$225*
*Tax: 17%, Meals available to guests only
Closed: Sep, Credit cards: all major
Region: Beach–Pacific Coast
www.karenbrown.com/mex/laquintatroppo.html

The Villa Carolina, a well-designed, family-owned, all-suite, small luxury hotel, is located atop a hill in the colony of La Ropa and within walking distance of Zihuatanejo's most popular beach, Playa La Ropa. The architecture creates a sense of space in the six sienna-colored, thatched-roofed, split-level, fully-equipped suites. Each suite has a king-size bed and a sitting area where you can catch the local news on CNN, enjoy a video from the office selection, or listen to music on the cassette player. All the tastefully decorated rooms have high ceilings, fans, and air conditioning along with full marble bathrooms, fully-equipped kitchens, and safe-deposit boxes. Each master suite has a partial ocean view, separate bedroom with terrace, private Jacuzzi, dining area, a hammock, lots of sea breeze, and ample space to move around. The garden suites, located in front of the swimming pool, are large and beautifully appointed. Guests can relax by the pool and in the afternoon enjoy hors d'oeuvres and a drink. Breakfast and lunch are offered from 8.30 am to 4:30 pm and, for more privacy, meals can be brought to the room. A special exit from the hotel leads down to La Ropa Beach. *Directions:* Located on the hill above Playa La Ropa.

VILLA CAROLINA
Manager: Tim Conti
Carretera a Playa la Ropa
Zihuatanejo, Guerrero 40880, Mexico
Tel: (755) 554-5612, Fax: (755) 554-5615
6 rooms, Double: $195–$350*
*Tax: 17%
Open: all year, Credit cards: MC, VS
Region: Beach–Pacific Coast
www.karenbrown.com/mex/villacarolina.html

What began as the dream of a German engineer 25 years ago has turned out to be one of Mexico's most distinguished boutique hotels. He started with just a few casitas on the beautiful beach of Playa la Ropa in Zihuatanejo, slowly adding more over the years, as well as extra amenities that you would find at any small luxury hotel. Today the complex includes four swimming pools, tennis courts, a day spa, a beauty salon, and a fitness center. There are now 70 finely decorated rooms and suites, with Mexican colors and furnishings. Although all the rooms are special, the beachside units, some with terrace pools overlooking an expansive view of the bay, are certainly the best. But for that special occasion, the upgrade is well worth it. Playa la Ropa, right outside your door, is perfect for long evening walks or morning runs. Villa del Sol also offers gourmet cuisine, beginning with breakfast on the beach with linen tablecloths and the sand at your feet, to casual and fine dining in the evenings at sunset. Zihuatanejo, with its beachside cafés, restaurants, and market, is just a few minutes' ride away by taxi and is well worth a visit. *Directions:* Ten to fifteen minutes by taxi from Ixtapa-Zihuatenejo International Airport. Directly on Playa La Ropa.

VILLA DEL SOL
Owner: Helmut Leins
Managers: Jonathan & Nicole Wise
Playa la Ropa s/n
Zihuatanejo, Guerrero 40880, Mexico
Tel: (755) 555-5500, Fax: (755) 554-2758
70 rooms, Double: $360–$1170*
*Includes breakfast & dinner, Service: 5%, Tax: 17%
Open: all year, Credit cards: all major
Region: Beach–Pacific Coast
www.karenbrown.com/mex/villadelsol.html

Hidden away in a corner of the small beach town of Barra de Potosi, a tiny fishing hamlet south of Zihuatanejo, sits a cute, two-storied, orange cottage with a palapa roof. This is the guesthouse of your gracious hosts, Anabella Martinez, a Mexican actress, and her husband, François Heritier, who is a specialist in Mexican culture. There is a relaxed, bohemian, carefree ambiance to this secluded property. The guestrooms, all with a view of the ocean and direct access to the beach, are spacious with king-size beds and roomy, well-appointed bathrooms decorated with Talavera tiles. Ocean breezes and ceiling fans cool the rooms, which are decorated in Anabella's unique, colorful, Mexican style. The beds come equipped with mosquito netting that can be tucked in at night. Hammocks beckon you to take a nap or spend a lazy afternoon with a good book. The whole compound is surrounded by an 8-foot fence that encloses a wonderful sandy walkway and beautiful gardens. The watermelon fish painted on the inside of the fence are whimsical and create a wonderful South-Pacific atmosphere. A breakfast of fresh juice, a mixed fruit plate, croissants, and coffee or tea is included in the room rate. Lunch and dinner are offered by reservation. Meals are also available just a short walk away in the village of Barra de Potosi, where there are several seafood restaurants. *Directions:* Located south of Zihuatanejo. Ask for directions when making reservations.

☎ ⚓ 🍺 🐎 P ⚍ 🏊

CASA FRIDA B&B
Owners: Annabella Martinez & François Heritier
Zihuatanejo–Barra de Potos
Guerrero 40880, Mexico
Tel: (755) 556-3944, Fax: none
3 rooms, Double: $70
Open: Nov-Apr 15
Region: Beach–Pacific Coast
www.karenbrown.com/mex/casafrida.html

Tres Puertas is in a residential area with a tropical atmosphere. The owners, Guillermo and Gabriela Brana, were living and working in Mexico City when they decided to move to the coast and get away from the noisy hustle and bustle. They bought land near Palma Real golf course in 1986 and started building their dream, with Guillermo riding the red-eye bus from Mexico City for 12 hours every Friday night to arrive in Ixtapa on Saturday in time to pay the workers who were building their house. In the beginning there were only three villas and the library: the fourth villa, their home, and the swimming pool were finished in 1995. The delightful outdoor kitchen near the pool is fully equipped and it is here that Gabriela offers her cooking classes featuring authentic Mexican cooking. The guest villas are large, with king-size beds, two couch/beds, a fully equipped kitchenette, and a terrace from which to watch the birds and garden wildlife. The baths are all tiled and offer ample room. There is no need for air conditioning as the villas are hidden in the trees and tropical vegetation and there are ceiling fans in all the rooms. Meals are served on request for guests only, while on Thursdays, Fridays, and Saturdays Gabriela opens her dining room to the public (you must call a day in advance). Dinner, served by the pool, is always a great experience. *Directions:* Ixtapa is just northwest of Zihuatanejo. The inn is near the Palma Real Golf Club.

TRES PUERTAS
Owners: Gabriela & Guillermo Brana
Colina de las Palomas No. 325
Zihuatanejo–Ixtapa, Guerrero 40880, Mexico
Tel & fax: (755) 553-0610
4 rooms, Double: $150*
*Tax: 17%
Open: all year
Region: Beach–Pacific Coast
www.karenbrown.com/mex/trespuertas.html

Over a rough and sandy road, fifteen minutes from Ixtapa-Zihuatanejo International Airport and five minutes from the fishing village of Barra de Potosi, we happened on the Hotel Las Palmas. This romantic hideaway is owned by Shari and Scott Crawford who, while on an around-the-world tour, conceived the idea of leaving their careers in Phoenix and opening a small luxury hotel. After a visit to Playa Blanca, near Zihuatanejo, they knew they had found the perfect secluded spot and commissioned one of Zihuatanejo's premier architects to build their dream. The design is excellent, featuring a thatched palapa roof and high ceilings that allow ocean breezes to cool you as you sit in the lobby or bar and enjoy the quiet evening. The four downstairs bedrooms are air-conditioned while the ones upstairs are cooled by ceiling fans and sea breezes. The king-sized beds are draped in mosquito netting and the rooms all come with wooden shutters to keep out the early-morning light and the harsh afternoon sun. Bathrooms are well designed and are open to sea breezes. All bedrooms face the ocean and you can watch the sunset from your private deck or by the pool. The infinity swimming pool sits just below the outside dining room and from here you can watch the pelicans as they skim over the water. A complete breakfast is included in the room rate and lunch and dinner can be had upon request. *Directions:* Ask for directions when making reservations.

HOTEL LAS PALMAS
Owners: Shari & Scott Crawford
Manager: Doug Davis
Calle Playa Aeropuerto
Zihuatanejo–Playa Blanca, Guerrero 40880, Mexico
Tel: (755) 557-0443, Fax: (602) 253-3487 USA
6 rooms, Double: $150*
*Tax: 17%
Open: all year
Region: Beach–Pacific Coast
www.karenbrown.com/mex/laspalmashotel.html

Don't be deterred by the dusty road that winds out of the tiny fishing village of Troncones—your reward lies just 3 kilometers north, in the oasis-like setting of the Inn at Manzanillo Bay, mere steps from a dazzling white-sand beach. Mike Bensal, a native Californian and honors graduate of San Francisco's California Culinary Academy, and his Mexican wife bought the inn in 2000 and offer warm hospitality in ten palm-thatched casitas, each with a king-sized bed hung with picturesque but requisite mosquito netting. There is no air conditioning; instead, ceiling fans and the sea breezes cool the rooms. Eight casitas surround a stunning free-form pool but the ones nearest the beach are the most private, so request one of those. Sit in the dining room-bar and watch as your meal is prepared in the unique open kitchen or enjoy a tasty snack from the beachfront grill and watch the perfect waves wrap around Troncones Point. Michael designed the menu, an innovative and deliciously spicy fusion of classic and modern Mexican cuisine. You can order all day from the menu and enjoy it poolside or on the beach at a palapa-shaded table. The dual attractions of the inn are relaxing and surfing. You can rent surfboards, mountain bikes, and kayaks from the Inn surf shop, which carries a full line of surf accessories and apparel and Internet services. *Directions:* Troncones Bay is 30 minutes north of Zihuatanejo. Manzanillo Bay is 3 km north of Troncones.

THE INN AT MANZANILLO BAY
Owner: Michael Bensal
Manager: Julio Chavez
Playa Troncones
Zihuatanejo–Troncones, Guerrero 40880, Mexico
Tel: (755) 553-2884, Fax: (755) 553-2883
10 rooms, Double: $88–$108*
*Tax: 2%
Open: all year, Credit cards: all major
Region: Beach–Pacific Coast
www.karenbrown.com/mex/manzanillobay.html

When visiting Mexico's incredible Monarch butterfly sanctuary, Rancho San Cayetano is definitely the place to stay. But don't limit your visit to migration time—the Rancho San Cayetano offers a tranquil retreat year round. The hotel has a superb setting in 12 parklike acres that encompass manicured gardens, exotic trees, wide expanses of lawn, and even a river cutting a gorge through the grounds. This delightful inn, reminiscent of a mountain lodge with large windows accenting walls of stone and wood, also hints of a Mexican hacienda in the verandas that stretch in front of the rooms. The main building houses the reception office, a lounge with a huge stone fireplace accented by tiles, and a cozy dining room. The guestrooms are decorated in a rustic style: brick and exposed-stone walls, beamed ceilings, and tiled floors are enhanced by hand-loomed fabrics, local artwork, and attractive wooden furniture. In addition to the standard guestrooms there are three separate cottages, my favorite being the Casita de Adobe, a romantic 100-year-old adobe cottage with a cozy wood-burning stove and a terrace overlooking the river running far below in a deep ravine. All the rooms are decorated by your charming hostess, Lisette, who also creates the exceptionally delicious meals. Pablo Span is marvelous at helping guests plan their excursions. *Directions:* Just outside town on the road to Huetamo. Ask for detailed instructions.

HOTEL RANCHO SAN CAYETANO
Owners: Lisette & Pablo Span
Km 2.3, Carretera a Huetamo
Zitácuaro, Michoacán 61500, Mexico
Tel: (715) 153-1926, Fax: (715) 153-7879
12 rooms, Double: $75–$170*
*Service: 15%
Open: all year, Credit cards: MC, VS
Region: Central–Near butterfly sanctuaries
www.karenbrown.com/mex/ranchosancayetano.html

Index

A

Acapulco, 202
    Cliff divers of La Quebrada, 204
    Las Brisas, 222
    Quinta Real Acapulco, 223
    Villa Vera Hotel, 224
Acapulco Bay, 202
Agua Azul, 141
    Cascadas, 141
Agua Azul La Villa, Huatulco, 261
Alamos, 190
    Hacienda de los Santos, 190, 225
Angahuan, 75
Angangueo, 172, 174
    Casa Parker Museum, 174
    Mural, 174
Antigua Villa Santa Monica, San Miguel de Allende, 331
Archaeology, 3
ATM Machines, 29
Aztecs, 4, 7, 46, 78, 146

B

Bacalar
    Rancho Encantado, 226
Bahía Concepción, 160
Bahía Magdalena, 152, 153, 156, 159
Bahías de Huatulco, 204
Baja Cruises, 34
Baja Peninsula, 192, 205
Balankanche–Sacred Cave, 130
Balboa Club, Mazatlán, 274
Bank Hours, 24
Barrancas, 183
Becán, 144
Bed & Breakfasts, 11

Benito Juárez, 109
Bottled water, 39
Buses, 34

C

Cabañas La Conchita, Riviera Maya–Tulum, 327
Cabo San Lucas, 192, 207
    Cabo San Lucas (Hotel), 227
    Casa del Mar, 228
    Las Ventanas al Paraiso, 229
    Twin Dolphin (Hotel), 230
Cabo Surf Hotel, San José del Cabo, 328
Cacaxtla, 100, 125
Calakmul, 143
Calakmul Biosphere Reserve, 143
Camino Real Oaxaca, Oaxaca, 295
Camino Real Puebla, Puebla, 308
Camino Real Zaashila, Huatulco, 262
Camino Real, Loreto, 269
Campeche, 132
    Fuerte de San Miguel, 132
    Museum, 132
Campeche-Uayamón
    Hacienda Uayamón, 231
Cancún, 126, 212
    Casa Turquesa, 232
    Villas Tacúl, 233
Car Rental, 17
Careyes (The), Costa Alegre–Careyes, 243
Casa Blanca, Puerto Vallarta–Bucerias, 314
Casa Brunson, Pátzcuaro, 305
Casa Buenaventura, Zihuatanejo, 347
Casa Cid de León, Oaxaca, 296
Casa Claudia, Puerto Vallarta, 312

Enhance your Guides—Visit us Online

www.karenbrown.com

- Hotel specials
- Color photos of hotels and B&Bs
- 20% online discount for book purchases
- Discount airfare, both business and coach class
- Direct links to individual property websites and e-mails
- Up-to-the-minute phone, fax, and e-mail information
- Rental cars, travel planning, trip insurance, itineraries, maps, and more

Become a Member of the Karen Brown Club

- Additional specials and offers from our travel partners
- Exclusive access to "new discoveries" from our current research
- An additional 20% savings on purchases from our online store

A complete listing of member benefits can be found on our website

Don't delay, join online today!

www.karenbrown.com

KB Travel Service

❖ **KB Travel Service** offers travel-planning assistance using itineraries designed by *Karen Brown* and published in her guidebooks. We will customize any itinerary to fit your personal interests.

❖ We will plan your itinerary with you, help you decide how long to stay and what to do once you arrive, and work out the details.

❖ We will book your airline tickets and your rental car, arrange rail travel, reserve accommodations recommended in *Karen Brown's Guides,* and supply you with point-to-point information and consultation.

Contact us to start planning your travel!

800-782-2128 or e-mail: info@kbtravelservice.com

Service fees do apply

KB Travel Service
16 East Third Avenue
San Mateo, CA 94401 USA
www.kbtravelservice.com

Independently owned and operated by Town & Country Travel
CST 2001543-10

Seal Cove Inn

Located in the San Francisco Bay Area

Karen Brown Herbert (best known as author of Karen Brown's Guides) and her husband, Rick, have put 23 years of experience into reality and opened their own superb hideaway, Seal Cove Inn. Spectacularly set amongst wildflowers and bordered by towering cypress trees, Seal Cove Inn looks out to the distant ocean over acres of county park: an oasis where you can enjoy secluded beaches, explore tide-pools, watch frolicking seals, and follow the tree-lined path that traces the windswept ocean bluffs. Country antiques, original watercolors, flower-laden cradles, rich fabrics, and the gentle ticking of grandfather clocks create the perfect ambiance for a foggy day in front of the crackling log fire. Each bedroom is its own haven with a cozy sitting area before a wood-burning fireplace and doors opening onto a private balcony or patio with views to the park and ocean. Moss Beach is a 35-minute drive south of San Francisco, 6 miles north of the picturesque town of Half Moon Bay, and a few minutes from Princeton harbor with its colorful fishing boats and restaurants. Seal Cove Inn makes a perfect base for whale watching, salmon-fishing excursions, day trips to San Francisco, exploring the coast, or, best of all, just a romantic interlude by the sea, time to relax and be pampered. Karen and Rick look forward to the pleasure of welcoming you to their coastal hideaway.

Seal Cove Inn • 221 Cypress Avenue • Moss Beach • California • 94038 • USA
tel: (650) 728-4114, fax: (650) 728-4116, website: www.sealcoveinn.com

Travel Your Dreams · Order Your Karen Brown Guides Today

Please ask in your local bookstore for Karen Brown's Guides. If the books you want are unavailable, you may order directly from the publisher. Books will be shipped immediately.

_____ *Austria: Charming Inns & Itineraries* $19.95

_____ *California: Charming Inns & Itineraries* $19.95

_____ *England: Charming Bed & Breakfasts* $18.95

_____ *England, Wales & Scotland: Charming Hotels & Itineraries* $19.95

_____ *France: Charming Bed & Breakfasts* $18.95

_____ *France: Charming Inns & Itineraries* $19.95

_____ *Germany: Charming Inns & Itineraries* $19.95

_____ *Ireland: Charming Inns & Itineraries* $19.95

_____ *Italy: Charming Bed & Breakfasts* $18.95

_____ *Italy: Charming Inns & Itineraries* $19.95

_____ *Mexico: Charming Inns & Itineraries* $19.95

_____ *Mid-Atlantic: Charming Inns & Itineraries* $19.95

_____ *New England: Charming Inns & Itineraries* $19.95

_____ *Pacific Northwest: Charming Inns & Itineraries* $19.95

_____ *Portugal: Charming Inns & Itineraries* $19.95

_____ *Spain: Charming Inns & Itineraries* $19.95

_____ *Switzerland: Charming Inns & Itineraries* $19.95

Name _____ Street _____

Town _____ State_____ Zip _____ Tel _____

Credit Card (MasterCard or Visa) _____ Expires: _____

For orders in the USA, add $5 for the first book and $2 for each additional book for shipment. Overseas shipping (airmail) is $10 for 1 to 2 books, $20 for 3 to 4 books etc. CA residents add 8.25% sales tax. Fax or mail form with check or credit card information to:

KAREN BROWN'S GUIDES
Post Office Box 70 · San Mateo · California · 94401 · USA
tel: (650) 342-9117, fax: (650) 342-9153, e-mail: karen@karenbrown.com, www.karenbrown.com

KAREN BROWN wrote her first travel guide in 1976. Her personalized travel series has grown to 17 titles, which Karen and her small staff work diligently to keep updated. Karen, her husband, Rick, and their children, live in Moss Beach, south of San Francisco. They settled here in 1991 when they opened Seal Cove Inn. Karen is frequently traveling but when she is home, in her role as innkeeper, enjoys welcoming Karen Brown readers.

CLARE STEVENSON BROWN was a travel consultant for many years, specializing in planning itineraries to Europe using charming small hotels in the countryside. The focus of her job remains unchanged, but now her expertise is available to a larger audience — the readers of her daughter's guides. When Clare and her husband, Bill, are not traveling, they live either in Hillsborough, California, or in Vail, Colorado.

JANE STEVENSON DAY, Ph.D., retired Chief Curator of the Denver Museum of Nature and Science, now serves as Curator of Latin American Archaeology in their Department of Anthropology, and is an adjunct professor of archaeology at the University of Colorado and the University of Denver. Jane is an immensely popular lecturer in the Denver community and has led many museum trips to sites around the world. She and her husband, Horty, live in Denver, Colorado, and have four daughters residing nearby.

JANN POLLARD, the artist responsible for the beautiful painting on the cover of this guide, has studied art since childhood, and is well known for her outstanding impressionistic-style watercolors, which she has exhibited in numerous juried shows, winning many awards. Jann travels frequently to Europe (using Karen Brown's Guides) where she loves to paint historical buildings. Jann's original paintings are represented through The Gallery, Burlingame, CA, 650-347-9392 or www.thegalleryart.net. Fine-art giclée prints of the cover paintings are also available at www.karenbrown.com.

BARBARA TAPP, the talented artist who produces all of the hotel sketches and delightful illustrations in this guide, was raised in Australia where she studied in Sydney at the School of Interior Design. Although Barbara continues with freelance projects, she devotes much of her time to illustrating the Karen Brown guides. Barbara lives in Kensington, California, with her husband, Richard, their two sons, Jonothan and Alexander, and daughter, Georgia

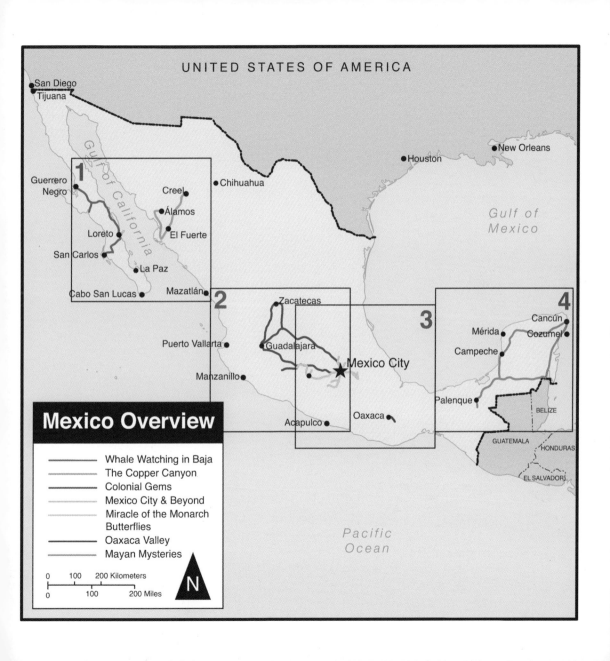

UNITED STATES OF AMERICA

San Diego
Tijuana

Guerrero
Negro

Gulf of California

1

Creel
Álamos
El Fuerte

Chihuahua

Houston

New Orleans

Gulf of
Mexico

Loreto

San Carlos

La Paz

Cabo San Lucas

Mazatlán

2

Zacatecas

Puerto Vallarta

Guadalajara

Manzanillo

Mexico City

3

4

Cancún

Mérida

Cozumel

Campeche

Palenque

BELIZE

Acapulco

Oaxaca

GUATEMALA

HONDURAS

EL SALVADOR

Mexico Overview

Whale Watching in Baja
The Copper Canyon
Colonial Gems
Mexico City & Beyond
Miracle of the Monarch
Butterflies
Oaxaca Valley
Mayan Mysteries

0   100   200 Kilometers

0   100   200 Miles

N

Pacific
Ocean

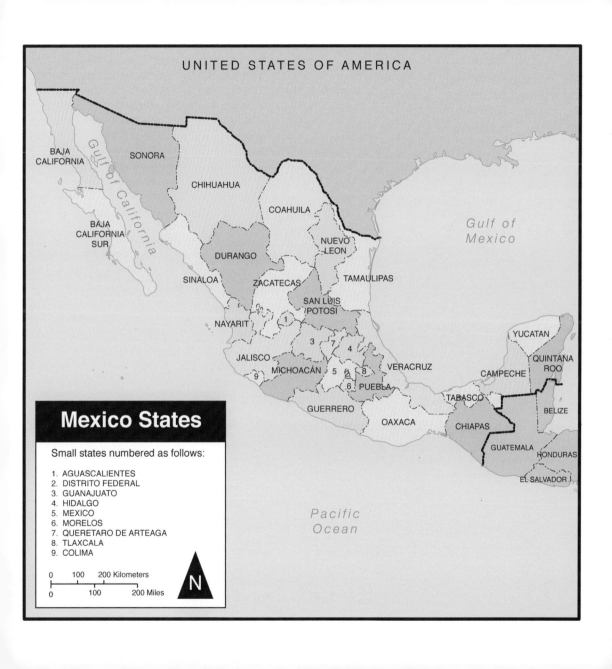

UNITED STATES OF AMERICA

BAJA CALIFORNIA

Gulf of California

SONORA

CHIHUAHUA

COAHUILA

Gulf of Mexico

BAJA CALIFORNIA SUR

NUEVO LEON

DURANGO

SINALOA

ZACATECAS

TAMAULIPAS

SAN LUIS POTOSÍ

NAYARIT

1

YUCATAN

3   7   4

QUINTANA ROO

JALISCO

CAMPECHE

9   MICHOACÁN   5   2   8   VERACRUZ

6   PUEBLA

TABASCO

BELIZE

GUERRERO

OAXACA

CHIAPAS

GUATEMALA   HONDURAS

EL SALVADOR

Pacific Ocean

Mexico States

Small states numbered as follows:

1. AGUASCALIENTES
2. DISTRITO FEDERAL
3. GUANAJUATO
4. HIDALGO
5. MEXICO
6. MORELOS
7. QUERETARO DE ARTEAGA
8. TLAXCALA
9. COLIMA

0   100   200 Kilometers

0   100   200 Miles

N

Mexico Map 2

- ● Places to Stay
- ─── Colonial Gems

0   25   50 Kilometers

0   25   50 Miles

N

To Mazatlán

15

Zacatecas

La Quemada

57

49

San Luis Potosi

70

85

Tepic

15

54

Aguascalientes

Dolores Hidalgo

San Miguel de Allende

Punta Mita

Bucerias

Puerto Vallarta

Majahuitas

Yelapa

Tlaquepaque

Guadalajara

80

45

Guanajuato

Querétaro

57

90

La Cruz de Loreto

Quémaro

80

Laguna de Chapala

15

Costa Alegre

Cihuatlán

Careyes

54

Angahuan

Uruapan

Pátzcuaro

Morelia

55

Mexico City

Texcoco

Isla Navidad

San Antonio

Colima

Zitácuaro

15

Toluca

Manzanillo

200

37

Cuernavaca

Taxco

51

Amacuzac

134

Ixtapa

Zihuatenejo

95

200

Acapulco

Pacific Ocean

Mexico Map 3

Legend:
- ● Places to Stay
- ⚛ Archaeological Sites
- Mexico City & Beyond
- Miracle of the Monarch Butterflies
- Oaxaca Valley

0 25 50 Kilometers
0 25 50 Miles

N

San Luis Potosi
Ciudad Madero
Tampico
70
85
180
Dolores Hidalgo
San Miguel de Allende
Poza Rica
Querétaro
57
Tula
Tulancingo
Teotihuacán
140
Chincua Butterfly Sanctuary
Mexico City
Texcoco
Gulf of Mexico
Morelia
Cacaxtla
Tlaxcala
Veracruz
Zitácuaro
Toluca
Puebla
150
Malinalco
Cuernavaca
Orizaba
Xochicalco
Taxco
Amacuzac
51
Coatzacoalcos
134
180
Zihuatenejo
190
175
95
San Felipe del Agua
Oaxaca
Teotitlán del Valle
Monte Albán
Yagul
Mitla
Acapulco
175
200
Salina Cruz
Pacific Ocean
Gulf of Tehuantepec
Huatulco

Icons Key

This year we have introduced the icons listed below in the guidebooks and on our website (*www.karenbrown.com*). These allow us to provide additional information about our recommended properties. When using our website to supplement the guides, placing the cursor over an icon will in many cases give you further details.

❄	Air conditioning in rooms	🏊	Swimming pool
☕	Breakfast included in room rate	🤸	Tennis
👶	Children welcome	📺	Television
♨	Cooking classes offered	🔔	Wedding facilities
CREDIT	Credit cards accepted	♿	Wheelchair friendly
☎	Direct-dial telephone in room	🏛	Archaeological site nearby
🐕	Dogs by special request	🏌	Golf course nearby
🛗	Elevator	🚶	Hiking trails nearby
🏋	Exercise room	🏇	Horseback riding nearby
🍸	Mini-refrigerator in room	⛷	Skiing nearby
🚭	Non-smoking rooms	⛵	Water sports nearby
P	Parking available	🍇	Wineries nearby
🍴	Restaurant		